THE POWER PACK

101 POINTS

TO

SOCIAL AND ECONOMIC JUSTICE

Elmore Richmond Jr.

909-420-7338

Victory Publishing Company
4017 Palmyra Road, Suite #2
Los Angeles, California 90008

International Standard Book Number: 1-886636-50-8
Library of Congress Catalogue Card Number: LCN 94-90762
Printed in the United States of America

Edited By: Linda Broadous Miles
Cover Designed By: Richshell Allen

ACKNOWLEDGEMENTS

I thank the Urban League for the outstanding work over the years to provide "The State of Black America" annually. A special thanks to all the writers; their research truly helped me tremendously in preparing this book.

Special thanks to the NAACP, SCLC, CORE, The National Rainbow Coalition, ACLU and other civil rights groups for their efforts to help make social and economic justice to become a reality in America.

Thanks to all the authors who have work so hard to bring the problems of America's poor to the national agenda. I am indebted to each of you.

Special thanks go to William C. Taylor, Earl J. Wilson and George P. E. Pearson. I thank my family and friends. I'm also indebted to two officials of IBS, Ms. Pala Lawson and Mr. Lou Brooks for their support and encouragement. Most of all, I thank God, for giving me the opportunity to make a difference.

DEDICATION

This book is lovingly dedicated to the remembrance of the late Dr. Martin Luther King, Jr., all the young people who have died in senseless killings, and the young people who are looking for hope and direction to become more productive citizens in the 21st Century.

CONTENTS

FOREWORD

By: Charles E. Henderson, D.D.

We live in a world that is steeped in crime, violence, hunger, poverty, indifference, and intolerance. As members of this present society, we need to take a second look at the deplorable conditions that have our world in a death grip. In every world age, societies have broken up from within. The reason is people lose respect for law and order, then they lose respect for one another. As we view this spectacle with awe and amazement, one cannot help but wonder when will this madness end?

Are there solutions to these massive problems? Let us take a look. It has been said that we can tell the future by looking at the past. History tells us that disregard for law and order, whole-sale destruction of human life, and zero tolerance among the races is a recipe for chaos. Be sure that destruction is knocking at humanity's door. Who can stem this tide of madness? Will the new crime bill change things? Will putting more law enforcement officers on the streets of our cities be a deterrent to this madness? I am afraid not!

What we need is a master plan that can address these problems on a broad base. Today we have such a plan. It is in the form of a Book called: "The Power Pack: 101 Points To Social And Economic Justice." This book was written by Elmore Richmond Jr. This book is nothing less than a treatise. It has been thoroughly researched and the data has been compiled in a very articulate and timely manner by Mr. Richmond. He has worked relentlessly in compiling a work wherein issues are raised, and with great skill he has given us great answers. These answers can and will bring about solutions to many of the problems that we face as a society.

I believe that this book will cause this great nation to take a second look at her stand on these issues; then rise up and live out her creed, "that all men were created equally" and that there should be liberty and justice for all. The results will be relief and restoration in our nation that will spread abroad.

I believe that this book can and will be used in the many classrooms of our schools, our institutions of higher learning, government agencies, libraries, and the general public. I highly recommend this book by all. This book will inspire you to rise and be about the task of restoring and rebuilding the infrastructure of the precious commodity, the family. The information contained within this book will surely serve as a crossroad to turn the lives of millions from crime to concern, and from poverty to provision. This book will bring about healing among the races. It will help to promote peace and harmony among the peoples of the world. It will help bring about social and economic justice as well as new vision and insight. It will heighten the awareness of all who are seeking truth about one of the world's greatest problems, **RACISM.**

INTRODUCTION

This book develops a plan of action to address the problems facing African Americans, Hispanics, Native Americans and the poor, to include "poor Whites" by mobilizing the Community (U.S.) to work together in creating a new conscience, direction, spirit of togetherness, and team effort that will lead to a more caring, sharing, and loving people. The by-product will be a People with self control, and respect for one another, and a People having the sense of urgency and awareness to carry out their responsibilities to this end.

This spirit of unity will enable every organization, formal and informal, to work together developing a sense of unity, unmatched in the history of this country. This team will allow African Americans, Hispanics, Native Americans and poor whites to become focused and to do the work required to take charge of their destiny. Consequently, it will force the nation to join in and address the needs of the African Americans, Hispanics and poor whites.

A dream? Yes, it is a big dream. It has been visualized. For it is said: If you can't visualize it, you can't make it happen. Moreover, the blueprint has been prepared to include detailed planning. Your involvement will make it all inclusive because you will enlist others to include organizations throughout the United States. Together, with the grace of God, we will refine our plans to meet the needs of our specific communities.

To effect the Power Pack, action must be taken to inform the following of this effort:

1) All organizations that address people concerns

2) Every religious organization and institution

3) Every American

4) Corporate America

5) The Governments of the United States, Federal, State and Local

Next, empower African Americans, Hispanics and the poor through a sense of unity and develop a plan to raise their sense of awareness of this fact: We, the people must make a significant difference and show our resolve to the nation, now.

This book is the first step in effecting this plan. This book capitalizes on the knowledge of many and creates a means of identifying and addressing the problems that are negatively impacting Black Americans and to some extent, the Hispanics and the poor.

Implementation of this plan will require all available resources to work together by finding common ground. This book provides a plan of action that creates the foundation to eradicate the conditions that plague Black, Hispanic, poor white communities and the nation, as a whole.

CHAPTER 1

AWARENESS

The current conditions in America that keep African-Americans, Hispanics, Native Americans and poor whites at a disadvantage and at odds with each other are unacceptable and very destructive. Action must be taken to stop this cycle of destruction, discrimination, violence, and injustice, both social injustice and economic injustice. There are a number of organizations currently addressing certain aspects of these conditions, however, there is not a united effort to this end. Consequently, without a united effort, we will fail to eradicate these conditions.

The Power Pack is the vehicle that will cause us to come together, reassess, mobilize, restore our cultural values and then protect them. Moreover, through this plan, we shall re-enact an effective socialization process, eliminate discrimination and injustice, restore a sense of pride, rebuild self-esteem for all of our people, to include the very young to the very old. Finally, we will reduce homelessness, the sense of hopelessness, and then create trust and respect for one another.

Today, in America we find recovering from a deep recession from the Reagan and Bush eras quite difficult. In fact, it won't happen without a united effort. Consequently, we are faced with a decline in the Black family income, increased poverty rate, high unemployment, racial inequality in income, increased school drop-out rate, increased violence, increased gang activities, increased homelessness, increased sense of hopelessness among the masses, substance abuse problems, AIDS, and Black, Hispanic, and "poor White" underclasses. The underclass adds another dimension to the traditional class structure being "upper class," "middle class," "working class," and "lower class".

To address these conditions and problems, we must effect these 101 Points as outlined in this book. Though many of these Points target African Americans, some Points can be used to address poor White Americans and other minority groups who are facing similar conditions. Most of these Points are thorough commentaries, with specific actions, challenges, and recommendations. On the other hand, at times you will discover just the Point and very short commentary. This is done to get you involved in the process. You have ideas and even effective programs that are just as important as Points made in this book. We must work together and not get hung up on process. Let's look for common ground and work this plan.

We suggest as you read this book, have a pencil and pad to record your thoughts. This document is not designed to be placed on the shelf. It must become a working document. It can be used in a number of ways. For example: It can be used at home when you're discussing issues with your family, at church meetings, workshops, seminars or preparing sermons, speeches or lectures. Moreover, it will assist you to correct some of the problems within your community. In fact, it serves as a vehicle to create interaction and action throughout the nation. One of our aims is to make each Point common language in such a way, that Point 19 in Los Angeles will also be Point 19 in New York, Tennessee, Ohio, Texas, etc. Every household should have a copy of this book.

If you write proposals, this book is an outstanding source of information. It will also provide much needed information to foundations or corporations that fund grants by identifying areas that need funding and recommending specific actions.

Remember, get a pencil and pad and proceed to read and explore your mind. We must change these conditions now and your personal involvement is key to making our streets safer, developing our youth, and gaining social and economic justice for many hopeless people.

POINT 1 - ENDING PSYCHOLOGICAL WARFARE AND RACIAL DISCRIMINATION

The United States Government must stop engaging in "Psychological Warfare" against Black Americans. Psychological warfare is being waged in a way to weaken the will of African Americans to fight for what is right and it puts Blacks against Blacks and other groups against Blacks. Some governmental officials are introducing measures that make it appear that their objectives are in harmony with the prevailing ideas of society. However, in their efforts to persuade people to their beliefs, they don't allow fair consideration to the opposing views.

It is apparent that a measure like "Three Strikes You are Out" is another attempt to appeal to the desires, fears and prejudices of most Americans. (A measure of sentencing individuals to life in prisons after three felony convictions, when these felony convictions fall in certain categories.) However, this is an act of psychological warfare, a device to create favorable political opinions. Moreover, "Three Strikes You are Out" doesn't address the basic problem.

We all want safe streets, and a place conducive to raising our children; however, at what expense? At the expense of someone being locked behind bars for the rest of his or her life because the system didn't give him or her a fair chance.

What is a fair chance? An opportunity to work, learn and to develop their minds. An opportunity to go to school in an environment that is conducive for learning. An opportunity to have positive role models in their lives. An opportunity to become employable.

Many individuals get out of prison and look for work, only to discover that they are not employable because they became criminals, when they were young and undeveloped. Some will try to go straight. However, they face much disappointment in their job search. Consequently, they end up hanging out on street corners, being bums, and some will even pump gas in your car or wash the windows of your car for a few pennies. These individuals need jobs, however, our current system isn't designed to give them jobs, only prisons. Nevertheless, it creates jobs for thousands by keeping prisoners in prisons. **This must change.**

These individuals aren't receiving a fair chance. In fact many of them have not received a fair chance since their birth, like other Americans who live in poverty. They don't receive a fair chance to be all that they could be in this land of plenty.

In fact, one must question the action of the Reagan's Administration and Congress for failing to heed the advice of the National Advisory Council on Economic Opportunity in 1981. In 1981 the National Advisory Council on Economic Opportunity, before it's demise due to a budget cut - issued a grim warning: "the economic policies of the Reagan administration, Congress, and budget cuts aimed at the poor, if continued, would plunge the nation into social chaos. About 32 million are officially poor, another 30 million hover just above the poverty level. Continued budget cuts will devastate about one-fourth of the nation's population, particularly the elderly, women, minorities, and the young. The results are predictable: more crime, physical and psychological illness, broken families, racial division, and potential for violence." [1]

Today, in 1994, we are living this nightmare, a nightmare that was predicted in 1981. Though the overall official poverty level is not at 25%, for Black America it's above 33% and we are experiencing the by-products of those budget cuts. It appears that we have attempted to address the by-products of this failure or "criminal act" of Congress and the Reagan Administration by passing a bill that says: "Three Strikes You Are Out". Clinton's administration and Congress must rethink this "Three Strikes You Are Out" measure.

There is a better way. The measure "Three Strikes You Are Out" is not the solution. Each case is different. We are not playing baseball. However, under this bill we play with these human beings as if we were playing a game of baseball. God did not make people to live in fear - nor did God make people to be locked in cages for life. Today we have over 900,000 prisoners in our state and federal prisons. This is an outrage and a waste of human lives.

A recent visit to Los Angeles County Jail, near Valencia, California on one Sunday evening was truly a nightmare for me. I observed hundreds of Black and Hispanic women and children in line or waiting in a large staging area to see their brothers, husbands or their fathers. At first I thought I was visiting a segregated jail until I noticed a few white visitors. I could count the white visitors on both hands.

There were children who should have been outside enjoying a walk through the park, or playing baseball or something with their parents, spending their Sunday afternoon, waiting in line or a large staging area at the county jail. It reminded me of going to a large amusement park or zoo. However, unlike the zoo, there were no animals in these cages, only people. On a side note, I discovered that one man was in jail for 72 days because he failed to pay several traffic tickets. However, he couldn't pay these tickets because he was unemployed. This was a sad, sad experience to see so many minority children waiting at the country jail to share a little time with there fathers who were confined in jail.

There is a better way. We don't need "Three Strikes You Are Out". We must restudy this problem and work harder to find real solutions, not quick fixes.

Other past acts of this warfare include the Justice Department's war on affirmative action. This war was waged through a powerful disinformation campaign to convince the public that affirmative action is actually "reverse discrimination". For example the cases of Weber, Fullilove and even Bakke. As Cited by Dorsen:

> "First, the very fact that the Supreme Court took these cases for review, with all the media coverage and public debate that attends such grants, tended to foster a distorted sense of what was really happening in the field of racial discrimination. Based upon the Bakke suit, some were undoubtedly led to conclude that blacks were entering other medical schools at such high rates as to begin squeezing out white applicants in large numbers. The truth, blacks accounted for less than 5 percent of medical school enrollments as the Bakke Case reached the Supreme Court, despite a significant expansion in the number of seats available in medical schools during the late sixties and early seventies."[2]

In respect to Weber, Dorsen stated: "One would have thought from the arguments Brian Weber made that Kaiser Aluminum's Gramercy, Louisiana plant had provided unnecessary assistance to black workers at the expense of whites. Instead, the Gramercy plant, located in an area where the labor pool was almost 40 percent black, employed only a 15 percent black workforce and a less than 2 percent black craft workforce."[3]

Regarding Fullilove, Dorsen added: "And because an association of white contractors sought to have the 10 percent Minority Set-Aside provision declared unconstitutional, many were probably led to believe that minority contractors had succeeded in cornering the market on federal construction contracts. As of 1977, however, minority firms were getting less than 1 percent of the federal public works budgets; white contracts were getting the rest,...In sum, though the evidence of the continuing unaddressed effects of deep-seated prejudice Bakke, Weber, and Fullilove tended to skew public discussion away from how to remedy "just plain old discrimination" to the questions of so-called "reverse discrimination."[4] Consequently this caused prejudiced public attitudes and encouraged hostility toward African Americans. Unfortunately, until this date, there has been very little effort to dispel these counterproductive perceptions.

Psychological warfare is also heavily embedded in the mass media, radio, television, the movie industry and newspapers. The federal government must enact laws to stop this psychological warfare and take appropriate action to counter negative activities that impact human relations. The general public must become educated to recognize the difference between propaganda used in psychological warfare and education.

Late in 1994, in a book titled the "Bell Curve", Richard Herrnstein and Charles Murray concluded that Black Americans are inferior to White and Japanese Americans in respect to the Intelligence Quotient (I.Q.). Herrnstein and Murray should be commended for his efforts, research and hard work. However, often people like Herrnstein and Murray make discoveries and fail to realize the essence of their findings.

These failures occur for a number of reasons; for example (1) when one overlooks or ignores the limitations of the data (2) when one is biased and has a faulty premise which lead to a misinterpretation or an unjustified comparison (3) or is unaware or uninformed of other factors.

Herrnstein and Murrary are like a few other psychologists, contends that a person's innate ability limits improvement and argues that compensatory education has not been successful. On the other hand some psychologists agree that a person's intelligence level is determined by both heredity and environment. Some believe that the environmental factor is most important and consequently the intelligence test scores reflect social, economic, and cultural influences in addition to innate ability.

I agree with the latter viewpoint. Moreover, I submit to you that the essence of the findings of Herrnstein is not that Black Americans are innately inferior, but it demonstrates the impact of discrimination on the expression of innate ability. Consequently, the effects are measurable by the general I.Q. results.

Nevertheless, their conclusions are becoming heavily embedded in the mass media. In fact, the media is involved in perpetuating this myth. If appropiate action is not taken, tax payers will eventually pay for this myth to be taught to our children. This act of psychological warfare is based on racism and will cause people to discriminate. When this occurs, it has a number of negative impacts on its victims.

We have studied the roots of prejudice. However, now we must explore the impact of discrimination and psychological warfare on its victims. Let's start by looking at the impact of this psychological warfare and racism on the African American Male. We can begin with the work of Allen-Hagen (1993) Cordes (1985), Devart (1988), Sickmund (1993) and Swinton (1989) which cite numerous independent reports and studies, delineated a wide range of issues and high-risk activities confronting the Black American male. These findings include:

- For centuries Black men worked hard in the nation's most back-breaking jobs.

- Of all gender and race groups, Black men are the workers most displaced by automation.

- Motivation and personal choices may distinguish those who cope from those who are victimized by what is actually a structural problem of the labor market.

- Through the last two decades, black male income fluctuated between 57 and 63 percent of white male income (economically, the black man is still treated as 3/5 of a white man).

- According to the Urban Institute of Washington D. C. after adjustments for inflation, the average disposable income rose 4.1 percent for White families but fell 2.1 percent for Black families.

- Income inequality existed in every region of the country in 1989.

- In 1991 the average rate of unemployment for black males was 12.9 percent and 6.4 for white males. The rate of unemployment for black males in the age group 20-24 was 22.4 percent.

- Black men represent less than 5 percent of the U. S. population but they make up 46 percent of all individuals arrested for violent crimes, 40 percent of the inmates in local jails, and 50 percent of all prisoners in state and federal prisons.

- Poverty is at the center of the plight of the Black man and afflicts about one-half of the unemployed, the jailed, the disabled (due to job injuries or substance abuse), and the victims of homicide or suicide. Some Black men enlist in the armed services, often at last resort.

- Infant mortality is more than twice as high for Black males as for White males.

- Black males leave school early, twice as often as Black females because of discipline problems.

- Conflicts between Black males and school personnel have led some observers to contend that many Black males are really "pushouts" rather than dropouts.

- In 1979 about 30 percent of low-income Black households with children reported a child being suspended from school in the previous year.

- In 1991 the nearly 50,000 juvenile weapons arrest accounted for more than 1 out of 5 weapons arrests. Black youth were arrested for weapons law violations at a rate triple that of white youth.

- The 1991 violent crime arrest rate for black youth was 5 times higher than that of white youth (1,456 per 100,000 compared with 283 per 100,000).

- Nearly one in five Blacks ages 18 and 19 dropped out of school in 1981.

- Lower achievement scores, et cetera, are part of the legacy of centuries of education discrimination.

- Inferior schools are preparing Black men for inferior roles and systematic confinement to the lowest-paying jobs available.

- Low motivation interacts with such factors as age, education, and past job experience.

- In 1981 there were about 123,000 more Black females in college than Black males.

- The total Black enrollment in higher education declined from 9.4 percent in 1976 to 8.8 percent in 1984. Black undergraduate enrollment declined over the same period from 10.5 percent to 9.5 percent.

- Since 1976 the proportion of Black high school graduates who go on to college has declined from 33.5 percent to 26.1 percent. In terms of absolute numbers, there were 15,000 fewer Black high school graduates entering college in 1985 than there were in 1976.

- A four-year graduation rate of 35 percent and lower is not uncommon for Blacks at predominantly White institutions.

- Only 42 percent of Black students who enter college continue through graduation.

- Black men are both physically and emotionally less healthy than White males.

- African American males live only 65.7 years, a life span that is almost a decade shorter than the 73 years average for white males.

- Black males are most likely of any group to die from injuries on the job.

- Blacks die at a higher rate than White males from such causes as heart disease, hypertension, cancer, stroke, cirrhoses of the liver, tuberculosis, diabetes, and lung diseases.

- In 1975 Black males had the highest admission rate of any sex or racial group to state and community mental hospitals as in-patients and were admitted at younger ages.

- They were most likely to be diagnosed as having alcoholic disorders, drug disorders, and schizophrenia.

- At outpatient facilities, the largest diagnostic category for Black males was that of no mental disorder - 28 percent compared with 10 percent of White males.

- More Black men in technical to semi-professional occupations are now turning to psychotherapy.

- Depression, anxiety, and work-related problems were their most frequent complaints.

- Neurotic symptoms increase for Blacks as they ascend the social ladder.

- Black men seek help with such work-related problems as lack of assertiveness, anxiety about assessments of their performance, handling others' aggression, feelings of alienation, and interpersonal and interracial conflict.

- The suicide rate among Black males rose faster than among any other group in the 1970's and is currently at record-high levels.

- The suicide rate for Black males peaks between the ages of 25 and 34 - years when most people are building careers, and beginning independent adult life.

- Black males also suffer the highest rate of deaths from accidents and violence, including a homicide rate more than six times that of Black female or White males.

- The link between poverty and crime is obvious - nearly 60 percent of young Black prison inmates reported an annual income of less than $3,000 according to a 1975 report of the U.S. Bureau of Census.

- The leading cause of death for young Black citizens between the ages of 16 and 34 is homicide.

- Ninety-five percent of Black murder victims (5,128) were slain by a Black offender.

- The treatment of racial and ethnic minorities by individuals, institutions, and cultural expression may be viewed as constituting a severe form of mental cruelty to the extent that racial and ethnic minorities are denied equal access of goods and services of the broader society. They suffer the psychological perils attendant to being the victims of structural inequality and overt forms of racial and ethnic discrimination and racism.

- In 1989, blacks had an income deficit equal to 6,149 for every man, woman and child. In the aggregate, the income of the African-American population was $186 billion short of the income required for parity.

- A four-month investigation by Money magazine shows in dollars and cents that racial discrimination still prevents middle class (and upper-class) black families from earning as much as whites; lowers their access to mortgages, business loans, and other financial services; retards their homes' rate of appreciation; prevents them from increasing their wealth effectively; and deprive them of the economic well-being enjoyed by their white middle-class counterpart.

The President, governors, mayors, corporate America, the people and the media must understand that African Americans will no longer allow this to happen. Our government and the media must develop a plan of action to stop this Psychological Warfare and ensure that the government will never again engage in Psychological Warfare against its own people.

In addition to the plan by the government and media, African Americans must develop a plan to ensure that action is taken that will end this warfare and discrimination. Action must be taken to monitor these efforts, until the end of this warfare is realized. In the book entitled: "State of Black America", 1992, John E. Jacob, President, National Urban League Inc. made the following observations in his overview.

"Our failure to see beyond the narrow confines of the present to build for the future and our terrible failure to develop all the resources represented by all our people have led not only to economic decline but also serious erosion of the bonds that tie our society together. [5]

Those persistent negative racial stereotypes have sapped too much of our energies, undermined our self-confidence, retarded risk-taking, and led too many of our young people to see academic achievement as a "white thing" and failure as a "black thing". [6]

Mr. Jacob challenged African Americans to use its resources to develop Black Children for the 21st Century. We have the strengths and resources to meet this challenge. However, I don't believe we have the awareness needed to effect this undertaking. We are fortunate that the Urban League has a nineteen-year published history of "The State of Black America." Unfortunately, we have not taken full advantage of this information. Through this information lies the answers to end this psychological warfare and racism and to pave the way to develop the black children for the 21st Century.

In 1994, John Jacob retired from the Urban League and he left behind a treasure trove that will give the new president, Mr. Hugh B. Price the needed tools to continue the quest for social and economic justice.

The psychological warfare is very real and it must be addressed now. However, in addition to the psychological warfare, there are a number of other factors that must be addressed. Mr. Price gave the following warning in his keynote address at the National Urban League's convention in Indianapolis: "We must not let ourselves - and especially our children - fall into the paranoid trap of thinking that racism accounts for all that plagues us,..." [7] Mr. Price also noted that the culprits include economic trends that transcend race, though inner-city blacks may be disproportionately victimized.

A closing note: Like the fall of the Berlin Wall, like the fall of Communism in the U.S.S.R., and the fall of the government of apartheid in South Africa - let this wall of psychological warfare infested with prejudice and discrimination come down in America. Let's have a revolution of thoughts and build a new America, where peace and prosperity abound.

POINT 2 - EDUCATING THE PEOPLE

Educating America on the State of Black America - The National Urban League and the National Association for the Advancement of Colored People (NAACP) and other pro-human rights organizations must take a more active role in educating the nation through their annual reports, workshops, community forums, rallies, town hall meetings, and etc.

In addition to this book, I recommend that the National Urban League's Annual "State of Black America" be used as a tool to educate African-Americans and the country in general. The Urban League's Annual, "State of Black America" is well-written and could be a powerful tool, however, it has little or no real impact if it is not read by the general public. Therefore, immediate action must be taken to help ensure that these documents are read by at least ten million blacks and millions of non-blacks, annually.

In addition to these books, a training program should be developed to help facilitate the learning process across America. This training program should consist of manuals, videos, and slides/overhead transparencies. Churches throughout the country should obtain copies of the training program. Moreover, recommend that the Urban League sell the most recent volumes of "The State of Black America" in a set, for example volumes from 1987 through 1994. This is an excellent source of information and it is needed to help facilitate the increased awareness that is required to equip Black America and the nation on how to address these problems.

Recommend that this training package be developed by the National Urban League. Pastors of local churches should select instructors from their congregation to train all church members.

In addition to conducting this State of Black America Awareness training through the churches, training should also be conducted through community forums, workshops and seminars. The mandate should be to educate America on the State of Black America and to afford solutions to eradicating these unhealthy conditions.

Hugh B. Price, the new president of the Urban League expressed the need to educate young people and called for the league's affiliates to mount a "house-by-house, living room-by-living room" drive to "help parents understand, in laymen's terms, exactly what their children must know and be able to do in order to meet 21st Century standards of competency."[8]

This action will help bring about a more informed community - when the community becomes informed, the people of the community will be in a better position to use their talents, time, and resources in more productive ways. The Hispanics should use a similar approach to educate its communities regarding the flight of Hispanics.

POINT 3 - "THE POWER PACK" MOBILIZING THE NATION

The "Power Pack" creates a sense of positive thoughts and affirmations that will move the nation. On June 19th, 1990, I was inspired to write the " Power Pack". I felt a surge of energy that took control of my pen for about five minutes. This revelation is key to addressing the problems of this nation.

The Power Pack

Objective: The Power Pack Objective is to mobilize the community (U.S.) to work together in creating a new conscience, direction, spirit of togetherness, and team effort that will lead to a more caring, sharing, and loving people. The by-product will be a People with self-control, and respect for one another, and a People having the sense of urgency and awareness to carry out their responsibilities to this end.

This can be realized through a plan that will shock the nation. Every channel of communication must be activated. This can be done through churches, gospel singers, rappers, soul and rock stars, entertainers, the stars of Hollywood, politicians and every citizen.

The Power Pack will become the means in which everyone can become involved. I can envision the messages being carried through dances, songs and raps. I can see people wearing and producing rings, tee shirts and other garments - carrying the message. I can see people registering to vote and becoming members of the power pack. I can see people, to include Blacks and Hispanics, buying stores and organizing businesses in their community in the name of "The Power Pack".

I can see young men allowing young ladies to develop into mature women in the name of "The Power Pack". I can envision teenagers with a new sense of pride in themselves rejoicing and enjoying the feeling of love all around them. I can also see teenagers who will stop seeking love that result in early pregnancy. I can see young people learning with a renewed sense of responsibility. I can envision gang members awakening and crossing over from their current gang affiliation and becoming an active force - part of "The Power Pack". The country will be shocked when this occurs.

I can envision the reluctant ones joining the bandwagon when it begins to roll. It will move with much force and there will be no turning back.

The United States Government must join in. Initially, I can see efforts to undermine the "Power Pack" by the U.S. Government and other opposing forces. However, in the end, I can see the U. S. Government supporting the effort. The "Power Pack" will become so powerful that we will experience a revolution of thoughts.

I can see welcoming signs to the "Proud Community of South Central Los Angeles", "Watts" and the "South Side of Chicago". I can see trash being cleared from the streets of the ghettos, and sanity being restored to the insane. I can see an effective EEOC, taking swift action to end discrimination in the workplace. Moreover, I can see the end of Black on Black crimes and the end of the plot that allowed Blacks to kill off one another.

If you believe this will happen - it will. Who is in charge? God is in charge. Therefore, the movement will not stop when individuals are killed by those who will try to stop this movement. The "Power Pack" will continue to move forward.

Who will be the community leaders? They will come from all around you. They will be recognized by their action. People will follow them and work on one accord. The community leaders will do whatever is necessary to address the needs of their community. God is in charge.

The basic plan is simple. It is already written - the only thing we must do now is to follow it - "The Greatest Commandments" - "To love the Lord your God with all your heart, with all your soul, and with all your mind and to love one another as you love yourself."[9] When this occurs, everything else will follow.

This will seem too simple to most - but this is the answer. Make an affirmation that will renew the spirit and intent of this Affirmation - For God so Loved the World ...". Now, your love for God and one another will be the force that will make it impossible to stop this movement. This is the "Power Pack."

Now is the time for this energy to flow. There is not much time left in the real sense to get this done. So I'm calling upon you to take action now!

First, write down all thoughts that come to your mind at this point. More will be revealed to you later. However, now it is important that you record these thoughts.

Contact people who are currently in the position of power and influence and let them know about the "Power Pack".

Amen.

Note: This power regarding love is a belief of Hindu-Moslem-Christian-Jewish-Buddhist believers. For it is recorded: Let us love one another: for love is of God: and everyone that loveth is born of God, and knoweth God. He that loveth not knoweth not God; for God is love....If we love one another, God dwelleth in us, and his love is perfected in us.

Chapter I Notes

1. National Advisory Council On Economic Opportunity, Thirteen Report (Washington, D. C.: 1981), Cited in Henry Weinsten, ("U.S. Cuts Will Devastate Poor Panel Charges," Los Angeles Times, September 21, 1986 pt.1 P.3.

2. Dorsen, Norman, (1984) Our Endangered Rights:The ACLU Report On Civil Liberties Today, p. 89

3. Ibid. p.89, 90

4. Ibid. p.90

5. Dewart, Janet, 1993, The State of Black America, p. 2, National Urban League, Inc.

6. Dewart, Janet, 1993, The State Of Black America, p. 6 National Urban League, Inc.

7. Los Angeles Times, July 31, 1994. "Black Americans Must Rescue Black America", Quoted by William Raspberry.

8. Los Angeles Times, July 31, 1994, "Black Americans Must Rescue Black America", Quoted by William Raspberry

9. The Holy Bible, Matthew 22:37-40.

CHAPTER II

SOCIAL

This chapter focuses on social issues that are interconnected and provides insight on the course of actions to resolve these conditions. Some of these issues are very complex, however, a serious attempt has been made to breakdown each issue in a way to effect solutions.

POINT 4 - ELIMINATING POVERTY

In 1991, more than two-thirds of all African American children living in female-headed household were poor, at a poverty rate that was about 20 percentage points higher than the rate for white children in similar households. However, the majority of the poor in America are white.

In 1991 - the poverty rate for African American children in married couple families was 15 percent.

African American juveniles are greatly over-represented as tenants of public facilities, accounting for 42 percent of the total population.

There is a number of factors that cause poverty i.e. unemployment and underemployment. By official estimates, the overall African American unemployment rate in 1991 was more than double the rate of white.

Poverty also affects the rate of infant mortality among African Americans which continues at more than twice the mortality rate among whites. African American infant females are 2.5 times likely as white female infants to die before their first birthday.

The gap between the poor and the non-poor is widening. There are a number of reasons for this, among them are inflation, reduction of government programs for the needy, and discrimination.

In 1981 the National Advisory Council on Economic Opportunity, before its demise due to a budget cut - issued a grim warning: "The economic policies of the Reagan administration, Congress, and budget cuts aimed at the poor, if continued, would plunge the nation into social chaos. About 32 million are officially poor, another 30 million hover just above the poverty level. Continued budget cuts will devastate about one-fourth of the nation's population, particularly the elderly, women, minorities, and the young. The results are predictable: more crime,

physical and psychological illness, broken families, racial division, and potential for violence."
[1] Today, in 1994, we are living this nightmare, a nightmare that was predicted in 1981.

In the work of D. Stanley Eitzen, he posed this question: "Can poverty be eliminated?" He answered the question like this: "The answer is yes if by poverty we mean the condition of life that is intolerable because the necessities of adequate health facilities, diet, clothing, and shelter are denied certain persons."[2]

In 1989, an estimated family budget on poverty-level income allowed for $298 per month for rent and utilities, $20 per person per week for food, and $0.75 per person per day for transportation. It is extremely difficult to live under these conditions, however, the income poor, by definition, exist below this level of income.

Below is a summation of some of the assumptions and approaches as outlined in Eitzen's work.

Assumption 1. Poverty can be eliminated in the United States. America has the resources to eliminate poverty. The paradox of poverty in the midst of plenty need not exist if the people wish to make a commitment. It only requires a reordering of the nation's priorities. It is not a great commitment: Less than 2 percent of our gross national product, or less than one-fifth of what is spent annually on defense, would raise all impoverished persons and families above the poverty line.

Assumption 2. Poverty is caused by a lack of resources, not a deviant value system. Basic to a program designed to eliminate poverty is the identification of what keeps some people in the condition of poverty. Is it a lack of money power, or the maintenance of deviant value and lifestyles? Developing the social competence of the poor-not changing the system-would bring an end to poverty, some would suggest. However, this approach would not work because it is like treating the symptom, not the disease. The attack must be directed at the structural changes that will enable lower-class persons to earn a living to support their families adequately.

Assumption 3. Poverty is more than a matter of deficient income; it also includes other inequities in the society. Poverty reinforces a pattern of restricted opportunities, deficient community services, powerful predators who profit from the poor, prejudice attitudes, and unequal distribution of resources. These conditions can be eliminated by enforcing laws under the civil rights acts, regarding equal opportunity for jobs, advancement, schooling, and the redistribution of power at local and national levels.

Assumption 4. Poverty cannot be eliminated by the efforts of the poor themselves. The poor don't have the power nor resources to change the structure necessary to eliminate poverty.

Concerns for eliminating poverty is not a new concern. Huey Pierce Long, a United States politician from Louisiana expressed concerned during the 1930's. As a United States Senator, he promoted a "Share Our-Wealth" program, a plan for equal distribution of wealth. He planned to use this as a base in seeking the Democratic Presidential nomination. However, at the height of his power, Long was assassinated by Dr. Carl A. Weiss, son-in-law of a political opponent. Like Long, there were others that voiced concerns and were assassinated, such as Kennedy, King and the demise of the National Advisory Council on Economic Opportunity.

Fifteen years prior to the demise of the National Advisory Council on Economic Opportunity, the assistant director of the Office of Economic Opportunity, Hyman Bookbinder in 1966 stated: "The poor can stop being poor if the rich are willing to become even richer at a slower rate". [3] He further declared that it would require substantial sacrifice by Americans. If not we could expect further deterioration of the cities, increased antagonisms between races and continued disorders in the streets. Moreover, he asserted that people are not informed enough to give adequate support to antipoverty programs, and he leveled a share of the blame at the federal government because it "must do more to get people to understand the size of the problem." [4]

In 1967, the late Dr. Martin Luther King, Jr. summed the problem like this regarding the poor black:

> "When the Constitution was written, a strange formula to determine taxes and representation declared that the Negro was 60 percent of a person. Today another curious formula seem to declare he is 50 percent of a person. Of the good things of life he has approximately one-half those of white; of the bad he has twice those of whites. Thus, half of all Negroes live in substandard housing, and Negroes have half the income of whites. When we turn to the negative experience of life, the Negro has a double share". [5]

Today, when we look at some of the negative experiences, we find African Americans are still receiving more than a double share of the negative things in a number of areas as noted throughout this book. In addition to the problem confronting the African Americans, today we find 35 millions - 50 millions Americans are living in poverty. Poverty impacts upon both African Americans as well as the white poor. There are millions and millions of poor whites in the United States of America.

Prior to the death of Dr. Martin Luther King, Jr., he expressed concern about poor whites and blacks and made plans to march on Washington. Here are excerpts from his last Sunday morning services on March 31, 1968 at the National Cathedral (Episcopal) in Washington, D. C.:

> "In a few weeks some of us are coming to Washington to see if the will is still alive or if it is alive in this nation. We are coming to Washington in a poor people's campaign. Yes, we are going to bring the tired, the poor, the huddled masses. We are going to bring those who have come to feel that life is a long and desolate corridor with no exit signs. We are going to bring children and adults and old people; people who have never seen a doctor or a dentist in their lives.
>
> ....We are coming to demand that the government adds itself to the problem of the poverty." [6]

Four days later, Dr. King was killed.

King left these lessons learned for us:

> "...you cannot depend upon American institutions to function without pressure" and "the nation doesn't move around questions of genuine equality for the poor and for black people until it is confronted massively, dramatically in terms of direct action." [7]

Eliminating poverty is our responsibility. We have the resources, now we must demand that this government take action now to end this social misery. We must organize and set a new agenda for this nation. Eliminating poverty must be at the top of the list.

America, America.

Recommend that the NAACP, Urban League, SCLC, CORE, Rainbow Coalition, and other civil rights organizations schedule a poor peoples march in Washington D.C. in 1996 in an effort to force the president and Congress to enact an economic bill of rights. This effort must include the White poor, and we must build a powerful new alliance, a true alliance, whereby based on solid ground of honest conscience and proper self-interest.

King summarized the effect of the bill as follows: "This would guarantee a job to all people who want to work and are able to work. Some people are too young, some are too old, some are physically disabled, and yet in order to live, they need income." [8]

A study by Kenneth Keniston and the Carnegie Council on Children support King's position on full employment. In the book, "All Our Children", they state:

> "Jobs are, of course, only one component of a sound family policy. But the denial of jobs to people who are ready, willing, and able to work is a tragic waste of their potential and of the social and economic benefits their work would produce for the society. When families enjoy economic security from productive work, the social dividends reach far into the future, when children reach adulthood and can make their contribution.
>
> We believe that with conscious and sustained effort it would be possible, over the next decade, to combine a full-employment strategy with a system of income supports so as to yield almost all American families with children minimum income of at least half the current median in any given year-the line most Americans consider the true poverty line" [9]

Is full employment possible in the United States? Yes it is possible. Studies make it very clear that the federal government is able to make choices that drastically affect the job market and the number of people employed. We have the tools to reduce unemployment, however, they are currently not being used to a great extent.

Among the government options include: (1) designing tax policies that give businesses an incentive to hire more people within the United States and not cheaper labor outside the United States (2) undertake economic development programs (3) putting more money into circulation, by either lowering taxes or borrowing money to increase federal expenditures and (4) of course, the government itself can simply create more jobs, such as highway improvement, protecting the environment and preventive health.

Kenneth Keniston and the Carnegie Council on Children also made the following observation:

"Finally, with the federal government guaranteeing jobs at minimum wages to all those family heads who cannot find employment otherwise, the program will at times cost the taxpayers money. But quite apart from the fact that this program would be likely to produce better transportation systems, revived cities, cleaner parks, and needed goods and services not available now, creating jobs for the unemployed will save the taxpayers money as well." [10]

Like Kenneth Keniston and the Carnegie Council on Children, Senator Paul Simon believes that we can put America back to work. In 1987, he prepared a blueprint in his book entitled: "Let's Put America Back To Work". The plan has merit and Congress should give the plan serious consideration.

These measures will dramatically reduce the amount paid out as unemployment insurance, AFDC, and food stamps because many of these people would be employed. More money into circulation will beget more jobs from the private public sector. Family stability should be given high priority, full employment helps the children of this nation, who are the future. However, full employment can't be achieved as long as the federal government's highest priority to inflation control or policy makers choose to control inflation primarily by letting unemployment rise.

Professor Harvey Brenner of John Hopkins University conducted a study and found that a 1 percent increase in unemployment caused a 5.7 percent increase in homicides, a 4.1 percent increase in suicides, a 4.0 percent increase in prison admissions, and a 3.5 percent increase in mental hospital admission. When you consider these findings, you can see a direct relationship with problems in Black America. Moreover, you can see the deadly impact the high employment rate is having on America overall.

In a land of plenty, thirty-five million to 50,000,000 people are far too many people to live in poverty, especially when the most affected group are our children. Unfortunately, this is not a new problem for America, but it's an old one. America, a country with the resources to resolve this problem, however, lacks the leadership and determination to balance policy and to give higher priority to full employment.

Four days before Dr. King was killed he left this message for us:

"And I submit that nothing will be done until people of good will put their bodies and their souls in motion. And it will be the kind of soul force brought into being as a result of this confrontation that I believe will make the difference. Yes, it will be a poor people's campaign. This is the question facing America. Ultimately a great nation is a compassionate nation. America has not met its obligations and its responsibilities to the poor.

One day we will have to stand before the God of history and we will talk in terms of things we've done. Yes, we will be able to say we built gargantuan bridges to span the seas, we built gigantic buildings to kiss the skies. Yes, we made our submarines to penetrate oceanic depths. We brought into being many other things with our scientific and technological power.

It seems that I can hear the God of history saying, "That was not enough! But I was hungry and ye fed me not. I was naked and ye clothed me not. I was devoid of a decent sanitary house to live in, and ye provided no shelter for me. And consequently, you cannot enter the kingdom of greatness. If ye do it unto the least of these, my brethren, ye do it unto me." That's the question facing America today."[11]

Fellow Americans, allow me to make this sad commentary. What type of leadership do we have that will not act on this serious problem unless there is political pressure imposed on them? If the 35,000,000 to 50,000,000 people living in poverty were voters, our politicians would have resolved this problem many years ago. This state of poverty poses a threat to millions of Americans and the future of America. However, it does not pose a threat to these politicians because these suffering people primarily don't vote, therefore, they don't have a political voice. My fellow Americans, I call upon you as you read this book to become the political force that is needed to turn these conditions around. At Point 54, when we discuss our economic system, we will reiterate this need to eliminate poverty. Individuals in politics must remember that their political futures are personal and no ones political future is as important as the future of America.

POINT 5 - ENHANCING THE QUALITY OF LIFE

Enhancing the quality of life - the government must redirect money for programs outlined in this blueprint. Our current budget is insufficient to bridge these gaps that have been allowed to go unchecked far too long. Improving the quality of life of the people of this country must become a priority on this nation's agenda. It must receive the same type of funding consideration as our military defense. Hundreds of billions of dollars must be earmarked to social programs designed to empower people. Our current approach enables people to remain in a state of dependance on the government.

In the Urban League's State of Black America for 1990, John E. Jacob, President and Chief Executive Officer National Urban League, Inc. mentioned a newspaper cartoon that clearly shows how we are failing to keep the internal affairs of the United States in check. Below is a quote from Mr. Jacob's overview.

"During the heady days of winter revolts against Eastern Europe's totalitarian regimes, a newspaper cartoon appeared that provides a stunningly accurate commentary on the current state of urban and Black America.

The cartoon showed Uncle Sam looking over the Berlin Wall through binoculars. He says:

"Gee, isn't it fascinating to watch the way communism is disintegrating." Behind him, on the U.S. side, is an urban landscape of mugging victims, hypodermic needles strewn on the ground, drug addict, guns, potholed road, and crumbing houses."[12]

Elected officials must take the lead and turn this around. For this to occur, they must become acutely aware. Reading this document is a starting point, however, it must go far beyond that. They also must ensure that their staffs are also sensitive to these conditions. Furthermore, they must discover the community, the people's needs who elected them and who they represent. Politicians must take overt actions to discover these needs even if the people fail to convey these needs to them.

On the other hand, the public must take action now and demand action be taken to address all of these conditions in the inter-cities and rural America.

POINT 6 - EMPOWERING THE HOMELESS

A drive through some of the streets and alleys of America's larger cities is like driving through the streets of some Third World cities. In these cities you can find the homeless by the thousands, sleeping out in the rain, under cardboard boxes, under trees, and living lives of threadbare destitution.

In the work of Rossi, "Down And Out In America", he connects extreme poverty with homelessness. Here is an excerpt of his observation:

"Although there is clearly a line between those with homes and the literally homeless, that line is easily crossed. A life of extreme poverty is one of extreme vulnerability. For most Americans it is easy to roll with all but the major punches life can give; most of us can absorb the shocks of illness and unemployment up to a point. A few months of unemployment or a week in the hospital are serious, but most people have enough financial and psychological reserves to survive either without becoming destitute or deeply depressed. Among the extremely poor, however, the many untoward events that the rest of us absorb can be major shocks catapulting them across the blurred line between having a home and being homeless. For the extremely poor, with no reserves of savings, no safety net of entitlement, and no credit cards, losing a few days' wages or catching a severe cold can mean losing a job, going without adequate food, or getting evicted. Events of this sort can trigger an episode of homelessness. Being homeless is a considerable notch below having a home although being extremely poor. And getting back among the domiciled population is not easy for someone with essentially zero resources." [13]

The problem described above is not a new problem for America, there is a recorded history that dates back to the minutes of seventeenth century New England town meeting. However, never in the history of this country has the problem been as severe as it is today. Moreover, it appears that America at one time gave much consideration to assist the homeless. For example: In the late 1800's anyone could approach a New York City police station and be given lodging for the night without being arrested and booked for an offense. The New York City police reported in 1890 that over the pervious decade the department had provided lodging in jails and lockups to 150,000 person annually.

In the early nineteenth century Skid Row areas were established, consequently, transient homelessness became an institution and segregate in American cities. Individuals living in skid row were mostly men who did the dirty work for our society. They provided muscle power for industries, agriculture, lumbering, railroads, highway construction and many other jobs that mainstream did not wish to do.

Here I don't wish to give an history lesson on the homeless, only to provide a perspective. Homelessness, poverty and economics are all interrelated. We have problems with all three. If we resolve the economic problem, we would resolve the problem of the homeless. We had an opportunity to resolve the homeless problem when it was small and quite manageable, however, we didn't have the resolve to do so. Today, with about 3 million people homeless in America, it will be quite difficult to correct. However, if we fail to address this problem today, ten years from today, it will be even more difficult to correct, especially with the increasing number of homeless families with small children.

In 1986, a 25-city survey revealed that in all but one of the urban centers surveyed the number of homeless people needing shelter had increased.

A 47-city study found that children comprised the largest segment of homeless families. One forecast from a psychologist who has studied the children of homeless families is that such young people are likely to become "alienated adults, unable to forge relationships and tending toward anger, criminality and poor education achievement.

Addressing the problem of the critical shortage of affordable housing is interrelated with empowering the homeless. Over the years there has been a number of studies and approaches to addressing this problem of affordable housing.

Rossi recommended a number of measures to include: (1) fostering the retention and enlargement of our urban low-income housing stock (2) reversing the policy that has put personal choice above institutionalization for those so severely disabled that they are unable to make decisions that will preserve their physical well-being (3) enlarging our conception of disability to include conditions not purely physical in character (4) recognizing that chronic mental illness and chronic substance abuse are often profound disabilities (5) restoring the real value of welfare payments to the purchasing power they had in the late 1960's and (6) extending the coverage of welfare benefits to include long-term unemployed, unattached persons.

Another common recommendation is to compel government agencies to cease putting up massive complexes of housing in the ghettos where no jobs are to be had. Instead use vacant land in suburban areas for developing moderate-income family housing near centers of employment.

Moreover, many more have made sound recommendations that have not been put into effect. Without public pressure on our government the homeless problem will not be resolved. The homeless themselves will not put public pressure on the government because we have labeled them as bums, hobos, tramps, etc. over the years and today, unfortunately many see themselves in that light. Therefore, America this is our problem. We must empower the homeless by first recognizing that it is our responsibility to put this item on the nation's agenda. We must look into the future for a moment and realize that conditions like homelessness and poverty are direct attacks on America, unlike the attack on Pearl Harbor with bombs from planes. Nevertheless, the end result could destroy America. The by-products of poverty are increased crime, increased violence, increased racial hatred, etc. These conditions produce the same outcome as war, destruction of America, not by the dropping of bombs, but from within.

The destruction is visible today, if we take a closer look at our inner-cities. With a closer look you can bear witness to America's destruction; the ruins of some of America's greatest cities of the past is evident. Like after winning World War II, when the great cities in Europe were reconstructed, America must declare war on poverty and win, and then commence the reconstruction of its great cities, and the lives of all of its citizens.

If we fail to address these problems today, the money that you are saving for your children's future may be in vain. If you really want to invest in your children's future - you must invest in America today and stop these attacks, like the one on Pearl Harbor.

America, America.

POINT 7 - RESOLVING THE HUNGER PROBLEM

Hunger in the United States presents a paradox: hunger amid plenty. America is too wealthy for any American to go hungry.

Everyday there are new findings regarding the plight of the hungry in America, however, no one knows the extent of hunger and malnutrition in America. Nevertheless, the problem is serious and is getting worse. Here is an example of evidence of the extent of the problem from a Physician Task Force in a ten-month survey of four broad areas of the country, ranging from hospitals in Chicago to huts in the hills of Tennessee. It was discovered that the children and the elderly were hard hit. The most common symptoms of malnutrition among children were poor health and stunted growth. Here are some of the specific findings:

(a) children in Texas living on rice, beans and potatoes;
(b) children in Tennessee mountain country living on biscuits, butter, and neck bones;
(c) anemic babies in North Carolina's Madison County;
(d) babies in Mississippi with no access to milk;
(e) children digging for food in dumpers outside apartment buildings in St. Louis;
(f) stunted children in the Midwest in the heart of the nation's food producing region;
(g) nine-year-olds in rural Mississippi with the stature of six-year-olds;
(h) kwashiorkor and marasmus, normally associated with famines like that of Ethiopia, in hospitals in Chicago and on Indian reservations of the southwest.
(i) deficiencies among Memphis pre-schoolers in vitamins A, B1, B2, C and iron so widespread that the Chief of Nutrition and Metabolism at a local hospital spoke of "epidemic levels of marginal undernutrition.

Hunger in the United States, this should not be. Resolution of this serious problem does not call for quick fixes, but it must be interrelated with the resolutions for the high unemployment, poverty and the homeless. Nevertheless, when we revamp our economic system, we will resolve them all.

America, America.

POINT 8 - REDUCING THE LEVEL OF VIOLENCE

Today, we are living in a time of much anger in America. To stop the violence we must remove the sources of frustration inherent in social and economic inequalities. In other words, prejudice, poverty, unequal opportunity and all of the other injustices must be corrected.

Today we see hundreds of people marching, expressing hope, with signs that read **"STOP THE VIOLENCE"**. These marches are good gestures. In fact they may be good for the marchers because the marches allow the participants an opportunity to release some of their frustration. Nevertheless, these acts alone will not stop the violence.

African Americans were enslaved and oppressed for hundreds of years. Surely, they resented and hated their condition. However, any expression of violence was brutally suppressed. They learned from the many beatings how to deal with their hostilities in less violent ways, by withdrawing, and becoming apathetic and regressing their behavior. Often when anger became overwhelming, they would take it out on one another. Nevertheless, occasionally, they would take their anger out against the slavemasters and other whites.

Today there is a lot of frustration in America. We find Whites angry at Blacks, and Hispanics, Hispanics angry at Blacks, Korean-Americans, and other Hispanics, Korean-Americans angry at Blacks and Hispanics, while Blacks are angry at Whites, Korean-Americans, Hispanics and other Blacks. (These summations are not all inclusive nor do they imply that all members of a particular group are angry at all members of another group.)

The bottom line, there is a lot of anger and we must take measures to find the source of the frustration.

For example: Why are African Americans Angry?

Some African Americans will list these reasons:

1. They are angry at other blacks because of the past death of loved ones;

2. Continuous senseless killings of one another;

3. Acts of violence upon one another;

4. Gang violence;

5. Racism

You must ask other questions to find root causes. Some African Americans will tell you they are angry because of the prejudice, discrimination, and all the other social and economic injustices. How do most African Americans deal with these conditions? Unfortunately, the same way slaves dealt with them. Some withdraw, lock themselves up in bars at their homes, some become apathetic and develop a "There is nothing I can do attitude", and some regress and fail to take a stand for what is right. Some will take positive action. However, unfortunately, some resort to violent acts upon other African Americans.

In general, African Americans are not pleased with the social and economic injustices in the United States. The level of frustration is too overwhelming. America must take measures now and address these root causes, the sources of the frustration.

The anger problem in America is very complex because of its applications. We find poor whites angry because of inadequate food, unaffordable houses, poor housing, being homeless, poverty, high unemployment; Hispanics are faced with the same condition as African Americans. The Koreans-Americans are fearful that their livelihood is being threaten, and the Skinheads think their slice of the pie is getting smaller and they view Blacks, Jews and non-whites as a threat.

In respect to the Skinheads, they should be angry because the average median income for black and white males during the 1980's were $11,994 and 19,994 respectively, versus $13,341 and $22,121, during the 1970's. Yes, they should be angry at the system because it is not that their slice of the pie is getting smaller - the pie itself has become smaller.

The average white American is angry because they just don't understand the nature of this psychological warfare and yet they are so intimately involved.

America, America how long can this go on!

The leadership of America must take immediate action and address the right problems and establish a goal of removing the sources of these frustrations imposed by our society. The leadership of this country must do this as quickly as possible because we are at the blink of a level of violence worse than what we experienced during the "Hot Summers" of the 1960's and the Los Angeles riot of 1992.

When there are inequities, people have the right to become angry. These inequities will not be corrected overnight. However, there must be a clear and detailed plan to address each one of these conditions.

Recommend that the people of the United States of America give the leadership a mandate to correct these inequities now.

Recommend that the President adopt a new approach in dealing with violence and address the root causes.

Recommend mayors across the country take measures to discover the source of the frustration in their cities. As they research they must do an in-depth study, not only the fact people are frustrated because of gang violence, but they also must discover, why gang members are frustrated to the point their anger reaches full circle and erupts into violence. Moreover, we must not attack the Skinheads for their views, but explore their views, clarify, and offer solutions.

Recommend communities continue to march, however not just the small marches of one to two-hundred people, but marches on a large scale of hundreds of thousands. These marches should not just be about gang violence, but the other conditions that cause the level of frustration.

Large marches of this type will have an impact on gang members and it may have an immediate impact on the level of violence. Moreover, this level of community involvement will cause a number of the gang members to cross over and help the people who are trying to make a real difference in their lives.

A large scale march of 200,000 would make a difference. To effect this effort there must be a willingness to mobilize. This effort should began in Los Angeles, the scene of the Los Angeles riot/rebellion of 1992. All community organizations should participate in this effort. The media should televise the march with the same enthusiasm it gave to the Los Angeles Riot of 1992. After Los Angeles' demonstration, lessons learned should be shared with other cities, and demonstrations should be held throughout America at large.

However, prior to the commencement of these demonstrations, there must be a massive educational campaign. Organizations must work together. No one organization, however, big or small should attempt to receive all the credit or praises for this effort. Organizations must realize that this is not the time to be self-centered. However, now organizations must put the future of African Americans, Hispanics, social and economic justice and the future of America ahead of organizational goals.

POINT 9 - REDUCING THE SUBSTANCE ABUSE PROBLEMS

Before discussing reducing substance abuse among African Americans, let's consider the history.

- Slaves were given alcohol on weekends and holidays by their slavemaster to prevent uprisings.

- Blacks were perceived as subhumans who drank excessively, refused to work and very dangerous while drinking. Many people had this view about blacks during reconstruction.

- Certain drug acceptability has varied like marijuana and heroin historically. Opiates once were legal in the United States.

- The National Association of State Alcohol and Drug Abuse conducted a survey in 1990 and reported an estimate of 280,000 pregnant women nationwide were in need of drug treatment, yet fewer than 11 percent of them received care.

- The rate of infant mortality, sudden infant death syndrome, child abuse, and neglect, as well as HIV infection are significantly linked to maternal substance abuse -caused most often today by crack-cocaine use, followed by other illicit drugs and alcohol.

- There are a number of co-factors that contributed to excessive alcohol consumption of blacks, among them are: rural-to-urban migration, adjustment to urban lifestyle, agricultural to urban economy change, poor education, unemployment and a stressful life.

In order to reduce the use of drugs we must deal with the reasons people use drugs. Does drug abuse education really resolve the problem? No, it does not. However, it may deter some. Some people, like myself, never used drugs and never had the desire, though faced with similar problems that the average drug user is confronted with. What makes the difference? Values? Maybe to some extent. Money? No. Coping skills and high self esteem? These two factors are very important to reducing the use of drugs amongst any group.

The approach employed by our enforcement agencies and Congress is not working. As, McCagahy noted:

"With the exception of Prohibition, which was finally repealed, the approach has been unvaried. Pass a law, if that does not work make sentence harsher, get more policemen, get better, detection devices, loosen up laws to make arrests easier, and so. Whatever you do, refuse to recognize that making some behaviors criminal does not prevent them."[14]

We must rethink our approach to this issue of substance abuse and deal more with preventative actions by addressing coping skills and correcting these social conditions that produce undue stresses.

The substance abuse problem creates another problem. The illegal status of some drugs enables illicit economic interests to flourish throughout the United States and Central America. Drug laws are intended to deter crime by severely punishing both the seller and user, however, this approach is not effective. Eitzen summed it up as follows:

"There are three fundamental reasons why this approach does not work as intended. By making drugs illegal and therefore dangerous to produce, transport, and sell, society pushes the cost to many times what it would be if they were legally available. Thus, heroin users, for example, are often forced to crime to sustain a habit that costs over $100 a day. Crimes committed to produce money for drugs are typically nonviolent (pimping, prostitution, shoplifting, selling drugs, and burglars), but their cost is enormous. Suppose, for example, that there are 100,000 addicts in New York City with habits costing $100 daily. If they each steal $300 worth of goods daily in order to get the $100 (a 3-1 ratio is about the way fencing works), the amount stolen in the city would be $30 million daily or $10.95 billion a year!" [15]

Today in inner-cities throughout America we find neighborhoods under siege and the children who occupy them have been taken hostage by violence. Children form gangs as surrogate families and use automatic weapons as a symbol of their deep feelings of helplessness. Behavior is an indicator of a child's emotions and low self-esteem. Thus, the surface actions of drive-by shootings, selling drugs for profit with no regard for human life and living with no regard for consequence, indicate a deep-seated detachment from morals, values and caring. Moreover, this shows that these young people lack self-worth and self-esteem.

In 1973, the report of the National Commission on Marijuana and Drug Abuse expressed their concerns regarding the ineffectiveness of national leadership in response to drug abuse:

"We are convinced that public policy, as presently designed, is premised on incorrect assumptions, is aimed at the wrong targets, and is too often unresponsive to human needs and aspirations." [16]

Today, in 1994, some 21 years later, this decry should be resounded. The leadership of this country must take advantage of the lessons learned and develop a fresh approach in dealing with drug abuse.

Recommend that we take the following actions:

(1) Teach young people meaningful coping skills. The teaching must be culturally significant and taught at pre-kindergarten level with home enforcement.

(2) Accept addiction as a chronic disease with remission and relapses. Place more emphasis on the demand side of the problem. We must never forget, as long as there is a demand, someone will supply these drugs whether legally or illegally.

(3) Develop training courses that focus on coaching and coping skills and less emphasis on substance abuse. This initiative can be developed by non-profit organizations. Training should be administered throughout the nation, at churches, schools, and youth centers.

(4) The government, national and community based organizations must take immediate actions to reduce the stressful conditions in the lives of Blacks and Hispanics.

(5) Organize the community and develop a detailed plan. Define community goals. Convey them to the people who live in the affected community. Hold community strategy sessions. Mobilize and then effect the plan.

(6) Revise education and prevention programs in order to focus on coping skills and self awareness and stop popularizing the drug with scare tactics. These programs should begin in pre-kindergarten and continue throughout college and even graduate school.

(7) The government should rethink its approach - be objective and seek real alternatives to the current approach enforced. The current approach didn't work 21 years ago. It is not working today, and it will not work 21 years from today.

(8) If drugs are not legalized, there must be an all-out war declared, targeting kingpins, suppliers and pushers, both nationally and internationally. Take economic sanctions against countries who are supplying illegal drugs to the country. Enforce the current laws and ensure that funding is allocated to fund the Drug-Free School and Community Act, amended by P.L. 100-690 and the Anti-Drug Abuse Act of 1988 (P.L. 100-690) to insure proper treatment and prevention program. Establish more well-staffed and funded detoxification and empowerment programs throughout all inner-city areas.

(9) Establish an **Anti-drug Abuse/Corruption Hot Line.** The number to this line should be as common knowledge as 911, yet not traceable. This action is needed to get the* public involved in the enforcement aspect of the law without reprisals taken against them by the violators. This line should be staffed by a special group in the Department of Justice. The primary purpose of this net should be to report the selling/buying or plans to sell/buy illicit drugs or irregularities of law enforcement personnel. The net should be so designed that the special staff could immediately refer the calls to any local agency in the country within seconds.

POINT 10 - REDUCING THE DEMAND FOR DRUGS

We can reduce the demand for drugs by operating programs to teach children coping skills at an earlier age. Establish programs to increase the sensitivity of the general public on assisting abusers instead of enabling the abusers. There is an immediate need for more drug treatment programs throughout affected communities. Moreover, emphasis must be placed on increasing opportunities for counseling youth and other individuals who affect the lives of at risk youth.

More importantly, we must work to remove the conditions that create these stresses that lead people to use drugs. Effecting the Power Pack will help us to remove many of these conditions.

POINT 11 - UNDERSTANDING THE GANG PROBLEM

Gang activities pose a great problem for America. The symptoms of the problem are crimes. Currently crimes committed by gang members are being addressed by law enforcement activities. Nevertheless, the general public fears gangs and innocent people are being killed. America can't afford to allow gangs to control the streets of our cities. The following is a short summation of the problem.

Children form gangs as surrogate families and use automatic weapons as a symbol of their deep feelings of helplessness and hopelessness. Behavior is an indicator of a child's emotions and self-esteem. Thus, the surface actions of drive-by shootings, selling drugs for profit with no regard for human life and living with no regard for consequence, indicate a deep-seated detachment from morals, value and caring. Moreover, this shows that these young people lack self-worth and self-esteem.

There are tens of thousands of gang members throughout the United States. Driven by profits from the sale of illegal drugs or stolen goods, a societal underclass has been created. Thus, thousands of American youth are killed every year in gang-related incidents.

In addition to even more disabling and life changing injuries, there are innocent by-standers, non-gang members, and children-victims of gang initiated violence. Concurrently, car jacking is on the rise, often involving gang members targeting non-gang members and community residents. A 1994 report stated that black males are more subject to car jacking than any other group.

Consequently, innocent people are physically and emotionally killed in this cross fire. Danger has become a way of life for the young, but has driven residents to arm themselves, live behind bars and view the children of the neighborhood as the "enemy".

The "US" and "THEM" mentality allows the problem to grow deeper and larger and the symptoms of distrust, isolation, fear and lack of communication continue to permeate ever-increasing areas of neighborhoods throughout the country.

The very adults that could provide the attention, care, training, love and support become the victim and enemy. Our youth who need the guidance, protection, direction and boundaries become the victim and the enemy. The schism will continue to grow unless bridges are developed to re-establish that very natural bond between the young and the old.

The roots of the problem must be identified and addressed in order to eradicate the gangs. The main root of gang violence is low self-esteem and the supporting roots are high unemployment, lack of skills, poverty, the opportunity to commit crimes, minimum wage of $4.25 an hour, unstable home environment, a spiritual void, lack of adequate education, lack of positive influences and role models, the drug abuse problems of others (Demand), opportunity to sell drugs (The Supply and Jobs), "gang phobia" (fear of gangs), and the perceived power of gangs.

This problem of low self-esteem has evolved into violent activities which are out of control. Past actions have primarily addressed only the symptoms of the problems; therefore, the roots are firmly planted in highly fertile soil.

Gang members receive the following benefits from their participating in gangs: (1) sense of pride (2) sense of belonging (3) a means of making money (4) a false sense of security (5) higher self-esteem than previously experienced, although based on a false sense of security. Nevertheless, due to the criminal conduct of gangs they pose a direct threat to America.

To resolve this problem, we must realize that we have the power to correct these conditions. We must use an approach to eradicate these roots and then replace them with vital alternatives. Containment is not the answer.

An effective plan of action requires the involvement of the entire community. At Point 78, you will find a program entitled: Operation Root Up Gangs (Operation RUG) - Recommend this program be implemented throughout the country.

POINT 12 - REDUCING GANG PHOBIA (FEAR OF GANGS)

Reduce Gang Phobia (Fear of Gangs). The public believes that they are powerless against gangs. This fear must be overcome. An education campaign must be waged to expose gangs for what they are by explaining their makeup. There must be increased activities to teach the public how to deal with gang members and how to provide alternatives to gang members. Training must also be made available to the public on how to assist in helping gang members become more effective members in our society. Information must be given to the general public on how to refrain from engaging in activities that reinforce the perceived power of gangs or cause gang members to harden their criminal behavior.

These actions can be implemented under Operation RUG at Point 78.

POINT 13 - IMPROVING BLACK MEN AND BLACK WOMEN RELATIONSHIPS

Improved relationships between black men and black women is a must. It is important that we address this area in order to secure the future for our youth. The by-products of these poor relations are indicative by this set of facts.

- In 1991, more than two-thirds of all African American children living in female-headed households were poor, at a poverty rate 20 percentage points higher than the rate for white children in similar households.

- The birth rate among never married teenagers for African Americans are more than four times as likely as their counterparts to bear one or more children.

- Currently, only 34 percent of poor African American women who qualify for child support have a child support award. Of those child support awards only 50 percent receive partial payment or no payment at all.

As discussed earlier, black males and females are going through a lot of stresses, in which they have not learned how to effectively deal with. Coaching black young males is very important. Moreover, it is also important that the black males and black females know the nature of the connecting problems we must address.

The nature and severity of this problem must be given utmost priority. As we work to resolve the problem of the poor relationship of the black male and black female, it is important for us to realize that this complex problem is only one of the symptoms of a greater problem. Yet, this symptom is one of the most deadly conditions the African American males and African American females are facing. For if you can destroy the black male and black female relationship, eventually, you will destroy the race. Therefore, much attention must be placed on understanding and addressing the bigger problem because if we fail to address the bigger problem, we can't improve the male/female relations.

Before we discuss the bigger problem, let's look at some other symptoms. The problems of domestic violence, substance abuse, failing to pay child support payments, and crime are all symptoms of a bigger problem. The bigger problem must be addressed by eliminating conditions such as discrimination, high unemployment, lack of education and skills, and low self esteem.

During slavery, the black man was treated as if he was 3/5 of a white man. Today, on the average, he is paid as if he is 3/5 of a white man. This is a root problem. This is the bigger problem and it is kept alive by prejudice, discrimination, fear and apathy. This bigger problem allows low self esteem to become common place, consequently, the conditions of high unemployment, lack of education and the lack of skills are the by-products. We must work to end prejudice and discrimination, now.

We must not be afraid. The hanging ropes and the whips are put aside. Just because it appears that "you got yours" and your are enjoying life, don't think that this is a sound reason for apathy. The middle and upper classes must realize that this is also their problem. As the late Dr. Martin Luther King, Jr. said: "It is disappointment with the Negro middle class that has sailed or struggled out of the muddy ponds into the relatively fresh-flowing waters of the mainstream, and in the process has forgotten the stench of the backwaters where their brothers are still drowning." [17] We must never forget that the struggle for many still exists and we must be willing to help the less fortunate.

Due to the lack of concern for the less fortunate, today the tradition Black nuclear family is an endangered species. Now we must let America know that an African American man is not 3/5 of the white man.

If black males were paid at parity with the white males, could they buy more for their wife or "woman" (girlfriend)? Could they do more for their children? Would there be less divorces? Would there be less substance abuse? Would there be less crime? Would this help improve the black male/female relationships?

Frankly, I didn't know how I was going to approach this subject, but God knew and it was revealed to me. This problem of the male/female relations has caused a lot of pain and suffering, and destroyed a lot of lives. The hurts must be removed and the suffering must end. When this occurs, we can forgive and the healing process will commence.

Now I ask you to turn your attention to the Lord and ask the Lord for the answers to increase your understanding, and direct your involvement as you work to improve the black male/black female relationships. For it is recorded: "My thoughts," says the Lord, "are not like yours, and my ways are different from yours. As high as the heavens are above the earth, so high are my ways and thoughts above yours." [18]

We must combine our intellects. Share ideas and solutions on how we can improve the black male and black female relations. This should be done through forums, at churches, community centers and radio and television talk shows throughout the nation.

The current trend of television shows is to amuse by showing bad relationships. We must set a new tone and change the focus from putting each other down to building each other up. We must work for answers. If we seek solutions, we will discover them. We have produced plays in the past that addressed certain problems; plays also can be produced to help address this area. Recommend that this area be given top priority for playwriters and movie producers. We must use every means to turn this around.

Improving the Black men and Black women relationships will not be an easy task. However, if we fail to invest time in this now, tomorrow, the problem will be even greater and much more difficult to correct. It is predicted that by the year 2000, the proportion of African American children living with both parents will decline to 24 percent. If this should occur, we will face an even greater problem because this threatens our survival as African Americans here in the United States. We must remember that the family structure is key to our survival.

POINT 14 - EMPOWERING BLACK MEN

We must empower our young Black men by sharing success stories, being mentors, teaching and demonstrating. This requires a strong commitment from our elderly population as well as business owners, professionals and blue collar workers.

Today we have thousands of underdeveloped black men who are victims of an unjust system. Many didn't have positive male role models in their lives and received their formal education in the streets or in prisons. Dr. Frances Cress Welsing, the author of "The Isis Papers" made some interesting observations that we must consider here:

> "As Black males and females become more and more alienated, as our current rate of separation and divorce indicate, and as Black females being left to rear Black male children alone, the alienation, hate and disgust felt toward adult males are visited upon their son subtly. A female alienated from males is hard-pressed to reinforce patterns of conduct in male child that remind her of unhappiness and pain. She is more inclined to say, "There you go looking and acting like that no good nigger father of yours." The Black female teacher at school who also may be experiencing alienation from her Black man, if not inclined to make the same statement in such a direct manner, only says it more subtly, says nothing, or simply acts out her hate, disgust and distrust of Black males, achieving the same result." [19]

Dr. Welsing further states:

> "The dearth of adult Black males in the home, schools and neighborhoods leaves Black male children no alternative models. Blindly they seek out one another as models, and in their blindness end up in trouble - in juvenile homes or prisons. But fate and the dynamics of racism again play a vicious trick because the young males only become more alienated from their manhood and more feminized in such settings. They are given orders by men to whom they must submit; they wait passively to be fed three meals a day by men; and finally, they have sexual intercourse with men. It is no wonder that they are unable to play the role of Black men when they leave.

One ex-prisoner patient told me, "It is easier to endure the life on the inside than to try to put up with the pressures of being a man, a husband and a father in the street." The intent of racist programming had been achieved: "Give up trying to be a Black man. Why not be a woman?"

Many Black males have answered unconsciously, "Why not!" The braided and curled hair, the earrings and bracelets, the midriff tops, the cinch waisted pants, the flowered underwear, the high-heeled shoes with platforms and the pocketbooks are all behavioral answers to the above..." [20]

It is incumbent on us to assist our brothers so that they can become strong men and live more productive lives in this twenty-first century. In the gangs in the street and in prisons, we have some brilliant minds that are yielding for an opportunity. Many just want a chance to live a life from behind those prison's walls. A chance to be free from a life of crime. We must ensure that as many who are willing to change are given the opportunity to do so.

Empowering of black men also calls for educating black women on the real problems confronting the black men. In some circles, I have heard reports of black females saying: "A black man can't do nothing for me" or "I don't need a black man." Well, I understand how a black female could make comments like that, especially if she has a good paying job, never had a positive black male role model in her life, and if the black men she has encountered are being paid only 3/5 of what a white man is being paid.

If economics is their motive-why should they settle for 3/5? However, with this enlightenment, hopefully, the few women with this disposition, will realize that when black men are threatened, black women and their children are also threatened. Consequently, the black people as a whole are at risk.

Of course "abandonment" is an option. It's just another stress factor added to the many problems that confront black men. As mentioned earlier, the suicide rate for Black males peaks between the ages of 25 and 34 - "years when most people are building careers," and beginning independent adult life. For some, abandonment by the Black women may help to push them over the edge.

Abandonment, as used in this text is not merely interracial dating or marriage. It goes far beyond that. It is when the black female becomes so filled with illusions that she deserts, or forsakes the black man to the point that marriage, or dating does not become an option for her with a black man. When this occurs, the disposition held by the black female is openly expressed and its passed on to her off-springs and shared with her associates.

Understanding and supports are other options. These are the type of options that were taken by great black women in the past. These great Black women gave black men the type of strength they used to break the physical chains of slavery. Now, continued support will enable Black men to remove the psychological chains of slavery.

When we empower our young Black men this will also help to improve relationships between our Black men and Black women. Furthermore, it will help instill the sense of responsibility that is needed to father thousands of black babies. Black men are protectors and developers of Black people. It is best they learn that during the rearing process. Today, however, the positive Black male role models have a complex job. They must become role models to other Black males and role models to other black males' children.

POINT 15 - DEVELOPING PRE-MARRIAGE COUNSELING AND MARRIAGE LIFE SKILLS TRAINING

We must implement pre-marriage counseling and marriage life skills training programs that are designed to enhance understanding and communication. Collected data suggests that there is a need for building male/females relations among African Americans. Here is an example of the data studied.

- African American females are less likely than white female to be married

African American		White Americans	
Male	Female	Male	Female
Never married			
44.8%	38.7%	28%	20.8%
Married			
43.1%	38.4%	62.4%	59.0%
Widowed			
3.3%	11.9%	2.5%	11.2%
Divorced			
8.8%	11.0%	7.1%	8.9%

This data must be fully understood and its implications. This data suggests that the Black race as a people is endangered. We must work to stabilize the union of Black male and Black female relations. For this to occur there must be an increased understanding of what's going in from a larger perspective.

In the book entitled: "The Isis Papers", Dr. Welsing provides some interesting insight into the problem. Dr. Welsing states:

"Until now, we have attempted to function as united Black males and females with no knowledge of exactly how the white supremacy dynamic must drive the Black male and the Black female apart. Therefore, we have failed in the past and we continue to fail in this relationship. If we understood white supremacy, the number one priority for each Black male and Black female would not be to reach out for one another with designs of dependency, love, lust or marriage. Instead, we would seek to master specific patterns of perception, logic, thought, speech, action and emotional response that would counter the white supremacy dynamic scientifically. We would codify such behaviors and practice them day and night. We would become single-minded in our activity, knowing that unless global and local white supremacy is attacked continuously and effectively, the Black male/Black female relationship has no chance of surviving." [21]

I've talked to a number of people about "The Isis Papers". Some have never read the book and most of the ones who indicated that they read the book had not read beyond the first one hundred pages. The perspectives shared by Dr. Welsing should not be taken lightly, however, Black America should integrate this knowledge into their scene of understanding. Some of the information she shared is key to the survival of the black race.

Recommend that churches adopt policies of pre-marriage counseling prior to performing marriage. In addition, recommend that the subject of marriage become part of life skills training integrated into our high school curriculum.

POINT 16 - IMPROVING THE FAMILY UNIT THROUGH THE CHURCHES, VIDEOS, AND MOVIES

The state of the Black family in America calls for special attention. It is predicted by the year 2000, only 24 % of black children will be living in a two parent household. Action must be taken now to confront this problem directly. Every media must be used to address this crisis to include the church, radio and television talk shows and the production of videos and movies. There should be an educational campaign waged to preserve and restore the black family unit.

This should become a special interest item for churches and non-profit community-based organizations and educational television. The focus should be to develop products that are designed to strengthen the family unit and to keep well families, well.

At churches throughout the year much attention should be given to this area. It should not be done from a one Sunday sermon approach, the problem is just too severe. Some churches may opt to focus on it for a week, month, or a year, or maybe until the year 2000. Nevertheless, it should become part of the Church's agenda.

To reach as many families as possible, we must be very creative and develop videos and movies and plays to this end. Writers and producers must act now and produce products that have commercial value and also educational.

We must recognize that the breakdown in the family unit is directly related with a number of other conditions that have been addressed by several other points. We must work together and evoke a higher level of thinking throughout the land centered on empowering our people, bringing them together like never before in the history of this country. We must save our children and the future of Black America.

POINT 17 - DEVELOPING A COMPREHENSIVE DOMESTIC VIOLENCE PREVENTION/INTERVENTION PROGRAM

Families under stress, without support systems and isolated are subject to experience considerably more domestic violence. There is evidence that domestic violence may be even more of a problem amongst African Americans than any other groups in the United States. In 1980, Straus and others found that black husbands were four times more likely than white husbands to have assaulted their wives and that black women were twice as likely to have assaulted their husbands. Nevertheless, according to Block, black husbands are more likely than black women, or white men or women to be killed by a spouse, acting in self-defense, according to Okun.

According to Block, a review of homicide trends from 1965 to 1981 found that blacks, in comparison to Hispanic and whites, were more likely to be killed in the home with a handgun during a verbal argument. While most individuals have guns in their home to protect their families from intruders, nevertheless the weapon is more than 40 times more likely to be used to shoot a family member instead of an intruder.

Findings also support that sometimes stress may manifest itself as child abuse to include the murdering of young children or elderly parents. In fact, this is the second-leading cause of death for black kids ages one to four. Often it starts as physical abuse, elderly abuse and/or domestic violence.

Research on husbands known to be abusers of their wives has revealed that these men tend to be underachievers-less intelligent, less successful in their jobs or school, or lower in certain status characteristics-when compared with their wives. A common pattern is for the husband's occupational status to be lower than that of his father-in-law.[22] It is believed that the inability to be superior to one's wife in a male-oriented society apparently induces a tendency to prove one's superiority over her physical ways.

Various studies have found 40 to 95 percent of abuse cases involved situations in which the husband had a drinking problem. There may be a number of other factors that contribute to this abuse to include work, financial difficulties, sexual dysfunction, jealousy, and other activities.[23]

Other findings indicate: husbands who batter their wives most often come from homes where they were beaten by their parents or had observed their own fathers beating their mothers.

Another concern of domestic violence is child abuse. Data from a number of studies indicate that child abuse is more likely to occur in families of low socioeconomic status. Unemployment leads to poverty, low self-esteem from being a "failure' in a success-oriented society and depression. Other social factors apparently related to increased stress are job dissatisfaction, marital conflicts, large family size, crowded and substandard housing, single-parent families, and isolation (membership in few organizations, lack of a telephone, and great distance from the extended family).

America, America, how long can we allow this to go on?

It is our duty as Americans to correct these conditions that foster this high level of stress. It is also our responsibility to help individuals who are experiencing stress to cope with these stresses. Churches and community-based organizations must take the lead in addressing this problem. Stress management training centers should be as common as barber shops throughout the black community. The establishment of these centers could also have a significant impact of reducing substance abuse as well as domestic violence. There must be other support systems for the families. Services should include drop-in day care programs, elderly respite-care programs, parenting classes and family counseling and therapy. These programs should be funded by the federal, state, and local governments and private foundations.

The staff of the programs must be qualified and paid commensurate with the services provided. Volunteers are needed to help run these programs, however, volunteers must not be the primary workforce. These programs must be presented in a positive sense, like programs designed to keep "well families, well". Emphasis must be placed on prevention and not waiting until a family gets into trouble. Pastors and community leaders must take the lead by attending these programs themselves to help promote these programs in the most positive light.

It will take time to correct all of these conditions that create stress in the black communities, however, as we work on these conditions that create these stresses, we must bring about effective programs to show our black sisters and brothers that killing one another is not the way. We must increase our awareness of what's going on around us and become involved.

POINT 18 - REDUCING THE RATE OF DIVORCE THROUGH COMMUNICATION

A number of factors affect the rate of divorce. It is believed that money problems are at the top of the list. However, there are other problems that create marital conflicts, such as children, in-laws, religious differences, sex, and the low earning of husbands. Sometimes a better economic situation of women may also lead couples to divorce.

When young people are able to find jobs they are more optimistic about their ability to support a family. This fact explains why the rate of black males who never married is at 44% and white males who never married is at 28%. Consequently, this also helps to explain why 62% of white males are married and only 43% of black males are married. We must work very diligently to resolve the economic problem. However there is another problem that we must address.

Some of the reasons cited, a couple may not be able to change them on their own. However, what compounds these problems is lack of effective communication. This lack of effective communication is one of the factors that helps contribute to many of these divorces. Common phrases that are often used are: (1) I can't talk to that woman (2) He doesn't listen (3) He thinks he knows everything and (4) She doesn't understand.

The following example is a true story that clearly shows the impact of ineffective communication:

I can recall a situation when a young married couple were engaged in an argument. The wife started yelling at her husband while he had his back turned as he folded clothes. The husband was trying to terminate the argument by ignoring his wife. The wife was also preparing spaghetti and she continued to argue; occasionally the husband would make a comment in a rather calm manner. However, the husband had no eye contact with his wife. The wife became so upset, she threw the boiling spaghetti water on her husband's back.

The husband was hospitalized for about thirty days and a divorce followed shortly thereafter. There were three boys who were also impacted as a result of this failure to communicate. There are countless stories like this one. Nevertheless, on a whole, we have not really addressed this problem centered around ineffective communication in our homes or in our interpersonal relationships.

Effective communication is critical in a marriage. Though, communication alone will not solve all problems; it is required to resolve any problem. If problems are discussed, they can be understood. This understanding can lead to a resolution.

One of the basic problems that confronts us today is the fact that we have not been taught how to communicate effectively. Therefore, we allow problems to build until they become crisis and then we attempt to address them. Sometimes, we take communication for granted and think we don't need training. This is a serious mistake. There is a direct relationship with how effective we communicate with our spouses and the stability of our marriages. Immediate action must be taken to improve our communication skills. This must become a special interest item for churches and social service organizations. Instead of approaching this concern from a crisis perspective, after abuse has occurred, a more proactive approach must be taken. This proactive approach should be designed to improve relationships and to help keep "well families well." As we address the economic factor, we also must give attention to improving our communication.

Training in effective communication should not be limited to married couples, it should also be given to their children. Sociologists believe parent-child conflict cannot be avoided in a society that is undergoing rapid change. Nevertheless, effective interpersonal communication will help improve these relationships and help facilitate the change process.

Training should be conducted at churches and community centers. These programs should be funded by the federal, state and local governments and private foundations. Moreover, interpersonal communication should also be a life skill subject taught to youth throughout the public school system, community centers and youth centers throughout the nation.

POINT 19 - REDUCING HEALTH PROBLEMS THROUGH EDUCATION AND TREATMENT

Poverty, racial bias, ignorance and a lack of access to quality health compound the health issues for African Americans. Today, statistics show a persistent negative disparity between the health status of blacks and other minorities and that of the population as a whole.

In general, African Americans' rate of death is one and one-half times that of white, and black life expectancy is declining - from 69.7 years in 1984 to 69.4 years in 1986. However, during the same period the entire population remained constant at 75 years.

The Journal of the American Medical Association reports the following:

- Twenty-eight percent of adult blacks suffer from hypertension, compared with 17 percent of adult whites.

- Severe hypertension is five times more common in blacks.

- Black have a stroke morality rate 65 percent higher than whites.

A study of cancer rates shows over a thirty year period, black male cancer deaths rose by 77 percent compared to 10 percent increase in black females. Nevertheless, the overall cancer incidence rate for blacks went up 27 percent, while for white it increased 12 percent.

Many of the factors that are suspected to be contributing to the excessive cancer rate in blacks are controllable. Here is a summary of these factors: cigarette or smokeless tobacco use; tobacco combined with heavy alcohol use; exposure to occupational hazard; poor nutrition; more limited access to medical resources; less patient knowledge about diagnosis, treatment, and prevention; and greater vulnerability to histologically aggressive tumors.

In addition to cancer and hypertension, we find the rate of other health conditions considerably higher in blacks than whites. Some of these conditions include:

- **Infant mortality.** In 1986, the infant mortality rate for whites was 8.9, for nonwhites overall 15.7 and for blacks 18.0 (twice the rate of whites).

- **Chemical Dependency.** In the "State of Black America," 1990, an article entitled "A Common Destiny" by Beny Primm sums it up as follows:

"The true dimensions of drug use for blacks may be under reported. This hypothesis is supported by a 1979 survey that found mortality from drug-related deaths increased steeply in nine major metropolitan areas, and about one-third of those fatalities occurred among black youth in the 15 to 24 age group (National Institute on Drug Abuse, 1990). Currently, cocaine and its potent derivative "crack" show increased use among all youth. In 1986, the first national data report of high school seniors found that 4.1 percent had used crack in the past year, and 17 percent had tried cocaine (Johnston et al, 1987). By any measure, drug problems have greatly increased over the past 40 years, and although that increase may now have slowed, a majority of adolescent blacks and whites have experimented with illicit drugs. The drug problem is potentially far more serious now because of the AIDS risk associated with the sharing of needles or "drug works." Although heroin use is minimal among adolescents, there is an increasing trend toward intravenous injection of cocaine. Cocaine injection poses a higher risk of HIV infection because cocaine's effects are of short duration, and so user inject far more frequently than do heroin users." [24]

- **Injuries.** Blacks make up 12 percent of the U. S. population, however in 1984 they accounted for 15.3 percent of all death due to injury.

- **Homicides.** In 1984, the homicide rate for black was 29.0 percent per 100,000 - over five times higher than the rate for whites.

- **Diabetes Mellitus.** The rate of diagnosed diabetes are 50 percent higher in black males, and 100 percent higher in black females, compared with their white counterparts.

- **Sickle Cell Anemia.** About 50,000 people in the United States are affected by Sickle Cell Anemia. There is a need to continue national support for research efforts to attain a definitive cure for this serious, painful and disabling illness.

- **Glaucoma.** The prevalence of blindness from glaucoma in the U. S. black population is 7:1 to the white population and 15:1 for the age group aged 45 to 64 years.

- **Kidney Disease.** Blacks with untreated hypertension has a kidney failure rate 17 times that in whites. Research also disclosed that 50 to 70 percent of all dialysis patients listed with the Southeastern Organ

Procurement Foundation were black, yet fewer than 10 percent of the organ donors in that group were black. Calendar review the reasons for black not wanting to donate organs to be as follows: (a) lack of awareness about transplantation; (b) religious myths and perceptions (superstitions); (c) distrust of the medical community; (d) fear of premature death; (e) racism; and (f) lack of trust and confidence among physicians, hospital and black organ and tissues donors.

In the Urban League Annual "State of Black America" for 1990, LaSalle D. Leffall, Jr. M.D. has an article entitled: Health Status of Black Americans. Below is a summation of his recommendations:

- Inform the black population of the special health problems and measures to improve their health by developing educational programs

- Ask for funding through local, state, and federal governments for health care systems for the socioeconomically disadvantaged to eliminate obstacles to access for this group.

- Emphasize prevention of disease and healthy lifestyle as a major health strategy.

- Develop cost-effective screening programs for common cancers and hypertension

- Develop special programs emphasizing the critical problems of drug abuse and AIDS in the black community and offer counseling and treatment.

- Identify intervention techniques (medical and psychosocial) for drug abuse victims.

- Develop clinic programs for newborns to detect sickle cell disease and to detect drug withdrawal symptoms and to provide long-term management for them.

- Develop programs to ensure adequate prenatal care and counseling, thus, decreasing the incidence of low birth weight and infant morality.

These recommendations from Dr. Leffall are sound. We must commence an educational campaign to address these medical conditions that are reducing our life span. The poverty factor, we must work on it together. However, some of these factors become our direct responsibility to change and control i.e. lifestyle, eating habits, and exercising.

I will never forget a turning point in my life, about 12 years ago when I was over weight and suffering from hypertension. My doctor spent about 30 minutes with me discussing my health. I remember him asking me a series of questions about my family medical history.

He asked. "Is there anyone else in your family with hypertension?" I responded? "Yes, my father has hypertension." My doctor asked another question. "Anyone else?" I replied: "My mother has hypertension." And then he asked me his final question? "Anyone else?" I answered: "My brother could not enlist in the military because he had hypertension!"

At that point, my doctor broke it down to me and explained the condition itself is not hereditary, but, habits are passed down. He further explained how the use of salt was working against me. He stated: "Salt helps you to retain your body fluids and it also hardens your arteries." That was truly a turning point for me and I have not added salt to my food since that encounter. Today, I don't have hypertension. On a side note, my mother died at 65 from a stroke; my father died at 65 due to kidney failure and my brother is still alive today at 48. However, he has had an unsuccessful kidney transplant.

African Americans, we must get busy and experience some turning points in our lives and turn these health factors around through education and a change in habits. To help evoke these turning points, we must turn our attention to community based organizations and churches. Recommend we develop plans to create a more healthier Black America by using the resources we have and solicit grants from insurance companies and foundations to fund real solutions. The plan should include nutritional/dieting education and physical activities that African Americans enjoy, such as sports, running clubs, dancing clubs, walking clubs, bike riding clubs, swimming clubs, hiking clubs, bowling leagues, etc.

Medical doctors, this is your calling. Prevention is the key to good health. Entrepreneurs, you must make it fashionable, trendy, i.e. his and her running suits, and other fashionable garments. Some entrepreneurs will start health clubs to make money as they ensure people in their community exercise at least two hours a week. (According to a recent study two hours a week of exercising helps reduce the risk of heart attacks). Physical fitness counselors, dance teachers and health food store owners, this is your market. Make it come alive and save people in the process.

These initiatives must be given enthusiastic support from the on-set. It will require education and the involvement of the entire African American community. The recording industry could play an important part in promoting this movement.

Hopefully, these thoughts have planted seeds that will grow into a national effort. Remember, you have the power to initiate this action.

As you read this message or listen to this message on tape, you will know what you must do.

POINT 20 - REDUCING THE RATE OF AIDS

The following data clearly shows why an extensive education campaign is needed on reducing the rate of AIDS for Black America.

- African Americans were 3.2 times more likely than whites to die from HIV infections in 1991.

- African American females were 8.1 times more likely to fall victim to the ravages of the AIDS virus in 1991. The most recent data indicates in 1992, African Americans Females were 10 times more likely to fall victim.

- In 1989 African Americans males' death rate from HIV infection was over four time the national average.

Recommend that this education be accomplished through every possible media. The movie industry should play a major role in educating the community. Writers must take on this responsibility to produce products with commercial value and educational. Recommend that the focus includes the epidemic of AIDS in Africa and the spread of AIDS in America. The impact of AIDS in the black community must be clearly conveyed. Black America can't depend on any other segment of America's population to convey this message. Suggest the products show some of the most beautiful African American women with AIDS. These movies can be used as a shock effect to clearly convey the severity of this epidemic.

POINT 21 - CONDUCTING STRESS MANAGEMENT CLASSES

Living in Black America is very stressful. These stress factors are numerous and include: high unemployment, job dissatisfaction, marital conflict, large family size, crowded and substandard housing, single-parent families and the list goes on. Unfortunately, the stresses Black Americans face are long-term, which is very devastating. It is not like bouncing back after a hard day at work. Most of us are able to deal with that. Far too many African Americans are faced with these conditions day after day. Under long-term stress, our personalities may seem to change. We may suffer from depression and feel hopeless and helpless (substance abuse). Occasionally we may feel tense and explosive; this level of frustration sometimes lead to spouse abuse and child abuse.

Sometimes we find ourselves compulsively repeating meaningless tasks in an attempt to control our lives. At times we act impulsively without thinking about the consequences (robberies, murders and assaults). At other times, we have exaggerated fears of such simple acts as leaving our house (afraid of gangs - placing iron bars on our doors and windows), and fear of walking the streets.

There has been much study on how to manage these stresses. However, African Americans have not been afforded real opportunities to take advantage of this training. Today, this training is needed to help cope with these realities of living in Black America.

Recommend training centers be established throughout America. These centers should be well staffed and funded by the federal government, state, and local government and foundations. These centers should be designed to help individuals receive maximum well-being and to enjoy a richer and more rewarding lifestyle as they work to change their current conditions.

POINT 22 - RESTORING A SENSE OF PRIDE AND CONCERN

"Say it Loud, I'm Black and I'm Proud" was the cry of the 1960's. Today, this sense of pride is not common place. Today, there is a need to enhance a strong ethnic identity. It is believed that this sense of identity could decrease the destructive black on black violence and other destructive acts that blacks commit upon one another.

Recommend African American professional and business people sponsor events, and programs geared to helping the least fortunate and the ones that are most subject to violence acts. In addition, recommend the churches become more actively involved in the community where its church services is held. Often, churches are located in communities, but, the memberships have very little interaction with the people who live in the surrounding community. The Church must become the heartbeat of the community. Therefore, there must be more interaction with the people who live in the community.

Like James Brown had an impact promoting racial pride in the 1960's with his recording "Say It Loud, I'm Black and I'm Proud", rappers today could play an important part in enhancing racial identity. Today, there is a real need for a movement of this type.

There are a number of programs designed to regain the sense of pride. However, there is not a united effort. Before there can be a united front, there must be a renewed sense of hope, a sense that we are on the move, and a spirit of working together to that end. It is important that African Americans as a whole experience the sensation of a sense of pride. For this to occur, it must be addressed at every level. A plan must be designed to involve the nation as a whole.

An unorganized approach will not have the same impact as a unified effort. Though individual action will be critical to the overall effectiveness of increasing this sense of pride.

Here is an example of an individual act: The president of a black hair care company in Chicago established the "Black-on-Black Love Campaign," which was designed to create love, discipline, and respect. The campaign consisted of adopting a building in a public housing development and investing in a library, computer lab, ceramics shop, and an outdoor mural exhibiting black pride. According to Griffith and Bell, since this program has been in place, there has been decreased gang activity, fewer fights, and less graffiti on the walls of this building. This success occurred in the midst of the police district with the highest homicide rate in the city of Chicago.

In Los Angeles, in the heart of Watts, a gang truce was organized in 1992 shortly after the Los Angeles riot. Black pride and respect for one another are at the center of this movement. There has been very little money to help these black brothers and sisters keep this truce going, however, it is stilling holding. These young people have discovered that they are not one another enemies and are now working together for solutions. Nevertheless, with a unified effort, the City of Los Angeles would be firmly supporting this effort by providing these African Americans with all the resources that are needed to bring this dream to fruition.

Recommend that the recording industry, NAACP, SCLC, CORE, the Urban League, the National Rainbow Coalition, and community based organizations join forces and organize and effect a campaign to help enhance black pride throughout America. Under any campaign, there will be many slogans. Remember, it's okay to have slogans, however, the campaign must be based on solutions for a brighter tomorrow. We who are faithful, must let our light shine and let it radiate our pride and love for each other. We must ask God to help us all along the way. Since we are fighting to counter a psychological warfare that is being waged upon us, we must be psychologically prepared. I believe that the best way to be psychologically prepared is to be spiritually prepared.

Let's remember the Word as it is recorded in Ephesians, Chapter 6:11 -18.

"Put on all the armor that God gives you, so that you will be able to stand up against the Devil's evil tricks. For we are not fighting against human beings but against the wicked spiritual forces in the heavenly world, the rulers, authorities, and cosmic powers of this dark age. So put on God's armor now! Then when the evil day comes, you will be able to resist the enemy's attacks; and after fighting end, you will still hold your ground.

So stand ready, with truth as a belt tight around your waist, with righteousness as your breastplate, and as your shoes the readiness to announce the Good News of peace. At all times carry faith as a shield; for with it you will be able to put out all the burning arrows shot by the Evil One. And accept salvation as a helmet, and the work of God as the sword which the Spirits give you. Do all this in prayer, asking for God's help. Pray on every occasion, as the Spirit leads. For this reason keep alert and never give up; pray always for all God's people."[25]

Let's meditate on these thoughts. Make a commitment now to use your talents and resources to make a difference. Walk with the sense of pride; the pride of being a child of God, realizing that if God is for you, who could be against you. Let's inspire others by our actions and our deeds. So "Say it Loud, I'm Black and I'm Proud, Say it Loud, I'm African American and I'm proud. Say it Loud, **I'm somebody**, yes, I'm somebody, a child of **God**.

POINT 23 - MAINTAINING A SENSE OF PRIDE

It is unfortunate that most Americans believe that the poor are poor because they have a deviant system of values that encourages behaviors leading to poverty. It is also sad that some people have the disposition of the view expressed by Edward Banfield, a distinguished professor of urban government at Harvard and chairperson of President Nixon's task force on model cities. His view is as follows:

"The lower-class individual lives from moment to moment. If he has any awareness of a future, it is of something, fixed, fated, beyond his control: things happen to him, he does not make them happen. Impulse governs his behavior, either because he cannot discipline himself to sacrifice a present for a future satisfaction or because he has no sense of the future. He is therefore radically improvident: whatever he cannot consume immediately he considers valueless. His bodily needs (especially for sex) and his taste for "action" take precedence over everything else - and certainly over any work routine. He works only as he must to stay alive, and drifts from one unskilled job to another, taking no interest in his work." [26]

I don't agree with this view expressed by Banfield. However, over the course of my lifetime, I have met a number of poor people with a sense of pride. However, I have only met a few individuals who had lost their sense of pride. These individuals fit the stereotype that casted above.

America must learn that we can't continue to stereotype a class of people and blame the poor for being poor. For this learning to take place we must speak out because speech is a God's gift. We must realize that through words we reveal what we are. When we have something to say - Do we have the right to remain silent? Speaking out is a serious matter, and we must weigh our words in the sight of God.

When can you speak out? There are many opportunities to speak out especially on radio talk shows. However, to be effective you must be well informed on the issue being addressed. Reading a book like this will help prepare you in having a greater impact. Take advantage of every opportunity to speak out when there is an effort to attack African Americans. However, you should be prepared, well informed and maintain your sense of pride.

POINT 24 - LEARNING FROM THE ELDERLY

We can learn much more from the elderly. African American's roots teach us that we must respect our elders and hold them in high esteem. The approach in America toward the elderly is sort of a "put out in a pasture's approach" (senior citizen homes and other institutions.) Senior citizen homes are not necessarily bad for seniors. However, when we fail to interact with them, this poses the real problem. This is not the best way to allow the elderly to use their talents to help address the concerns of today. Let's give them their rites of passage - this will enable them to see a new and distinct stage of life while helping us tackle the many problems that are facing us.

Recommend community-based organizations effect programs that gain the elderly populations involvement. First, discover from the elderly how they would like to assist. This group has unlimited resources and time.

Some of the tasks may include working with young people, volunteering, and as counselors, tutors, storytellers, mentors, financial counselors, management consultants, or just being friends.

POINT 25 - REDUCING THE NUMBER OF UNSTABLE HOMES

Reducing the number of unstable homes is essential to addressing the problem of our youth in Black America. First, let's give clarity to what is an unstable home. In this text we are referring to homes that experience any of these types of problems: (1) Families living in poverty, (2) Families experiencing the aftermath of divorce (3) Single-Parent Families with a limited outside support system (4) Families where there is domestic violence (5) Families where there is substance abuse problems (6) Families with money problems (7) Families where parents lacks parenting skills that are essential to raising children. There are a number of factors impacting on each of these families, however, there must be an effort to help identify needs and provide services to that end.

In many unstable homes a common factor is a problem of not having enough money. Action must be taken to change the level of employment, income, and family support services. Full employment would help stabilize many of these families that are in trouble. When there is trouble in the home no one has to tell the children. Their daily experiences show an African American, Hispanic, Native American, a Poor White American child that the adults with whom he or she lives, are having trouble, and no matter how capable, have difficulty in gaining education and work. What can he/she conclude about his/her own future. Children of unstable families develop concepts about their own future and ask questions. Why should I study hard in school - my mother is on welfare - my father can't find a job - what's the use in me trying?

Throughout the Power Pack, there are a number of Points that address conditions designed to help make families become more stable. Nevertheless, this must be addressed as a main point because the family is the chief agent of socialization in our society. In the family, children acquire much of the knowledge they need to play adult roles. Today, the undeveloped youth are products of unstable families. Moreover, the unstable families are products of our society.

Therefore, to resolve these problems that are confronting our youth we must stabilize the families. Regardless of whether the families are (1) One career families (2) dual-career families or (3) Single-parent families, they all have their own set of problems. Nevertheless, our responsibility is to ensure that these families needs are continuously assessed and every opportunity is made available to help these families become stable. There must be increased opportunities to assist these troubled families, through workshops, training programs and printed information.

POINT 26 - SHOWING OUR YOUNG PEOPLE THAT WE CAN GET ALONG

We must educate our young people and show them how to get along. Aggressive action must be taken to improve relations of young people - this could be enhanced by first improving the relationship between parents. More community functions are musts and parents, neighbors and community leaders must create more interaction among themselves and among the youth in the community.

Parents must not engage in "small destructive talk" about other members in the community, especially in the presence of their children or other young people. We must create a new resolve to work together and recognize that our young people are looking to us for leadership and direction.

Welsing suggests by the age of six-years old, all Black children should be taught the following in Black self-respect by Black adults examples in the home, school, church and neighborhood:

1. Stop name-calling one another.
2. Stop cursing at one another.
3. Stop squabbling with one another.
4. Stop gossiping about one another.
5. Stop snitching on one another.
6. Stop being discourteous and disrespectful towards one another.
7. Stop robbing one another.
8. Stop stealing from one another.
9. Stop fighting one another.
10. Stop killing one another.
11. Stop using and selling drugs to one another.
12. Stop throwing trash and dirt on the streets and in places where Black people live, work, and learn. [27]

These are more than just good thoughts. This is a sound behavioral foundation. You realize this should occur. But who's going to initiate it, because you don't have the time. We don't have time before a crisis. However, after a crisis, we have time. This is a common way of thinking; it is the most costly. I have planted seeds throughout this book. This is one of them. Hopefully, this one will produce a fine harvest for you.

Let's re-enact community and show our young people that we can get along. What we do will show them how they should and can get along.

POINT 27 - REDIRECTING OUR TALENTS FROM SELF-CENTERED TO CONCERN FOR ONE ANOTHER

"It often seems futile to try to change a system, or even to bring people together to talk about the need for change, but this kind of involvement is essential to the life of any system. The people who stand out in every profession are those who use their knowledge and experience to shape their working environment on both a small and a large scale. They teach and share and encourage others to do the same; they work to enrich themselves, their professions, and their communities. They seek out opportunities to participate, to give to themselves and develop relationships with others, and they are successful because they are involved in an active and ongoing exchange with their world." [28]

Adele Scheele, Ph.D.

America needs your help today as we move into the 21st Century. We have made a number of accomplishments. However, there is a lot of work to do, especially in the areas of social and economic justice. Nevertheless, America is a nation that is composed of professionals, like yourself, who are talented and willing to help in any way to make this world a better place to live.

There are a number of people in America that are less fortunate than you and they need your help now. By helping them now, you will also be securing the future of America for yourself and your loved ones for many years to come.

During my research, while preparing to write this book, I was able to take a good look at America, and its strengths, which are many, and its problems. Today, we are fortunate that America's strengths out weigh its problems and America's strengths can resolve all of its problems.

I'm glad that you are one of America's strengths.

POINT 28 - EDUCATING OUR YOUNG PEOPLE ON HOW TO DEAL WITH ANGER

Many lives are lost every years because people don't know how to deal with anger. This is not only a problem that confronts the young people, but adults as well. To counter domestic violence, this is another factor that must be addressed. We must educate both the young and the old. In respect to the young, we must educate them on how to deal with their anger and the anger of others. This training should be integrated into our school system as life skills.

In addition to the schools, life skills training should be made available throughout the community through churches, community forums, workshops and seminars. This training should be designed to reach all age groups and all segments of our population.

Until this training is put in force, allow me to share some helpful hints on how to deal with anger. This information can be put in effect immediately and positive results can be realized.

Definition And Concept

In order to effectively deal with anger you must understand it, know what drives it and how it develops. Webster's New Universal Unabridged Dictionary defines anger as "Strong feeling excited by real or supposed injury; often accompanied by a desire to take vengeance or obtain satisfaction from the offering party; resentment, wrath, ire." Anger has been described as the first emotion felt by human beings.

Gestalt viewed anger as resentment, an experience accompanying a demand or expectation that has not been made explicit. It is also believed demands or expectations which are not met trigger the anger cycle. The anger cycle is depicted below.

Study the drawing of anger. As you can see the anger cycle can be stopped by making appropriate assumptions and deciding that you have enough power to effectively address the threat. However, in reality, we can't manage it in that manner all the time and we do become angry. The aim here is to address dealing with personal anger. This approach to managing anger is a reprint from Richmond's Guide to Effective Human Relations and Problem Solving.

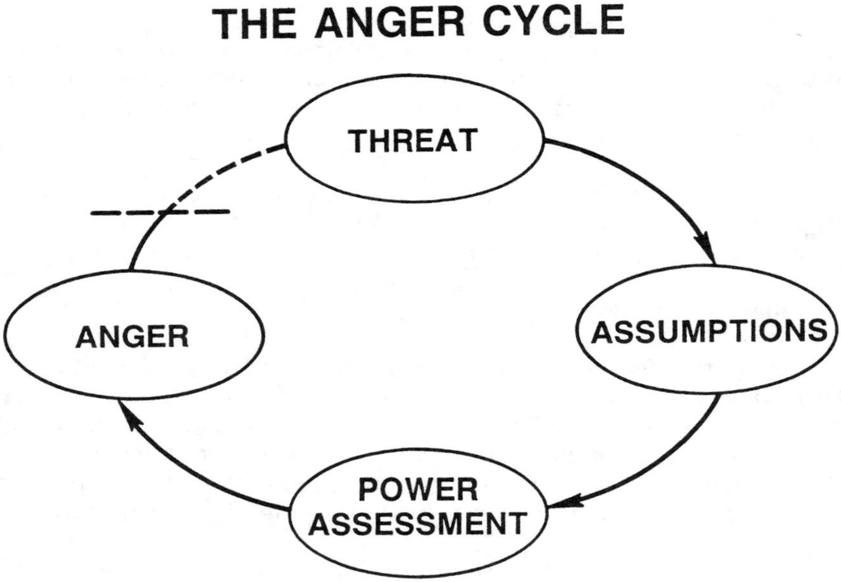

THE ANGER CYCLE

Figure 16.1   The Anger Cycle

(Reprinted from: J. William Pfeiffer and John E. Jones, (Eds.), *The 1976 Annual Handbook for Group Facilitators*, San Diego, CA: University Associates, Inc., 1976. Used with permission.)

Ownership

First, take ownership. Taking ownership of your personal anger increases awareness. Remember, nobody makes us angry; we allow ourselves to become angry. It comes from within.

Regulate Your Response

Next, you must be able to regulate your response. Your response could be a mild reaction, i.e. "I don't agree with you" or a hostile reaction. Until structure training classes are held in your community, training using this concept can be conducted in homes or at churches. Create scenarios that will help young people and couples to learn how to regulate their responses.

Assess The Threat

Third, you must assess the threat. Ask questions such as "How can this hurt me?" "What is so fearful about this experience?" When you ask yourself these types of questions, you can clarify what's really impacting you and this places you in a better position to deal with it.

Share The Perceived Threat

The perceived threat must be shared. This makes the anger interpersonal and diffuses the intensity of the feeling. This of course, leads to clarification of perceptions.

Forgiveness

Lastly, you must forgive. Let go of the anger. This cancels the charges against the other. It also frees you from the anger process; in other words, it cleans the slate and paves the way for future interaction.

The process works. Though it is not all inclusive, it provides a means to effectively deal with your anger, so you can maintain control of the communication process.

Transactional Analysis As A Means Of Dealing With Anger

Transactional Analysis is another effective means of dealing with anger. This concept theorizes when you become anger you are in the "child ego state". Transactional Analysis suggests the best way to deal with anger is to allow yourself to move into the "adult ego posture". Here is some background on this concept.

Dr. Eric Berne the originator of Transactional Analysis points out in his book "Games People Play" that every individual carries around three ego

States: Parent, Adult and Child. His study suggests that people carry their parents around inside of them. Everyone has an Adult, and everyone carries a little boy or girl around inside of him/her.

An "ego" state is a particular set of ways of thinking, feeling, and reacting that go together. A summation of each ego state is below.

Parent-When a person automatically acts, thinks, and behaves like those who raise him/her, the person is in the parent ego state. While in the parent ego state, the person deals with feelings and emotions. They also can be critical and full of opinions, prejudices, "shoulds," "should nots'" and able be to express love.

Child-When a person is in a child ego posture, he or she acts, thinks or feels the way he or she did when he/she was a child. While in this state a person may be loving, spontaneous, or rebellious, frightened, angry, etc.

Adult-When a person is in an adult ego state, he/she is totally unemotional, acts like a computer, and is concerned with "what fits" and what is most expedient and useful.

When managing anger, I think it is very important to understand this concept. There are a number of books on Transactional Analysis. My two favorite are "I'm OK-You're OK" by Thomas A. Harris, M.D. and "Games People Play" by Eric Berne, M.D.

Regardless of the method used, you must master your own anger before you can deal with the anger of another person.

Dealing With Another's Anger

Sometimes we allow ourselves to become hooked by the anger of others. Use the technique in the foregoing to control your anger, because it doesn't make sense to become angry just because someone else is angry.

There are several things you can do to deal with the anger of another. The process described below may help.

Affirmation of Others' Feelings

You must acknowledge you are receiving the communication and express a willingness to respond. Often people attempt to ignore or disallow another's anger. When this occurs, the anger may become more intensified.

Acknowledge Your Own Defensiveness

It is important to let the other person know what you are feeling. Again, you must become aware of how the anger is affecting you. For example, when we fail to acknowledge our own defensiveness, we may find ourselves becoming rigid and enforcing standards to the letter.

Clarify And Diagnose

You must stick to the issue by giving and requesting specific feedback. Find out expectations, needs and wants. Separate the needs and wants. Work together in this process. Communication can be restored and the anger could possibly be resolved. During this process think "Adult Ego" and control your "Child Ego" and "Parent Ego" throughout the process.

During the anger cycle a lot may be said and feelings may be hurt; therefore, it is important to forgive and renegotiate the relationship.

Renegotiate The Relationship

Review the situation which brought on the anger. Develop a plan to prevent similar situations from recurring. Take the lead and acknowledge regrets; if warranted, exchange apologies. Remember, you must live with people, play with people, go to school with people and work with people.

This process is not all inclusive; you may need a third person to serve as a mediator. Agree on one to help restore productive communication.

Since anger interferes with the communication process, it also interferes with the home life, learning in school, playing in the community and working with people.

Now if you are thinking: (1) You would like to share this information with your spouse and family, that's good. (2) If you are thinking, you would like to learning more about these concepts so I can share it with members of your church, that's good. (3) If you are thinking, you would like to make a video on the concepts to help train gang members, that's good. The market is wide open, for plays, tapes, workshops, and seminars and even more books.

Hopefully, I have planted some seeds that will be cultivated and produce good fruits.

POINT 29 - BUILDING MORALITY THROUGH RAP

Rap is a very effective way of communication among black youth. It is an art form that will be with us for many years to come. Often it conveys feeling, emotion, pain, and hurt. Some raps can be compared to the blues, but, with a different beat.

Some raps put women down; some put men down, mothers, fathers or our society at large. Attack! Attack! Attack! Often these raps contain expressions of pain and suffering of years gone by or conditions confronting the rappers today.

An outcry, stop the negative rapping!!! Another outcry, stop the negative rapping!!!

This is the rapper freedom of speech and expression. The rappers must not be denied these rights. However, we must assist the rappers by addressing the conditions that create the hurts, the pains, and the sufferings.

Personally, I don't like the negative messages, but more importantly, I don't like the conditions that cause rappers to express so much pain and suffering.

African Americans, we have a job to do, so let's get busy.

We must turn the ghettos into a vast school. We must make every street corner a forum, not a lounging place for trivial gossip, petty gambling, dealing drugs, where life is wasted and human experience withers to trivial sensations. We must make every current gang member, every unemployed black man and woman, a worker, an employer, a voter, canvasser or a student.

When this occurs, the conditions that cause the many hurts and many pains will be eradicated. At that point, I can envision rappers rapping new songs of love, happiness, togetherness, peace and prosperity.

In the meantime, let's give the rappers our love and let them know, that we understand their concerns and the sources of their pain. Coach them now. Hopefully we can help them express themselves without attacking others as we work together addressing the root causes. The rappers must understand your resolve to address the roots and not just their expressions of pain and displeasure.

Peace.

POINT 30 - EDUCATING THE MUSICIANS AND RAPPERS OF THE DAMAGING IMPACT OF THE NEGATIVE MESSAGES

At Point 29, we discussed that it is most inappropriate to prevent individuals from exercising their right to free speech and expression. Nevertheless, they should know the damaging impact of their action. Recommend that action be taken to develop videos and other training programs to this end.

Moreover, recommend that recording companies be encouraged to advise their artists of the possible impact of their action. Scholars in this area should prepare perspectives on this subject and make it available to recording companies. There also may be a need for videos on the effect of listening to negative messages to help educate the young people who listen to this type of music. These videos could be shown in school, church, home and community forums. Grantmakers should also consider funding this area.

Rappers must be coached and shown a new way to express their frustration without hurting others. A Study should be done on how serious an impact these negative messages could have on the youth who listen to negative raps. Foundations should give fellowship grants to individuals who promote positive messages through raps. Radio stations could host "rapping for positive changes" contests. Producers and recording promoters could play leading roles in this movement by actively seeking rappers with a positive message and with a beat of high commercial value.

POINT 31 - TEACHING LIFE COPING SKILLS TO OUR YOUNG PEOPLE

For many years, I have wondered why do we wait until a person becomes involved in drugs, or becomes a child abuser, before we teach them about themselves and equip them with some life coping skills.

This must become an item on our national agenda, to integrate life coping skills into our public school system to prevent/reduce drug abuse, divorces and other social problems. Unfortunately, under our current system, in general a person must become a child abuser, substance abuser, spouse abuser, or a social outcast before they are taught about themselves.

We must not wait until a person becomes a victim or a criminal. They must be taught when they are young, and as early as the first grade. The teaching must be modulated throughout the education system. For this to occur soon, the public must put pressure on the policy makers until this is realized.

Nevertheless, immediate action must be taken now to provide the needed coping skills for our young people. Recommend that churches adopt this as one of their initiatives. Moreover, workshops could be given at community centers, youth centers and other meeting places throughout the country. Some of this effort must be volunteer effort.

Lack of funding is not sound reasoning for not having vital programs to teach our young people life coping skills.

POINT 32 - MORE EFFECTIVE SOCIALIZATION PROCESS

Sociologists define socialization as the way in which people learn skills and attitudes relevant to their social roles. In light of the continued undue stresses that black families are confronted, with, it is having a serious impact on how African American youth see themselves in society. For example: boys who don't have male role models have a difficult time with discovering their rightful place in the family or in society.

To put it in very simple language, it is hard to become a father if you've never been fathered (to be treated or cared for by a father). With the increasing number of single-parent families where fathers are not present, there are some serious consequences that we are experiencing in Black America.

There is a growing number of black male youth who disrespect black women and black men, as well. If you are not trained when you are young how to conduct yourself, how can you be held accountable for your behavior when you become older? Let me use a phrase from a friend of mine, Frank Simmons: "Before you tell individuals what not to do-first, first, you should tell them what to do."

In some troubled families, the street has more influence on the children than their parents. In other words, other underdeveloped individuals, such as gang members, pimps, and prostitutes have become greater influential factors in the lives of many of the Black youth.

Immediate action must be taken to turn this around. However, for this to occur it will cause many of us to move from our safety zone. When we move from our safety net, this will allow us to look at the problem from a new perspective. We must recognize that these are our children who are in trouble. We must recognize that these children are the future of Black America. If they remained underdeveloped, they will produce underdeveloped fruits. Therefore, we must become fathers and mothers to all of them. We must discover their needs and make ourselves available for them.

Black men and Black women, you first must begin with your nature child and make sure you are giving that child what he or she needs. Although your nature child may be thirty years of age, that child could use your support. Your involvement with nature children could help to create the condition that is needed to cause them to have more positive impact on the lives of their children.

Next, there is a responsibility to the other children in the community and you must make yourself available for them. Volunteer at youth centers, or at your church to work with the youth.

Black Americans have worked hard over the years to earn their rightful place in America. However, we have not reached parity in a number of areas. In fact today in some areas, we are in worse condition than we were twenty years ago. Yes, there have been shattered dreams and the persistence of grinding poverty that have driven many to the feeling of hopelessness, a life of crime and despair. On the other hand, there have been successes that have driven some to a false sense of security, to the point, they forgot that someone helped them along the way.

Our task now is to become involved with these young people who are at risk and help them overcome their fears of insecurity and doubts that clouds their futures. We must become the ones to help them to develop the confidence and the vision of a brighter day. We must help them to become excited about tomorrow. Our involvement in their daily lives is the answer to the current weak socialization process of so many African Americans.

In addition to becoming involved with the youth, we must train and coach parents through workshops, seminars, and community forums to make them more effective in the socialization process of their children.

POINT 33 - ESTABLISHING TEEN PARENTING AND SKILL DEVELOPMENT PROGRAMS THROUGHOUT THE COUNTRY

In the central-city and suburban Black America, the fertility rates are particularly higher than for most Americans, especially for teenagers and young adults. Overall, the rate of fertility was 32 percent higher for blacks than for whites in 1988. Of which 64 per cent of the black babies were born out of wedlock, compared with 18 percent of the white babies. Black unmarried teenagers ages 15 to 17 bore 74 per 1,000 girls, while unmarried white teenagers ages 15 to 17 bore 17 per 1,000 girls. Of course, the young ladies are undereducated, unskilled, have few life skills, few parenting skills. However, they are responsible for raising a larger proportion of urban African American children.

Again, these young underdeveloped youth are responsible for raising a larger proportion of urban African American children. Children raising children, often with very little outside support system. We must work to turn this both dramatic and alarming rate of child birth around amongst our black youth. However, while we are working to accomplish that, we also must assist these young mothers in properly caring for and developing their children.

While black girls are having babies, increasingly young black men have dropped out of school, joined gangs, deserted all vestiges of work ethnic, developed a false notion of manhood, become heavily involved in drugs, crime and often many years spent in and out of prison.

Our challenge is to assist both, the mothers and the fathers, to carry out their responsibilities. Though these individuals are not married, both of these individuals have direct responsibilities to these children. Here we must develop programs that will help provide both the parenting skills needed to take care of the children and education and training for both the mothers and the fathers. However, we must not kid ourselves and these young people with these parenting classes. As we attempt to address these current problems with courses lets also consider these vital points made by Dr. Welsing:

> "The ability of parents to provide high-level emotional support for a child cannot be obtained from anyone's crash course designed to prepare the already pregnant teenage mother and father for their new responsibility. These highly complex tasks cannot be prepared for by course work or book-reading alone. These tasks must be learned through the child's own developmental experience over a period of years. It is a sham to allow these teenagers to believe that they can somehow learn to be long-term, effective parents when they are only emotionally immature children." [29]

Currently, the traditional nuclear family is an endangered species for Black America. Our current approach has not been effective in providing this much needed assistance. We must continue to provide support to these young parents long after parenting classes. However, the most effective approach to teen pregnancies is prevention, which is covered at Point 34.

Nevertheless, we must assist the current families and the teenagers who are already pregnant. It will take much more support from community based organizations to help deliver services to address this real problem and threat to Black America. Moreover, funds must be made available through both governmental and private sources. But we can't sit back and wait on these funds, we must act now.

POINT 34 - PROVIDING SEX EDUCATION FOR YOUTH 11 TO 13 YEARS OF AGE

At Point 33, we address the rate of childbirth among our black teenagers, therefore, there is no need for a long elaboration to convince you of the extent and severity of this problem. At this Point, we are focusing our attention of actions that we can take to reduce the rate of pregnancy.

Abstinence is the best way to reduce the rate of pregnancy. Teaching young people how to say no is very important and it should become a way to teach girls in the age group from 11 to 13 years of ages. Recommend this training be conducted by other teenagers at high school and junior college level. There should be videos developed to this end and training should be conducted in school, churches, and youth centers. In regard to the videos, since children often relate to cartoons, cartoons could serve as an effective approach to help facilitate this training even at an earlier age.

On a side note, the phrase "Just Say No" is a good phrase. However, I believe the phrase **"Respect My No"** is more powerful and can be used in a more effective way.

Abstinence must also must be taught to the teenage boys. I suggest emphasis be placed on the responsibility of raising a child.

In addition to teaching abstinence, teaching sex education to both the 11 to 13 year old males and females is very important. Often young people have sex for a number of reasons from "I want to do it" to "I felt pressured." If you look closely, sometimes youth are looking for the feeling of love, a feeling that they have not experienced at home. Some have not taken a serious look at what they want to do in life, therefore, they don't realize what it takes in life to achieve these goals.

Today, it is becoming quite clear that adolescent pregnancy is not always a mistake. Some teenage girls choose pregnancy because their options are limited and to become a mother for them is a sign of adulthood and independence. On the other hand, some adolescent boys use pregnancy as a way to establish identity with manhood.

Often when youth believe they have limited opportunities and don't have positive expectations about the future, it has a negative effect on their lives. Here is columnist William Raspberry's comments on a National Academy of Sciences report:

> "Youngsters who believe that they have a bright future ahead of them find it easier to make positive decisions, easier to resist peer pressure, easier to make the sacrifices necessary for academic excellence and easier to say no to drugs, sex and other future-threatening temptations... our major task is to see to it that our children have, and know that they have an opportunity for a decent, fulfilling life. We have to help them understand that, to a far greater extent than many of them imagine, they have the capacity to create their own success. What they need, in short, is not merely the means for avoiding pregnancy but a reason for doing so." [30]

A study of "locus of control" among pregnant teenagers reports that pregnant white teens generally have an external locus of control, while pregnant black teens have an internal locus of control. In plain talk, pregnant white teenagers are often influenced by others, while pregnant black teenagers are choosing pregnancy. In respect to abortions and pregnancies, black teens, on the average, have more pregnancies than white teens, but black teens have fewer abortions. This can be reasonably interpreted that black teens see pregnancy as a legitimate path to adulthood and opt for pregnancy from their limited set of opportunities.

Young ladies as well as young men need positive role models. Indirectly, the lack of positive role models, lack of goals, and the search for love, may impact a person's decision to become sexually active and even opt to become pregnant. Therefore, it is recommended that the sexual education programs also include role models who accomplished their career goals and then elected to have children. Moreover, we must clearly show our black youth at an early age, that they can excel. We must give them the support they need to this end. This message is not just to parents, but it is directed to every concerned citizen because often the parents of these youth can't provide the needed directions to these young people.

For effective sex education training, excellent training aids are very important. Children relate to cartoons. Recommend that videos be developed as part of this training program.

We must place more emphasis on sex education programs and provide a positive outlook for our young people. Let's set a goal and reach young people between the ages of 11 to 13 years old. Today the birth rate among never-married teenagers for African Americans is more than four times as likely as their counterparts to bear one or more children.

The bottom line, controlling teen pregnancies must be controlled by the teenagers themselves. Teenagers are very intelligent. We must educate them when they are young about what's going on in America. They must be given enough factual information about the real problems of raising a child as a teenager, the impact on that child's future. They must become acutely aware of the unfair chance that their child will have to experience a bright future in America.

These young people are the one who ultimately make the final decisions regarding their sexual behaviors. Our job is to train them when they are young and coach them along the way. Another way of coaching them is to encourage Black teenagers to develop initiatives to address teen pregnancies of their own. For example, clubs or groups could be established by teens who have to decided on "Abstinence Now - Sex When I'm Married", "No Sex Until After I'm 18", "Respect My No"- "I'm Going to Give My Baby A Future - I'll Wait", "Wait, Secure Our Future Now". These groups could start a movement that could greatly reduced the rate of teen pregnancies. There could be teen clubs established, raps recorded, forums, workshops, and lots of non-sexual fun activities. With the right coaching and support, this movement could become very powerful and reverse the sexual behaviors of our young people. Through this effort, we could develop a five-year plan to eliminate Black child-parenting.

Our immediate action should be to educate, using every available avenue. The record industry must be informed of these initiatives, along with the Church, and community groups. Grantmakers should request for proposals to promote these initiatives and this Point.

POINT 35 - ADDRESSING THE NEEDS OF OUR YOUNG PEOPLE WHO HAVE BEEN INSTITUTIONALIZED

In the foregoing we discussed underdeveloped children raising children. One of the sad consequences of this problem is many of the children are eventually institutionalized. And when they are released from these institutions they go back into the same home environment and back to the same outside influences.

Here is a summation of the crimes committed by juveniles according to information from the FBI's Uniform Crime Reports.

a. Between 1987 and 1991, the number of Violent Crime Index arrests of juveniles increased by 50% - twice the increase for persons 18 years of age or older. Most alarming, juvenile arrests for murder increased by 85% compared with 21% for those age 18 and older.

b. The estimated 22,900 Violent Crime Index arrests of juveniles in 1991 was the highest number in history, with 3,400 arrests for murder, 6,300 for forcible rape, 44,500 for robbery, and 68,700 for aggravated assault.

c. Juveniles accounted for 17% of all violent crime arrests in 1991.

d. Three of every 10 juvenile murder arrests involve a victim under age 18.

e. Juveniles' use of guns in homicides increased from 64% to 78% between 1987 and 1991, during which time juvenile arrests for weapons violations increased 62%.

f. In 1991 the nearly 50,000 juvenile weapons arrests accounted for more than 1 out of 5 weapons arrests. Black youth were arrested for weapons law violations at a rate triple that of white youth.

g. The 1991 violent crime arrest rate for black youth was 5 times higher than that of white youth (1,456 per 100,000 compared with 283 per 100,000).

This data clearly shows that there is far too much juvenile crime, especially among black youth. The problem that we are addressing is how do we reduce the number of repeat offenders so they can become more productive members of our society. We have looked at the internal support system of these young people. Often the ones from the black community are from single-parent families, a troubled family, where there is a parent under a lot of daily undue stress.

We discussed that often these parents need to have enhanced parenting skills. We also pointed out that many of these young people do not have the proper role models, and the streets often have more influence in their lives than the parents in their homes. Often when these individuals are released from these juvenile institutions, they go back into the same homes, communities, and find the same influences.

In order to address these problems, we must use appropriate strategy. Community-based organizations and churches should play very important roles in providing the much needed support systems for the juveniles who have been institutionalized. In addition to these formal organizations, the general public must be made aware of this problem and the action being taken to address it. The primary reasons for informing the general public is for awareness and to solicit the community involvement.

The public can provide the best assistance when there is a detailed plan available and when they can see how they can be of benefit.

The Department of Justice, Office of Juvenile Justice and Delinquency Program issued guidelines for a grant under Federal Register/Volume 58, No. 86, Thursday, May 6, 1993. Though the period for submitting proposals for this particular grant has closed, I believe it is important to share some of the Department of Justice's thinking on this subject.

The Department of Justice offered the following program strategy:

a. Support and assistance to families and core community institutions;

b. Delinquency prevention programs and services for at-risk;

c. Immediate interventions;

d. Intermediate sanctions;

e. Community-based correctional facilities;

f. Training schools and other correctional institutions.

This sounds like a good strategy. Now the key to this is program development. What type of assistance do you give to the families and institutions? What type of delinquency prevention programs? Who will intervene, the police department, school, parents, concerned citizens, or the elderly? When creating the program, thoughts must be given to getting the community involved to a great extent.

Most correctional facilities are in confined environments and are used as a form of punishment. However, redirecting training would be more effective for some offenders. Redirecting training is quite different from job readiness training. Correctional facilities is a form of punishment and is in a confined environment. The type of redirecting that has been suggested would not be in a enclosed environment, nor will it be a form of punishment.

While studying and working with ex-gang members, I discovered that redirecting training could be quite effective. This training allows current gang members to reassess values, clarify values, overcome grief, adopt new habits, and set new goals. This training also afforded participants gang relapse prevention education.

I strongly recommend redirecting training be afforded to offenders to include non-serious offenders and non-serious repeat offenders. In fact, this redirecting training should be given to all offenders. If they are already institutionalized, recommend that they enter into a transitional program, quartered in a less restricted environment and provide this training at least two to four weeks prior to the day of their release.

Building more prisons is not the answer, nor is "Three Strikes You Are Out." At Point 35, it was pointed out: Youngsters who believe they have a bright future ahead of them find it easier to make positive decisions, easier to resist peer pressure, easier to make the sacrifices necessary for academic excellence and easier to say no to drugs, sex and other future-threatening temptations... We must show them bright futures and focus more on solutions like those mentioned at this point. Community involvement and awareness are important components to providing the needed support to the at-risk or underdeveloped youth.

POINT 36 - EMPOWERING THE INTER-CITIES RESOLVE

In the news recently, there has been talk about the "urban crisis syndrome" a condition that causes individuals to commit violent act. Is this a myth or is it possible? It is not our intention to resolve this thought at this point. However, we will take a close look at some of the inter-cities conditions and discuss ways as to empower the people who live under these conditions. These conditions, in a sense link cities throughout the countries, therefore solutions also must be shared and we must never forget that what happen in one city affect us all.

In cities throughout the country you can find bread lines, soup kitchens, and people living under bridges, in doorways, beside boxcars, in parks, tents, emergency shelters, subways, and abandoned cars. By some counts, two to three millions have no place they can call home. In other words, there are millions of homeless and hungry people in America. They are the Poor Whites, African Americans, Hispanics, Native Americans, and other minorities. These are America's poor, 35 to 50 million.

Even when you visit Washington, D.C., for example, near the White House and the Capitol is a food kitchen that fed 175,000 hungry men, women, and children in 1984. Nevertheless, at costly French restaurants nearby, one meal can cost $100.00 (executives can write these meals off for tax purposes). However, in the same general area, but out of sight, men, women, and children dig into garbage cans for leftovers. Similar conditions can be found in major cities throughout the United States.

When you focus on the inter-cities life, you must mention the problems of the homeless and the poor. However, at this Point, we will not examine the hunger or the homeless factor any further, but we will see how the inner-city live, from day to day. In addition, we are focusing on other urban problems, although, there are some happy people who live in these cities. This however, is not the point of our discussion. There are many urban-dwelling families who are well adjusted to the urban live. There are some advantages and some disadvantages in living in urban America. Nevertheless, the closer you get to the inner-cities, the more social problems you will discover.

Often these problems are caused and perpetuated by the political and economic organization of society. The larger the number of people living close together, the more social problems abound. The inner-cities face higher crime rates, racial tensions, poverty, unemployment, traffic congestion, air and water pollution and inadequate governmental services.

In some of the more troubled families in the inner-cities, today in 1994 you can find the same conditions as described by Dr. King in 1968. Excerpts from his last Sunday morning sermon at the National Cathedral (Episcopal) in Washington, D. C., on March 31, 1968.

"And I was in Newark and Harlem just this week. And I walked into the homes of welfare mothers; I saw them in conditions--no, not with wall-to-wall carpet, but wall-to-wall rats and roaches. I stood in an apartment and this welfare mother said to me "The landlord will not repair this place. I've been here two years and he hasn't made a single repair." She pointed out the walls with all of the ceiling falling through. She showed me the holes where the rats came in. She said night after night we have to stay awake to keep the rats and roaches from getting to the children..." [31]

Though this account is dated, today you can find many of the poor families living under the same conditions as described by Dr. King in 1968. If we are a people on the move, we must change this type of living condition in the inner-cities. One must not misunderstand this commentary, because all African Americans living in the inter-cities don't live under these deplorable conditions. However, for far too many, the American Dream has not been realized.

Borrowing some thoughts and findings from Dr. Henderson:

"The twentieth century has been an increasing urban century for African Americans, particularly since World War II. As O'Hare indicates, "1990, the percentage of blacks living in metropolitan areas stood at 84 percent, compared with 76 percent for whites" The 1990 Census indicates that 31 cities have African-American populations of 100,000 or greater, and 12 have at least 250,000 African Americans. ...New York, Chicago, Detroit, Philadelphia, Los Angeles, Houston, Baltimore and Washington, D.C.-would by themselves rank among the 50 largest cities in the country." [32]

African Americans migrated into these areas to find better employment (from the cotton patches to the auto's plants), social justice, more education opportunities, cultural opportunities and development, and a greater share of the American dream. In light of the failure of the system, these dreams for many never did come to reality.

In general, African Americans and whites living in the our cities concerns are different. First of all, they live in different parts of the cities. Often the suburban areas that Blacks move in are adjacent to central cities. Many of the areas have declining public schools, commercial infrastructure, young single parents households, chronic health conditions, poor housing, poverty and severe crime.

Under these conditions, the children suffer worse than any other group. In fact, it is like robbing them of their future. If we look closely at the problem, one can conclude that the system trains children to fail who live under these conditions. Children sense at an early age that mainstream America defines them and their parents as "bums", good-for-nothing, no-good, inadequate, dirty, stupid, and welfare chiselers. They hear this over and over. It is constantly reinforced. This becomes the children's reality. They have accepted the messages from society as being accurate, therefore, many don't perform well when they are in school. Its unfortunate that our society treats the youth at risk very cruel.

The African Americans and others who are living under these conditions must be empowered by other African Americans, the government, and concerned citizens. To change these conditions it will require effecting the 101 points offered by the Power Pack. Therefore, it is very important that you share this information with others. We must use an inter-cities approach; Point 19 of the Power Pack must be the same Point in Detroit, New York, Los Angeles, and Memphis. Empowering our inter-cities resolve to correct these conditions must come through sharing information, workable programs, and solutions from one city to the next. This is especially true for neighboring cities. It is very important to develop an inter-cities resolve to address these conditions.

Increased awareness is very important. Through this awareness, we can unify and take the measures that are necessary to change these conditions. The bottom line, it doesn't have to continue to be this way. In fact, it must not. We can achieve full employment now. We must not accept this undue pain any longer. We have too much as a nation to allow this suffering to continue. America, America how long are we going to allow this to go on.

Black America, how long are we going to be silent about conditions that are destroying us as a people? The poor who are suffering are in too much pain to ask for help. They just attack each other because it is a lot easier. They are in too much pain to lift up themselves, for the burdens are too heavy. In fact, they are in too much pain because we have failed to use what we have! Moreover, they have failed to use what they have!

It is often said: "If you don't have any money you can't do anything." Though, this statement is made often, it is not a true statement. However, it becomes a reality for the ones who believe it. I look at it like this: If you knew what you had and use it - you can get the money you need. In the same sense, I'm confident we have enough assets, both tangible and intangible, to change the state of Black America.

At Point 56, we discuss how we must use our tangible assets. Here, however, we must take a look at our intangible assets. Our intangible assets will be the real power that we will use to change these conditions around and ensure full employment for all Americans who wish to work and to change these inter-cities conditions and the problems confronting our suburban communities. Let's look at the power that we have with our intangible assets.

(1) Access to Credit

(2) Human capital, which is generally defined as intelligence, educational background, work experience, knowledge, skill, and health. Let's also include energy, vision, hope, imagination, services, and ideas.

(3) Cultural capital, in the form of knowledge of culturally significant subjects and cues, ability to cope with social situations and formal bureaucracies, including vocabulary, accent, dress, appearance, with earnings in the form of acceptance into rewarding patterns of association.

(4) Informal social capital in the form of family, friends, contacts, and connections, sometimes referred to as a "social network," with earnings in the form of tangible support, emotional support, information, and easier access to employment, credit, housing, or other types of assets.

(5) Formal social capital, or organization capital, which refers to the structure and techniques of formal organization applied to tangible capital, with earnings in the form of profits through increased efficiency.

(6) Political capital in the form of participation, power, and influence, with earnings in the form of favorable rules and decisions on the part of the state or local government.

After reading this list of intangible assets some of you will still not realize the power you have. Therefore, I call upon community leaders, especially the clergy to give farther insight to their congregations so we can be on one accord and develop a collective community resolve.

Some of you may ask, who is going to lead this effort? Some will say: "I'll help, however, don't ask me to lead." To the ones who hold this position, we need your help. The leaders in this area will say: "I heard you Lord, send me. I will lead this effort in my community. I will lead this effort throughout the nation." The initiatives are countless-there are opportunities for everyone to become involved.

POINT 37 - ENSURING SAFE COMMUNITIES FOR OUR YOUTH

Often it appears that certain communities don't receive the attention it deserves in enforcement of certain laws or enacting certain ordinances especially in areas where there are voters' apathy. Action must be taken to increase the political participation. (See Point 81) However, in addition to political participation, measures must be taken to ensure city ordinances are passed and enforced that ensure the safety of our young people.

The community must be kept abreast of what's going on in the community, to include the good and bad, i.e. trouble spots, gang activities, drive-by-shootings, other negative activities, needs of the youth centers, request for volunteers, community empowerment programs and other positive activities.

To complement the regular police, a community volunteer force should be considered. Similar to a volunteer fire department. This will place men and women in the community with uniforms and this will also help deter crime.

The people of communities should also put pressure on the cities to ensure that their regular police forces are properly trained in human relations. When a police department is received by the community in a positive light, it helps to improve the police department's effectiveness and the community will re-enforce the city's ability to deter crime. Police departments must work to earn the public trust and become involved in community affairs other than police concerns, especially in the communities they are paid to protect and serve.

The effectiveness of the police department is closely related to the trust that the people in the community have regarding that department.

The community will become safer as soon as we initiate the Points under the Power Pack. The effort will restore immediate hope not only to Black America, but America as a whole.

POINT 38 - MAINTAINING CLEAN COMMUNITIES

Ensuring our communities are kept clean, the streets, alleys cleared of trash, rundown vacated buildings, etc. should be a concern for everyone. For when these conditions are allowed to go unchecked, these conditions also have an impact on the minds of the people who live in the community.

When you find neighborhoods that are not maintained, this is a sure sign that the people who live in the neighborhoods are not exercising their political power. This serves as a clue for you to act because your involvement may help inspire someone else in the community to take action. A clean community has a positive impact on the residents.

Community based-organizations should establish initiatives to ensure ordinances are established and enforced to ensure clean communities become a reality. The community-based organizations should ensure that the people who live in the affected community are involved in the process. Actions of this type give the residents a sense of accomplishment and encourage them to become even more involved in the political process. Small measures of accomplishment are very important in stimulating political participation.

POINT 39 - ENSURING LANDLORDS MAINTAIN PROPERTIES THAT ARE RENTED TO THE ELDERLY AND OTHER LOW-INCOME FAMILIES

Do you rent or own your home? Have you ever rented an apartment or house? Do you have an idea what it is like to rent from a landlord who does not maintain the property? The failure of landlords to maintain rented properties is a problem that many elders and low income single-parents are faced with.

Often these tenants pay on time, but their landlords are irresponsible and fail to make repairs for days, months or maybe never. The properties look rundown, in need of painting, grounds not maintained. Inside you may find roaches, rodents and other pests. Often an irresponsible landlord will continue to make promises, however, he or she will not keep those promises.

A landlord's legal duty varies from state to state. However, in most states, landlords are required to maintain the building. This includes, maintaining the roof, heating facilities, and plumbing. In addition, the landlords must maintain those parts of the building and grounds which they control (such as the stairways, landings, and halls) in a clean, sanitary and safe condition, including getting rid of insects, rodents and other pests.

Often tenants need help to get landlords to carry out their duties. Of course, they can file a complaint with the health department, write the landlord a letter, pay for repairs out of the rent, sue, move out, or stay and live with the problems. Unfortunately, some tenants take the latter action, stay and live with the problems. These tenants need your help. Often these tenants feel so alone, powerless and don't know their rights or don't have the time to fight this battle because of so many other daily survival battles to fight.

Neighbors should help neighbors. Who is your neighbor? The next time you drive in a neighborhood and you notice apartments in need of painting, the old run down look, and yards that have been not maintained, don't jump to conclusions that the tenants don't care. Remember, you may be looking at pieces of properties whereby the landlords are not carrying out their responsibilities.

You can help. Recommend that community-based organizations adopt this initiative and help beautify the community by getting the landlords to address these needs. Show these victims they are not alone. Non-for-profit organizations may be able to seek funding for this effort.

Chapter II Notes

1. National Advisory Council: National Advisory Council on
Economic Opportunity, Thirteen Report (Washington, D.C.: 1981),
cited in Henry Weinsten, ("U.S. Cuts Will Devastate Poor Panel
Charges," Los Angeles, Times, September 21, 1981, pt 1, p.3.

2. Eitzen, Stanley E., (1983). Social Problems, p. 77

3. Washington, James M., (1986), A Testament Of Hope: The
Essential Writings Of Martin Luther King, Jr., p. 558, quoted by
King in his book: "Where Do We Go From Here"

4. Ibid. p. 558

5. Washington, James M. (1986) A Testament of Hope, The
Essential Writings Of Martin Luther King, Jr., p. 245, "Where Do
We Go From Here." This was Dr. King's last and most radical,
SCLC Presidential address.

6. Ibid. p. 274. Excerpts from Dr. King's last Sunday morning
service on March 31, 1968 at the National Cathedral (Episcopal)
in Washington, D.C.

7. Ibid. p. 188

8. Ibid. p. 67

9. Keniston, Kenneth, & The Carnegie Council on Children (1977),
All Our Children, p.85.

10. Ibid. p. 91

11. Washington, James M. (1986), A Testament Of Hope, The
Essential Writings Of Martin Luther King, Jr., p. 275

12. Dewart, Janet, (1990), The State Of Black America, p. 1,
National Urban League, Inc.

13. Rossi, (1989), <u>Down And Out In America</u>, p. 9

14. McCaghy, <u>Deviant Behavior</u>, (1976) p. 300, Etizen quoted in <u>Social Problems</u>, p. 493

15. Etizen, Stanley D., (1983), <u>Social Problems</u>, p. 493

16. Cited by Eitzen, <u>"Social Problems"</u> (1983) page 508. Source: Roger A. Rotyman, <u>"Addiction Concepts and the Vietman Experience,"</u> Urban and Social Change Review 9 (Summer 1976)

17. Washington, James M. (1986), <u>A Testament Of Hope, The Essential Writings Of Martin Luther King, Jr.</u>, p. 577

18. <u>Holy Bible, Isaiah</u>, ch. 55, ver. 8,9.

19. Welsing, Frances Cress, (1991),<u>The Isis Papers</u>, p.88

20. Ibid. p. 89

21. Ibid. p. 279

22. John E. O'Brien, "Violence in Divorce Prone Families," Journal of Marriage and the Family 33 (November 1971): 962-698. Quoted by Eitzen, <u>Social Problems</u>, (1983) p. 530

23. Reported in Roge Langley and Richard C. Levy, Wife Beating: the Silent Crisis (New York:Dutton, 1977). Quoted by Eitzen, <u>Social Problems,</u> (1983) p. 530

24. Dewart, Janet (1989), <u>The State Of Black America,</u><u>"A Common Destiny"</u>, by: Beny Primm

25. Ephesians, Chapter 6, Vers. 11-18, <u>Good News:New Testament</u>, The New Testament in Today's English Version, (1976), American Bible Society

26. Eitzen, Stanley D., (1983), <u>Social Problems</u>, p.70

27. Welsing, Frances Cress, (1991), <u>The Isis Papers</u>, p. 249, 250

28. Scheele, Adele, (1979),<u>Skills For Success</u>, p.93

29. Welsing, Frances Cress, (1991), <u>The Isis Papers</u>, p. 271

30. Raspberry, William, (1986) <u>Key To Teen Birth Is Self-Perception"</u>, St. Louis Dispatch, December 20, 1986, 3B. This view is also expressed in publications of the Children's Defense Fund; See Marion Wright Edelman, <u>Families In Peril: An Agenda For Social Change</u>, Cambridge: Harvard University Press, 1987

31. Washington, James M., (1986), <u>A Testament Of Hope:The Essential Writings Of Martin Luther King, Jr.</u>, p. 268. Excerpts from his last Sunday Morning Sermon at the National Cathedral (Episcopal) in Washington, D.C. on March 31, 1968.

32. Dewart, Janet, (1994) <u>The State Of Black America</u>, p.12, "<u>African Americans In The Urban Milieu: Conditions, Trends, and Development Needs</u>, by: Lenneal J. Henderson, Ph.D.

CHAPTER III

EDUCATION OPPORTUNITIES

This chapter focuses on current problems with our overall education system, to include the school, home, and community. More importantly it offers solutions on how we can make our system more effective in order to develop our young people for the 21st Century. In addition it provides insight on how to raise self-esteem, prepare for the new information era, establish redirecting training for gang members and much more.

POINT 40 - DEVELOPING BLACK CHILDREN FOR THE 21ST CENTURY

Developing Black Children for the 21st Century - Recommend that we adopt the approach outlined by Dr. Jeff P. Howard in his article entitled: "The Third Movement; Development of Black Children for the 21st Century", State of Black Americans, 1993. Here is a quote from Dr. Howard's article:

"Failure of development - Too many black children grow up without the skills, capabilities, and values they will need to function in this society. Underdevelopment is the most basic reality; it is the very heart of the problem. As long as black children remain underdeveloped, no other solution to the problems black people face will change the basic conditions of our communities. Failures of development are a function of failures of education and training, and these are remediable." [1]

It is very clear that our young people have not failed, but we have failed them. We have the resources and the means to correct this problem. Dr. Howard concludes with specific outcome targets entitled: "Efficacy 21st Century Education Objectives".

He suggests to attain status of true citizenship in the world they will inherit and full participation in the 21st century economy, by the end of high school, children must:

"Master calculus (or any substitute form of mathematics certified by mathematicians as equivalent)

Achieve fluency in at least one language in addition to English

Demonstrate a capacity to write a literate, well-structured, well-researched, twenty-five page essay on any topic deemed important by teachers and interesting to the student.

Demonstrate a capacity to live by strict, high ethical standards."[2]

The President of the National Urban League, John E. Jacob added the fourth objectives at the 1992 National Urban League Conference. These objectives are achievable. Recommend that we adopt this approach as outlined by Dr. Howard. Moreover, obtain a copy of the "State of Black America," 1993, the eighteenth edition. In the book you will find Dr. Howard's article which contains a process to teach children the Efficacy of Effective Effort, Step-by-Step.

POINT 41 - RAISING SELF-ESTEEM

When you find a child suffering from low self-esteem (not possessing a favorable opinion of oneself) - you will also find a parents who needs help in coaching that child. The level of self esteem, sense of purpose, and direction of a parent is directly related to the child's performance and how he/she feel about himself/herself. High employment and poverty impact upon some African American's parents. These factor also cause low-self esteem. Although these parents are at home and nearer to the children, their presence does not have a positive effect. These parents must be trained and need help to successfully guide their children.

Today with the number of single-parents and working two-parent households poses another problem and more burdens are now on the school to educate, console and to feed their children. Some teachers think that these parents do not care and resent the ever-increasing responsibility. In addition to this factor, there are some teachers who still believe that African American children can't learn, and they treat them as if they are not teachable, consequently their self-fulfilling prophecy becomes a reality.

We must remember that people discover who they are from the ways in which they have been treated by those who surround them as they grow up. Children are extremely sensitive to spoken and silent messages that are given by the people around them. They can sense the feeling of rejection and negative racial attitudes - these feelings affect their self concept. They may sense these feelings of rejection at home, from their peers, watching television, at school or at church.

Though self-esteem is one of the most important possessions a person can have, only few will admit that they have low self-esteem and fewer develop strategies to improve it.

Often, to raise the self-esteem of children, the self-esteem of their parent also must be raised. We have identified a problem, now let's look at some solutions.

Building self-esteem must start at home; therefore we must address the self esteem of the parents. Raising self-esteem of our young people must become a priority. There are a number of community-based programs that need volunteers who can provide training to parents or to coach children.

We must increase the number of effective community programs for the at risk youths throughout the communities. We must share lessons learned and workable solutions. Solutions, like youth education enrichment programs and other programs must be shared and continuously assessed throughout the United States.

The Church must play a more active role in building self-esteem of our young people. According to a survey at the University of Michigan in 1980, the church was ranked last in having major influences on children. The rank order of the factors is as follow: (1) home (2) peers (3) television (4) school and (5) the church.

Today, in some instances, peer groups have more influence than the home. We as a group of concerned parents and citizens must work together and turn this around. This will require a collective approach to accomplish this. Dr. Welsing summarized this collective approach as follows:

"The Black collective must find ways to surround all Black children and young people with sufficient emotional support, warmth, encouragement and constructive activity. When this is done, they will not have to abuse the act of self-reproduction, and they will mature to the point that they eventually will be able to dignify the birth of every Black child and lead those children toward full development. If Black people wait for grant funds to become available for this to be achieved, all will be lost." [3]

We can't afford to wait on grant money before we create and effect solutions. Grant money should be thought of in a sense to enhance our efforts in addressing the serious problems that are impacting our young. Grant money does not beget commitment - commitment comes from within.

POINT 42 - REDUCING SCHOOL DROP-OUT RATES

Action must be taken to reduce the drop-out rate for African Americans. As of 1991, 2/3 of African American youth 15 and older had completed high school. However, for white groups, 9 of 10 completed high school. Reducing the drop-out rate must become a priority. While African American females are having babies young black males are dropping out of school. These two factors pose real problems. Education must be made more attractive by integrating the latest technology. This will resolve part or the problem, however other actions must be taken.

We also must increase opportunities for our youth. We must allow them to sense positive expectations about the future. Though the following commentary was mentioned several Points ago, some comments are worth mentioning again. Here is columnist William Raspberry's comments on a National Academy of Sciences report:

"Youngsters who believe that they have a bright future ahead of them find it easier to make positive decisions, easier to resist peer pressure, easier to make the sacrifices necessary for academic excellence and easier to say no to drugs, sex and other future-threatening temptations... our major task is to see to it that our children have, and know that they have an opportunity for a decent, fulfilling life. We have to help them understand that, to a far greater extent than many of them imagine, they have the capacity to create their own success." [4]

It has been discovered that most poor and disadvantaged young people respond positively when they receive hope of future possibilities. Through our efforts, we must work together to create more conducive environments so these young people can experience the expectations of receiving a fulfilled lives.

Sharon P. Robinson wrote an article in the book, "State of Black America, 1987, the Article was entitled: Taking Charge: "An Approach to Making the Education Problems of Blacks Comprehensible and Manageable".

Ms. Robinson recommended that Black America reunite and organize a political coalition which transcends economic status, geographic residence, and other distinctions that may separate one black person from the plight of another.

Today, we need to establish these coalitions with an education agenda.

Here are the initiatives as suggested by Ms. Robinson.

(a) Community-based programs to assist black parents as effective advocates for their children a they negotiate the public educational establishment, and to assist black parents to establish conditions in the home to support student achievement."

(b) The establishment of early childhood development programs in every community. Such programs are essential if black children are to realize the full advantage of the traditional elementary school experience.

(c) Redefine compensatory education from remediation to acceleration. The old paradigm or remediation assumes deficiency rather than lack of opportunity. Black students deserve the assumption of potential and success as the guiding principles of curricular and funding decisions.

(d) Community-based efforts to work with the local schools of black students to define the standards of accountability, and to work with local school staff to achieve the conditions necessary to meet such standards.

(e) Community-based efforts to work with and support the teachers of black students such that these schools become attractive and desirable places to teach. Along with competitive salaries and real opportunities for post-secondary education, this approach represents an important aspect of efforts to recruit minorities to teaching as a career.

(f) Legitimate vocational education programs which provide an adequate academic foundation and viable, employable skills.

(g) Reconsideration of school finance plans such that resources required for the quality education of black students will be available."

These recommendations were made over six years ago. They were vital six years ago and they are still vital today. There are some programs in place today that address some aspects of these recommendations. Recommend you discover the type of programs that are in your community. Discover what the programs are doing, how effective are these solutions, what support it needs, and how you can help.

If there is no program in your community, and, you find students dropping out of school - your community needs a program. Take action now to start one.

POINT 43 - IMPROVING EDUCATION OPPORTUNITIES

Creating conducive environments for learning is key to improving education opportunity. Therefore, we must address this issue on at least these three fronts the home, school, and community.

Home Environment

Education must began at home and it must be reinforced in the home as well. Throughout this book, we covered the problems African Americans are facing in the home such as the distressing issues of hunger, unemployment, single parents, children raising children, poor health, poverty, parents with low self-esteem, uneducated parents, and parents in need of parenting skills. In addition substance abuse problems, domestic violence, children being left home alone, and excessive viewing of television.

To address this environment each one of these factors must be addressed and it will require the total involvement of the community. Parents must be encouraged to seek help to address these factors and help must be made available.

School Environment

In many school environments we find a shrinking pool of qualified black teachers, shortage of staff, and in some cases teachers who think that these parents do not care and resent the ever-increasing responsibility. In addition to these factors, there are some teachers who still believe that African American children can't learn, and they treat them as if they are not teachable. Consequently their self-fulfilling prophecy becomes a reality.

Moreover, the school environment is often not safe with daily violence, fear of gang activities, and teachers that are not equipped to address this new set of problems.

The school system must work with the parents and help them help their children. However, the problems are very complex. Oftentimes, the parents themselves were dropouts and need to be in school themselves. School must be staffed to evaluate the conditions that are impacting on the child's home environment and on their children's learning.

There are a number of approaches and studies regarding parent involvement and participation in the education process of their children. The Committee on Policy for Racial Justice has recommendations for "progressive educational reform". These recommendations include: (1) involving black parents in the education process, with schools welcoming parental participation; (2) striving to make schools less impersonal; (3) developing closer ties between school and social services agencies; (3) recruiting more black teachers; (4) developing sensitive and precise testing procedures for the diagnosis of students' abilities and needs; (5) abandoning rigid systems of tracking and ability groups; (6) expanding the curriculum to reflect the lives and interest of black and other minority children; and (7) providing adequate funding for Headstart and Chapter 1.

Male role models are essential to counter the problem of single-parents where in most cases there is not positive male role models in the child's life.

There must be a continued exchange of information of successful programs throughout the nation. This exchange should include lessons learned, success factors, and implementation strategies. This system of information exchange should be at the local, state and national levels.

Community Environment

The community environment must be safe for young people to walk streets, and to play in playgrounds and parks. This must become a high priority in every community. The local government must do its part, along with community leaders, the church, parents and every citizen.

There are a number of factors that impact on each community. These factors must be identified and action must be taken to address each one of them. Within this book among the 101 Points, approaches have been suggested to address many of the factors you will find in your community. One common question is: Where do I start?

A good approach is to discover what is going on. Let me give you some encouragement by sharing this story about a dear friend of mine and how she become involved with the youth of her community at a level that only a few people can match. On the next two pages is an article that featured her on the front page of the Wall Street Journal.

WALL STREET JOURNAL.

A Mother Channels Her Own Anguish Into Hope for Kids

• • •

Mrs. Rumph and Volunteers Teach Life Lessons in LA; Spelling Amid the Shooting

By SONIA L. NAZARIO
Staff Reporter of THE WALL STREET JOURNAL

LOS ANGELES—Three years ago, 35-year-old Al Wooten Jr. was killed in a drive-by shooting in South Central LA. He was no angel — he'd been in prison for a mugging and later became a crack addict before beginning to turn his life around—but his mother was torn apart by the loss of one of her three children. "When he died, it was like that bullet had pierced my heart," says Myrtle Faye Rumph.

Family and friends held stormy meetings in the Rumphs' living room about what to do. Some men in the family, which had already seen three relatives die by gunfire, wanted to find and kill the murderer. Others wanted to march on City Hall to demand the reopening of teen centers that dotted South Central's landscape after the Watts riots but were shuttered in the 1980s for lack of funds.

Finally, Mrs. Rumph spoke up. "I must help the next generation of children," she said. "I can't let another mother go through this." So the soft-spoken Mrs. Rumph, whose world had consisted of church functions, sewing her husband's clothing and keeping the books for his storage business, rented an empty 20-by-50-foot building next to her husband's office for $500 a month and opened the Al Wooten Jr. Heritage Center.

What Would You Change?

Since then, in a storefront in the middle of South Central, Mrs. Rumph and a bunch of volunteers, many of them black professionals who live somewhere else, have been tutoring 25 kids, ages 11 to 17, in reading, writing and life.

The Heritage Center isn't the biggest volunteer effort in Los Angeles, or the oldest. And its successes so far are simply small daily triumphs. Still, for those who watched the Los Angeles riots and said somebody ought to *do* something, meet Mrs. Rumph, now 61.

Or, better yet, meet Jason Wilborne, now 12. When he first came to the Heritage Center, he was asked: "If you could change something in your life, what would it be?" Jason's answer: "Everything."

That was 17 months ago, when Jason used to disguise his inability to read. Now he snuggles up to Mrs. Rumph with a book. "I want to read you this," he tells her. His is the first hand to shoot up when teachers seek a volunteer to read. "Faye doin' a good thing," says Jason, who wants to be a computer operator. "I've got to learn math, how to read and spell to be what I want to be."

Myrtle Faye Rumph

Mrs. Rumph herself once dreamed of being a teacher, but dropped out of school in Dallas after the ninth grade because she didn't have the bus fare to get to a segregated black high school. Instead, she washed glasses at a restaurant and, when her father died three years later, married the first man who asked. She left him six years later with her three small children.

Her new home was Watts. By day, she worked as a salad chef for $50 a week; by night, she took sewing lessons and finished high school. "My upbringing was, you take care of yourself," says Mrs. Rumph, straightening her hand-sewn green polyester pant suit. "I don't believe in handouts." Her father, a minister,

Please Turn to Page A4, Column 1

A Mother Channels Her Own Anguish Into Hope for Kids

Continued From First Page
delivered newspapers and scrounged for chores so he could feed his nine children. Although he had only a second-grade education, "there was not a word in the Bible he couldn't pronounce," she says.

Mrs. Rumph moved to South Central from Watts after the 1965 riots, which began near her sewing shop. South Central was a different place then. "It was so beautiful. This was the place to be," she says. The Heritage Center's block had three cafes and a bridal shop with tuxedos in the window.

She and her new husband, Harris, who has worked as a garbage truck driver, a gardener and now as a mover, put two of her children through college. But since the late 1970s, the exodus of 70,000 manufacturing jobs in the area crippled the neighborhood. The cafes and bridal shop failed, replaced by spots like the Love Trap Lounge. Even before the riot, Mrs. Rumph's husband had decided to close his H&M Moving and Storage Inc. "It's a depression," he says.

Healing the Wounds

The kids go to the Heritage Center for free, but Mrs. Rumph has gotten only one $8,500 grant for the school, so last year, the Rumphs sold their home of 13 years to get operating funds for the school.

Now it's a lifeline for more than two dozen kids. Its classes supplement an education system in which local schools have dropout rates as high as 70% and some teens reach high school unable to spell their own names. Its partitioned areas provide a safe place for play, and its field trips to museums and parks show a different world.

The six-day-a-week center isn't licensed as a school and its teachers are volunteers — professional men and women willing to give up an afternoon or evening a week to teach such classes as reading, spelling and black history. Every Saturday there's an entrepreneur workshop in which the students learn what it takes to start and operate a small business. It's taught by Frank Denkins, who grew up in South Central, opened a chain of dry cleaners and now owns an office furniture outlet. "Whatever I can do to help, I will do," he says.

Half the boys in Mr. Denkins's class told him they wanted to be athletes. He discourages that, telling them it is unrealistic they will be superstars. "I tell them everyone can become an engineer, a doctor, if they work hard at it." Indeed, Lamar Porter, 13, is setting up a lawn-mowing business with three other boys in the class. "I'm gonna make it on my own," he says.

"We constantly hammer at them: You can do anything you want to. You just have to ask how," says Naomi Bradley, executive director of the center and Mrs. Rumph's niece. She says a similar, government-funded teen center helped her leave behind a life of robbery and drugs.

Teaching by Example

"Faye opens the door and the children rush in" — albeit through two metal security doors — says volunteer Alice Lane, seated below the portrait of Al Wooten Jr. that hangs at the center's entrance. Ms. Lane, a student activities worker at a community college, drives in from the nearby Crenshaw area to teach the grammar and language skills class.

The students play learning games or read from about 3:30 until 5 p.m., when a teacher arrives for an hour-long class. On the pastel-green walls hang charts with the students' names and blue stars: one star for attending each of three classes a week, eight stars to qualify for a field trip. Attendance generally isn't a problem; in fact, Mrs. Rumph urges the students to come only on days when they have class. Otherwise, the tiny center gets too packed. Kids and parents hear about the center by word of mouth — Mrs. Rumph says she hasn't yet had to turn anyone away.

The teachers try to show by example. Frank Elmore, who owns a management consulting business and teaches the "learning to learn" class, tells his class that confidence and hard work got him this far. Wanda Ross, who teaches phonics, says the key to buying her own home was education. She is an ophthalmic lab technician at the hospital of the University of California at Los Angeles.

Classes are charged with enthusiasm, but sometimes interrupted by reality. "Ascertain!" Ms. Ross says to student Holly Woods, 12. "Spell it!" Holly rushes to the chalkboard, but a rat-a-tat noise outside breaks her concentration. "What's that?" she asks, as a police siren starts wailing. "They shootin' again," another youngster pipes up. Finally, Holly, an aspiring lawyer, spells the word correctly and reads the definition from her dictionary. "Very good," says Ms. Ross.

A Pledge

But all those lessons threatened to go up in smoke the night the riots broke out. Mrs. Rumph, facing her students, knew she had to say something — and fast. "The way to change future verdicts is to get an education, to vote," she told them.

"That ain't gonna work," several shouted back. Lamar Porter was so angry he spit out: "I'm probably going to jail tonight."

But then Mrs. Rumph went around the room and made each student pledge not to loot. She called as many parents as possible to pick up their children early and drove the rest home through the streets.

The next day, with trepidation, Mrs. Rumph returned to the center. Only a few doors down, the Western Swap Meet and a Bank of America branch were burned out. But the center was untouched.

Just four days later, the center was open again and Ms. Ross, the phonics teacher, showed up to teach. Now, more than ever, she says, "we must show that people care about them, that they can amount to something." None of the students were injured or arrested — including Lamar Porter, who stayed home.

"Faye tells me: There are a lot of people out there trying to bring you down," he says. "But if you stay away from them, you'll make it."

Since this story about Mrs. Myrtle Faye Rumph was printed, the center has expanded in programs and now serves as a safe haven for over 150 youth though in the midst of South Central Los Angeles, with mostly low income parents, underclass, and some not educated. These parents, grandparents, small staff, volunteers, active board of directors (multi-racial board to include citizens of Beverly Hills) - Harris, (Mrs. Rumph's husband) continue to work hard to fill a void that was in so many of these children's lives.

When the article was first published in the Wall Street Journal, but people donated from all over the country, to include Canada and Cuba. Today, however, the center is serving about 150 youth, but the conditions in the environment still exist. Some people still donate, but money is still a problem.

The community must support programs like this one by giving their time, money and other resources.

In the book "Hindsights", Mrs. Rumph sums it up like this regarding education:

"The schools were segregated in east Dallas where we lived, so I only went to school up through the ninth grade. Eventually we moved to west Dallas, but the all-black high school was in east Dallas. It cost money to go every day, and my father had nine kids. There was no money for bus fare.

I don't know what I could have done, but I just wish there had been a way. Now everybody who wants an education can get it - no matter how old you are, you can still get it, like I did later. I had three kids, but I went back to school through mail, and I also attended some classes at night.

People don't think it's important, but it is. I made sure my kids had every opportunity to go to school - college if they wanted to. Kids here at the center, hopefully I'll be able to influence them. That's the main subject around here: Get your education."[5]

I encourage initiatives like this one, moreover, I also encourage you to support the efforts of Mrs. Rumph. Send letters of encouragement and support to: the Al Wooten Jr. Heritage Center, 9106 Western Ave., Los Angeles, California, 90047. Mrs. Rumph is also willing to share her strategy. In fact, just listening to her talk is very encouraging.

POINT 44 - ADDRESSING THE NEEDS OF OUR CHILDREN IN THE PUBLIC SCHOOL SYSTEM

We must ensure the school system addresses the needs of our children. For this to occur, it will take the government, African Americans, Hispanics, teachers, and every other Americans involvement. These actions include: (1) dropout reduction programs (2) school officials working directly with parents of children with learning or disciplinary problems (3) community involvement in school management by pressing for more minority staff and ensuring school environments are safe and conducive to learning. (4) Addressing the mismatch between our education system and the needs of the new information society and (5) Restudy the special education programs and ensure that these programs actually address the needs of these students with learning disabilities.

POINT 45 - CREATING A SAFER PUBLIC SCHOOL ENVIRONMENT

To create a safer school environment we must do more than just keeping guns or weapons from the school grounds. We must raise the level of self-esteem, create a sense of security, trust and respect among the student body and faculty.

Instead of attacking the victims, we must approach this problem from a different perspective. In regard to the troubled children, we must address these conditions that cause so much chaos in their lives. The school system in itself can't resolve these problems, but, it can set the tone needed for this to occur by ensuring that the teachers are properly equipped to deal with today's youth.

Moreover, the school environment is often not safe with daily violence, fear of gang activities, and teachers that are not equipped to address this new set of problems.

Parents can play an important role in ensuring the safety of the schools. In fact, through the youth and pride in the school, the youth themselves can enhance security and help create a safer environment. Nevertheless, we must help change our young people's perspective on how they view themselves as well as how they see the school.

Therefore, we must build educational settings that can build their self-esteem, instill pride, their sense of identity, and provide opportunities to develop their natural talents. For this to occur, it will take community involvement and the development of our school staff.

In reality, to create safer environments in school, students must perceive it to be safe - then they will help keep it safe. However, in general we have not done enough of the right things to create this perception. If you reflect over the news on the past years, you must agree that there has been much talk about programs in schools being cut back, teachers striking for more money, cuts to sport and recreational programs, and increased racial violence on our school campuses. In other words, a host of negative things have been in the news regarding schools.

Students are aware of the world around them, regardless of their ages. Children can conclude that today some schools are unstable environments. What are some of the positive things that go on in schools? Have we allowed budget constraints to create unstable and unsafe environments? If the staff needs development training, can we afford not to train them? If teachers need pay raises for their personal security, can we afford not to pay them? If there are problems among the teachers and administration, would these problems impact on the environment? If human relations training is needed to improve human relations - why do we wait until we have an incident? All of these concerns have an impact on how stable and safe our school environment is.

Positive things regarding schools today very rarely make the news. In a large sense, news in the United States is primarily driven by negative activities. If the environment is perceived to be unstable by the students, they are more prone to act out their anger in this unstable environment.

Therefore, it become our responsibility to provide direct and indirect support and to create safer school environments. However, building fences and block walls around the school may not be the answer. Nor will bringing in the national guard or a large police force. This is only a false sense of security. Security can only be realized in school when the students feel safe and secure. Therefore, we must make sure that we identify current problems and address each one of them. We can't afford to allow budget constraints to put our education system in jeopardy.

We must address the teaching staff concerns, and the mental health concerns of the students, by helping to remove self doubts, fears and other anguishes, and integrate programs to improve human relations. On a side note, the budget for human relations should be viewed as an investment for a more safer America, therefore, I suggest a separate budget be established and used to address this problem. Although, the training will be conducted at the public school, however the budget should be separate from the than budget for traditional education. Schools must become the training ground to improving human relations in America. Recommend funding for human relations programs come from federal, state and local governments.

Students must look at the school grounds as a place that produces winners, successful people, a learning ground, and a safe and stable place for development. Therefore, in addition to keeping the guns and weapons off the school grounds much more attention must be placed on these other factors that help set the tone of the school environment.

The bottom line, if we put more attention on weapons being brought into schools than on these other factors that are needed to create a conducive learning environment, we will fail in our effort to effect safer school environments, and we also fail to secure the future of America.

POINT 46 - TRAINING PUBLIC SCHOOL TEACHERS ON HOW TO WORK WITH TODAY'S YOUTH

At Point 45, we've mentioned the need for development training for teachers. This training is not only needed to ensure a safer environment for the children, but, it is also required to ensure the proper development of our children. Today, more and more, I've been hearing reports on how some teachers have adapted their behaviors to that of the students who are in trouble, in order to establish rapport with these troubled students. When this occurs it's a good sign that these teachers need staff development training.

In addition to this factor, there are some teachers who still believe that African American children can't learn, and they treat them as if they are not teachable, consequently their self-fulfilling prophecy becomes a reality.

There is a continuing need for staff development training programs for public school teachers to increase their effectiveness in working with today's youth. Training must be afforded to provide teachers with much needed skills on how to stay in charge of the classrooms and not behave as one of the students. In addition, teachers must enhance their skills on how to have a more positive impact with all students who fall under their control. We can't allow budget constraints to keep us from affording the teachers, who help shape America's future through our youth, the much needed training that will enhance their effectiveness.

Point 47 - DEVELOPING EFFECTIVE MENTORS' PROGRAMS

When developing effective mentors' programs, much consideration must be given to the disproportional number of black male teachers. Black male role models are very important to correcting the problems with our black young men. Administrators, teachers, and parents should solicit men to speak in schools to improve the male presence and influence. Recommend that every concerned African American male make himself available to provide positive direction to at least one male child.

Action must be taken to create excitement regarding other career fields other than entertainment or sports. If we think hard enough, we could make designing a car very exciting to some young minds. If we think hard enough, we could make building a house very exciting to some young minds. If we think hard enough, we could make programming computers exciting to some young minds. If we think hard enough, we could make owning a business, delivering the mail and any other work exciting to some young minds. The basic problem is - we have not put enough thoughts into making these other fields exciting.

Now let's take a look at how we can create excitement about other careers using television commercials. For example let's create a commercial regarding Coke and Ford.

"A very excited engineer having just completed the design for the new Mustang drinking a Coke. Next we see the workers assembling the car and the car coming off the assembly line. Next, we see the workers drinking Coke as they watch the New Mustang speed from zero to 60 miles per hours. And, later, the workers, both males and females are shown enjoying themselves drinking Coke and having fun on the beach. (Good idea, maybe I should sell it to Ford and Coke as a "partnership commercial approach.")

It took me about one minute to create this thought. Hopefully you get my point. We must work together and create excitement about other career choices and role models.

Men must become more involved in being role models for the many black young people who don't have a positive male figure in their home. Recommend schools create more excitement during their career days by inviting role models to take part in their school programs through the year.

Recommend that churches and community groups assist these black men to become more effective role models. This is needed because many black men have not been casted in a positive light and some of their presentation skills need to be sharpened and their awareness of the psychological warfare being waged against them needs to be increased. Therefore, proper etiquette and awareness training of the black plight would be most appropriate. The Muslim community could assist in this area. Nevertheless, the new effort should be designed to inspire men of the community to have a more positive impact with the youth in the community. There must be on going interaction, both formal and informal.

Effecting this Point will mark the beginning of a new era of black men in the lives of youth in the community. Recommend social clubs also be established to evoke this level of involvement. Some of these clubs should be started by black women, to have a more far-reaching impact of soliciting the black man's involvement. This movement, should be a movement with a purpose, developing young black minds for the twenty-first century. From this pool of black men, every community-based youth program will also be able to obtain willing men of the community to enhance their programs.

POINT 48 - EFFECTIVE HOMEWORK ASSISTANCE PROGRAMS

In my research I discovered jewels on effective home work assistance. Now, I have a treasure trove and wish to share this discovery with you. I ask you to help me by sharing them with all parents of children in school.

1.   Let your child know that you consider school as stimulating and enjoyable.

2.   Since going to school is a job, encourage your children and show them that you are interested.

3.   Homework and family discussion are important items that will pay big dividends.

4.   Include your children in family projects and discussions. This helps stimulate their thinking.

5.   Create a climate at home that is conducive to learning.

6.   Let each child be himself/herself.

7.   Treat each child as an individual.

8.   Help the child to gain respect for himself/herself with your approval.

9.   Make sure you give attention to each child everyday.

10.   Receiving cooperation from teacher and family members is very important.

11.   Remember that success and failure are spirals. Once started they continue.

12.   Help your child become successful in something, because success in one field brings success in another.

13.   Give your child an early start on the spiral of success.

14.   Let your child know that he/she can achieve.

15.   Help your children make school a happy place.

16.   Remember your children need successes and your approval everyday.

17.   Show your children how to form good habits of preparing written assignments and arithmetic.

18.   Watch for signs of slow reading, poor handwriting, weak spelling and math skills.

19.   Know when to get help from an expert, then get it.

20.   Help your children develop the habit of focusing attention on each assignment or job until it is completed.

21.   Assist preschool and especially elementary school children, in developing habits of paying close attention to their work.

22.   Provide encouragement to older children to help them improve their studying and learning habits.

23.   Let your children know that habits are formed over a period of time. You must keep reminding them of this.

24.   Help your children learn how to concentrate. Encourage your children to try for greater speed in reading and in doing other homework.

25.   Provide your child an opportunity for failure without embarrassment.

26.   Work with your children and help them to develop muscle coordination. This is important for their development because children may develop a fear of writing or playing games.

27.   Help your child learn to plan action. This can help them overcome the chronic fear of failure in reciting. Fill their mind with plans and leave no room for fear.

28.   Make an effort to help children form new interests.

29.   Listen to your children's questions. Help them learn how to answer them. This will also help them develop new interests.

30.   Don't encourage cramming. Encourage them to organize the materials being studied.

31.   When your child finds interest in an area, don't try to eliminate it. Although, it is important that the child keeps his/her grades up.

32.   Parents should help their children establish new interest centers.

33. Choose a subject in school for your child - enlist his/her cooperation. Your child must try. Let your child know how the spiral of success works.

34. Encourage your child to bring up grades in other subjects one at a time.

35. Remember, asking questions is part of the learning process, therefore encourage your children to ask questions.

36. Help your children with projects. Remember it is their project. Don't take over.

37. Help your child learn how to make clear statements. Give them time to practice them. However, don't coach too much.

38. Get to know your children's teachers. Plan conferences and compare notes.

39. When you need outside help get it.

40. If you are a single parent it is difficult to do all of these things, but, you are the key figure in motivating your child to learn. Of course, the ideal situation is both parents working together, coaching their children.

41. Provide an environment that's conducive for studying.

42. Show your children the importance of planning. Remember planning is a habit, therefore, it must be practiced day after day.

43. When your child has difficulties in establishing goals, use counselors, friends, or professional help.

44. Make sure your children know what is expected of them. Develop your expectations of your children based on your understanding of their interests and ability.

45. Support your expectations with understanding help and help your child to understand you.

46. Children must see themselves as being capable. Help them to develop pictures of themselves as being successful.

47. Parents must ensure that they do everything possible to help their children get started in school on a positive note.

POINT 49 - DEVELOPING VIDEOS/MOVIES ON THE IMPORTANCE OF A GOOD EDUCATION

Develop videos/movies that clearly show the importance of school and obtaining a good education. Do it in the form of cartoons and films to reach preschool and our young people. Develop a series of these films depicting a "how to approach". Show how the children should act versus how they should not behave. Display the positive aspects. First show them what they should do before you show them what they should not do. The work should stress:

(1) Asking questions for clarity

(2) Practicing good listening habits

(3) Developing life coping skills.

POINT 50 - DEVELOPING EFFECTIVE WORKSHOPS FOR YOUNG PEOPLE ON VARIOUS LIFE SKILLS

In light of the many social problems we are facing today, it is becoming more apparent that we must better equip our young people with much needed life skills. The words of Malcolm X on December 31, 1964 regarding the youth were meaningful then and today these thoughts have even more meaning. Here is a portion of his message:

"One of the first things young people, especially nowadays, should learn is how to see for yourself and listen for yourself and think for yourself. Then you can come to an intelligent decision for yourself. If you form the habit of going by what you hear others say about someone, or going by what others think about someone, instead of searching that thing out for yourself and seeing for yourself, you will be walking east when you think you're going west. This generation, especially of our people, has a burden, more so than any other time in history. The most important thing that we can learn to do today is think for ourselves."[6]

Today, the inability to think is still a real problem for our youth and many young adults. In order to address the problem of substance abuse, gangs, crime, drop-outs, teen pregnancies, and the under-developed males, life skills must be integrated into our system of learning from preschool children to high school and then to college.

These life skills subjects should include: (1) Improving Self Image (2) Body Image (3) Family System (4) Interpersonal Communication (5) Dealing With Anger (6) Decision Making (7) Sex Education (8) The Skill of Doing (9) The Skill of Showing Belonging (9) The Skill of Learning How To Practice and (10) The Skill of Listening.

Often students will hold themselves back from demonstrating their talents and revealing insights because they don't wish to appear aggressive, or too ambitious. These young people must be coached to demonstrate their creativity, enthusiasm, special skills and hidden talents.

The school system must be supplemented with community programs to this end. We must conduct effective workshops for young people on various life skill subjects throughout the nation. These workshops should be conducted at no cost to the students. This must become one of America's real investments to our future.

Request For Proposals (RFPs) should be initiated from the federal, state, and local governments, as well as private foundations to ensure that these life skills training opportunities become a reality throughout America. But we must not wait on funding from these sources before commencement of these programs, but instead, seek funding to enhance these solutions.

POINT 51 - PROMOTING BASIC SKILLS DEVELOPMENT (REMEDIAL TRAINING)

There have been a number of studies to support the need to promote Basic Skills Development Programs to include reading, writing, and math skills. Here is some of the results of the findings:

- Twenty percent of 3,600 young adults who took part in a recent study read below the eighth-grade level. Of course this put them at disadvantage since most American jobs require reading ability at the high school level.[7]

- A 1987 California study of welfare recipients found that more than a third needed remedial education of the most basic type.[8]

- Half of the adults in federal and state correctional facilities have little or no ability to read or write.[9]

- In order to fill 2,000 job openings at New York Telephone, 90,000 interviews were conducted. Of the 90,000 candidates, 84 percent (75,600) failed the examination which required less than a high school education to pass.[10]

The foregoing clearly shows the necessity for funding remedial education. As we reflect back to the early 1960's, we can recall a number of federal-funded programs designed to provide work experience and training, both on the job and classroom instructions. These programs were designed to make the less employable more employable. The primary target groups were minorities, welfare recipients, and low income youth.

Under the Reagan administration some of these initiatives were discontinued (such as CETA). However, the Job Corps and the Work Incentive programs did survive. Nevertheless, a new initiative was launched under the Job Training Partnership Act (JTPA). Though this is in the area of remedial education, in 1980 funding for all programs combined has been slashed. Between 1981 and 1986, federal support for five major programs was cut by two-thirds. This decline in funding is unlikely to improve the effectiveness of JTPA. For example, under JTPA, stipends are not offered to individuals who need remedial.

There have been many debates regarding this problem to no resolve. However, in general it is agreed by all sides that participants in these various programs are but a small percentage of those needing help, and the general problem of skill deficiency among youth and young adults is not merely unsolved, but has yet to be seriously addressed. Like many other observers, the National Academy of Sciences Panel in 1985 summed it up like this:

"The employment and training system is trying in large part to do what the education system should be doing but, for some significant segment of the youth population, apparently fails to do. Yet the employment and training system has not attained stability of funding, professionalization of staff, and delineation of authority, in short, institutionalization of the sort that has given the educational system its accepted place in the mainstream of American life. As a result, in most communities, organizations involved in employment and training are considered marginal."[11]

Here is a blunt commentary from a "second chance" training program in the Southwest:

"If we really wanted to serve hard-core unemployed youth, we'd have to do a lot more than we've been willing to do. You wouldn't be looking for a payoff in less than three years, possibly four years. A reasonably stable nineteen to twenty-year-old with some work experience, we can brush him up and send him out on a job. But the other? We don't want to make the investment, so we forget about them."[12]

So we forget about them-So we forget about them. Let's build prisons. So we forget about them-So we forget about them. Let's build more prisons. So we......

We need funding and support to stop this cycle of wasting so many human lives. We need to train them and give them stipends as they prepare themselves for the job market.

We the people must demand that our government provide sites throughout the nation to effect this training. At these sites, participants needs must be assessed, provisions made for one-on-one tutoring, and adult education classes must be realized.   Other training should be offered to include stress management, interpersonal communication and how to deal with anger.

Individuals who need remedial training should be encouraged to ask for this training. They must be shown that they are not alone and they can receive help. The reduction of fear and reservation of individuals asking for help in this area is very important.   This effort can be supported through public service announcements, movies, and television and radio programs. Again, we must let them know they are not alone. They must be able to identify with the situations depicted in the sources of encouragement.

For example: A good friend of mine who is in business as a contractor shared with me the impact of his illiteracy. He shared that when he couldn't read and he feared going after big jobs. When he had to bid because he couldn't do the paper work. He said since he couldn't read, he developed other coping skills to compensate for his inability. He coped by not looking at the street signs, but by looking for landmarks. When he sought directions for a new job site, he would not only ask for the street address, he would also ask for landmarks. He became a keen observer. Since he was very intelligent, he hired someone to do the paperwork for him. Finally, he admitted to himself that this was a real problem for him and he taught himself to read. He also expressed: he took it a word at a time and he found delight in each word that he learned.

There must be more public service announcements, movies and talk shows that are creative enough to show these type of situations as described above. The illiterate must clearly see, that we understand their problems and that we are ready and willing to help.   People must understand they are not inferior, and, this is a condition that can be corrected. They must see that it is like learning how to drive a car and they must realize that they are not alone, because there are millions of Americans who are like them and they too have not been properly trained. We must make the training inviting. More importantly, when they ask for help, it must be available for them.

We all must make personal sacrifices to bring real initiatives on-line to provide remedial education to these people. Some of us can volunteer our time as instructors or counselors. However, this cannot be just an all volunteer effort. Some of us can give money and other in-kind resources. By understanding the severity of the problem and working together, we can help coach these young Americans as they become more productive citizens.

POINT 52 - ESTABLISHING REDIRECTING TRAINING FOR CURRENT GANG MEMBERS

We must provide personal redirecting training for current gang members. This redirecting training should consist of values clarification, education, counseling training, and goal setting.

In studying and working with ex-gang members, I've discovered that redirecting training could be quite effective. This training allows current gang members to reassess values, clarify values, overcome grief, adopt new habits, and set new goals. This training also afforded participants gang relapse prevention education.

I suggest that the training be given with the following blocks of instructions: (1) Personal Grievous Period (2) Self- Awareness (3) Here and Now and Your Life Picture (4) Value Clarification (5) Financial Planning (6) Establishing New Goals (7) Habits Awareness (8) Group Rap up. After the group is over, individuals should be given an opportunity to develop their skills, receive job readiness training, and then be placed on a job. Recommend a follow-up period of nine months to one year. While ex-gang members participate in follow-up, recommend that they also take part in a gang deterrence speaker program.

I've designed a gang redirecting program and suggest that the training contain some of the features listed below.

Block I. Personal Grieving Period. This block gives participants an opportunity to get acquainted and to overcome hurt and grief.

Block II. Self Awareness. A series of group exercises should follow: (1) Complete Thought Exercise (2) Self-Image Exercise (3) Look at Self-Exercise and (4) My Life Chart Exercise.

Block III. Here And Now And Your Life Picture. This block gives participants an opportunity to examine what is presently going on in their lives and it allows each individual to reflect on his/her life picture.

Block IV. Value Clarification. This block of instruction enables each participant an opportunity to clarify their value by using a series of exercises. Through this process participants will be able to reassess their values and decide on which to hold onto and which to discard.

Block V. Financial Planning. This block of instruction allows participants to take a close look at their current financial picture, provide information on financial planning and how to create financial budgets.

Block VI. Establishing New Goals. After participants are given an opportunity to examine their lives, values, and financial picture, it is important to establish goals and commit themselves to follow these goals once established. The following exercises will be conducted during this period. (1) Goal Commitment Exercise (2) Goal Setting Exercise (3) Global Goal Exercise and (4) Habits Awareness Exercise.

Block VII. Personal Dependency Exercise. The purpose of this exercise to determine if participants are depending on the gang life style for his/her survival.

Block VIII. Group Rap Up. During this period individuals complete personal disclosure and feed back exercise, group exercise and a Self-Image Inventory and a self-evaluation.

After the redirecting training, they must be given an opportunity to develop an education as required and develop job skills. After successful completion, job readiness training must be afforded, and finally, the individuals must be placed in meaningful jobs.

Follow-up and Support/Gang Deterrence Participation.

The training as described is taken from the concept that I developed entitled: Operation Root Up Gangs (Operation RUG).

A copy of the plan can be procured. For more information check in the back of this book.

POINT 53 - INCREASING COLLEGE ENROLLMENT/COMPLETION AND PREPARING FOR THE NEW INFORMATION ERA

To equip African Americans for the new information era, it will require more to enroll and complete college. Moreover, they also must major in subjects that are in demand by the market. In addition, African Americans must understand that we are shifting in strategic resource from an industrial to an information society. Consequently, to meet this challenge we must ensure that our young people are prepared to meet the job market. Naisbitt and Aburdene summarized as follows:

> "...In the industrial era, when the strategic resource was capital, the goal of the corporation could only have been profits. In the information era, however, the strategic resource is information, knowledge, creativity. There is only one way a corporation can gain access to these valuable commodities-that is, through the people in whom these resources reside."[13]

When we look at the state of our education system today, we must agree in order to prepare for the information era, our young people need computer training, training on how to think, learn, and training on how to become more creative. To meet these demands, we must revise our current education system.

We must ensure computers are available for our young people at school and they must be educated on the importance of becoming computer literate. For this to occur, we must ensure that they know what is going on in the job market centered around computers.

The ability to think is another important aspect for the information age. Thinking is an important skill that can be learned and than developed. In fact, thinking is just as basic as reading. However, there has not been enough emphasis on this subject in our system of learning. There are a number of models on the process of thinking that should be integrated into our system of learning.

To keep pace with this changing society, individuals must be taught how to learn. There are a number of models on this subject that could also be integrated into our school system.

Like learning and thinking, today, it is believed that creativity can be taught. And creativity is viewed as the corporation's competitive edge.

In addition to computer training, learning, and creativity, we must increase our college enrollment and completion as we prepare for this new information era. Research reveals the following:

Between 1982 and 1991, there were increases in the portions of the total African American population with four years of college or more (36.2 percent), one to three years of college (19.9 percent), and those who were high school graduate (13 percent).

Moreover, the proportion of African Americans 20 to 29 years of age completing four or more years of college decreased by 6 percent, while the proportion of their white comparative group increased by 13 percent. Immediate action must be taken to reverse this trend.

In addition to reversing these trends, we must develop our untapped talents. There are a number of professions in the United States where blacks find themselves lagging far behind whites. One area of concern is technology. In the work of Warren F. Miller, Jr., "Developing Untapped Talent: A National Call For African-American Technologists", The State of Black America, 1991, he concludes that Black America remains seriously behind White America in achieving parity in the overall development of technology. However, recently, the black students college enrollment is approaching parity, but the completion is about one half of the rate of enrollment. For example: in 1988, African Americans made up 7.5 percent of the total student enrollment, however retention rate is about half of the general engineering student population.

When an engineer graduates with a bachelor's degree in the industrial sector, salaries range from $28,000 to $36,000 immediately after graduation. At mid-career, salaries more than $75,000 a year is not unusual for these engineers. Young people must me made aware of this opportunity while they are in junior high and high school and be encouraged to take mathematics, and science.

Like the rate of college retention in the field of engineering, data regarding other fields are very similar. Data calculated by the National Urban League reveal the following: Between 1982 and 1991, there were increases in the proportions of the total African American population with four years of college or more (36.2 percent), one to three years of college (19.9 percent), and those who were high school graduates (13 percent). However, during the same period African Americans, 20 to 29 years of age, completion four or more years of college decreased by 6 percent, while the proportion of their white comparison group increased. On the other hand, the proportion of African Americans 35 to 44 years-old, completing college was 52 percent larger than the proportion of this same groups completion of college in 1982.

In studying the data related to African Americans in the age group of 20-29, for both males and females, there is a decrease in the proportion of those with four years of college or more.

The National Action Council for Minorities in Engineering (NACME) has studied the problem of the disproportionate number of Black engineers and offer suggestions on how to reach parity. The recommendations they made can be adapted to apply to just about any field. Here is an adaptive form of the recommendations made by NACME:

(1)   Identify obstacles to retain black students and recruit black students to the quantitative fields. Include in the studies experiences of African Americans at predominantly white universities and Historically Black Colleges and Universities.

(2)   Increase significantly the number and size of scholarships and grants.

(3) Reevaluate minority academic, psychological, and cultural support programs on university campuses.

(4) Widely disseminate information of past accomplishments of African Americans in various fields. This information should be shared to both the minorities and the whites on school campuses.

(5) Take action on several fronts to increase the number of role models.

- Sensitize the mass media of this need to portray to young people about science careers and other careers that are needed for the information era.

- Increase the number of black role models at all level-elementary schools through universities.

- Engage Black professionals in mentoring programs at all levels. Provide positive exposure to quantitative careers for black children.

Chapter III Notes

1. Dewart, Janet (1993), The State Of Black America, p.p. 16-17, National Urban League, "The Third Movement; Development Black Children For The 21st Century, by: Dr. Jeff P. Howard

2. Ibid. p. 18

3. Welsing, Frances Cress, (1991), The Isis Paper, p.273

4. Raspberry, William, Key To Teen Birth Is Self-Perception, St Louis Post Dispatch, December 20, 1986, 3B. The view is also expressed in publication of the Children Defense Fund; See Marion Wright Edelman, Families In Peril:An Agenda For Change, Cambridge: Harvard University Press, 1987. Quoted by Sherraden, Michael in Asset And The Poor, (1991)

5. Kawasaki, Guy, 1973, Hindsights, p. 161

6 X, Malcolm, (1985), Malcolm X Speaks, p. 137

7 McClelland, Peter D. (1990), The American Search For Economic Justice, p. 319, Quoted from Back To Basic, Newsweek (September 21, 1987) p. 54

8 McClelland, Peter D. (1990), The American Search For Economic Justice, p. 319, Quoted from National Governors' Association, Making America Work, p. 79

9 Ibid. p. 80

10 McClelland, Peter D. (1990), The American Search For Economic Justice, p. 319, Back To Basic, Newsweek (Sept. 21, 1987) p. 54

11 Committee On Youth Employment Programs, Youth Employment and Training Programs, The YEDPA YEARS (Washington, D.C.: National Academy Press, 1985), p. 33. Quoted by McClelland in the American Search For Economic Justice p. 320

12 Hahn & Danzberer, <u>Dropout In America,</u> p. 51. Quoted by McClelland in <u>American Search For Economic Justice</u>, p. 320

13 Naisbitt, John & Aburdene, Patricia, (1985) <u>Re-Inventing The Corporation</u>, p. 11

CHAPTER IV

ECONOMICS

In this chapter, we look at economics from a number of perspectives, to include personal, business and we examined our economic system in America. This information is designed to increase awareness and can help chart the path to economic justice, regardless of an individual current status.

POINT 54 - REVISING OUR ECONOMIC SYSTEM

We must take a critical look at America's current economic system because the system is designed for the rich to become richer and the poor to become poorer. This clearly explain why we have the persistence of poverty in America today. America as rich as it is, has from 35 million to 50 million people who live below the poverty line. We must learn from our history of the major depressions of 1893 to the great depression 1929-1940. Today, the state of unemployment, rate of poverty, lack of vital programs to address real people problems are similar to the conditions in 1893, some 36 years prior to the period of the great depression. At this Point, we present the facts and offer real solutions to secure a strong America.

The first area of concern are the wages and benefits. Employers pay their workers the least possible. Therefore, the laborers only receive a portion of the wealth created by them. The owner receives the balance for investment and profit. Often this is under a principle of profit maximization. Under profit maximization, owners believe it is in their best interest to pay the lowest possible wages for the labor.

The second concern is the price of labor. The cost of labor is determined by the supply. A marginal productivity theory is used to determine if it is cost effective to add more workers. In fact, it is in the best interest of the owner to have a surplus of laborers, who are under-educated and desperate people who will work for very low wages. A large supply of these workers enable the ownership class by depressing the wages for all workers in good times. When the economic downturns, these workers could be laid off without effecting production.

The third area of concern is the investment decisions. The primary of profits in capitalism is that employers make investment decisions without regard for their employees. If cost can be reduced by installing new machinery or having the products produced in a foreign country at a cheaper labor cost, it is the decision of the employers, regardless of the displacement of the workers. Today imports are killing many American jobs. We purchase most of the television-sets, videotape-recorders from Japan. Thousands of Americans will lose jobs under NAFTA. Dorsen asserts: "Further, workers' interests in their jobs have not received even the minimal constitutional protection afforded poor people's interest in subsistence."[1]

As Dorsen also stated: "Work is not organized to enhance productivity, quality, or worker satisfaction. Technology has made many jobs obsolete, and we have not developed the capacity to either spread work around or to expand opportunities for people to work providing needed social services. It is possible to solve these problems. But our history strongly suggests that solutions demand a popular political movement, and that movement is lacking."[2]

Etizen, summarized the politics of economy of society as follows:

"The fundamental assumption of capitalism is individual gain without regard for what the resulting behaviors may mean for others. The capitalist system, then, should not be accepted as a neutral framework within which goods are produced and distributed, but rather as an economic system that perpetuates inequality."[3]

Robertson summarized it like this:

"Poverty exists in America because the society is unequal, and there are overwhelming political pressures to keep it that way. Any attempt to redistribute wealth and income will inevitably be oppressed by powerful interests. Some people can be relatively rich only if others are relatively poor, and since power is concentrated in the hands of the rich, public policies will continue to reflect their interest."[4]

The assistant director of the Office of Economic Opportunity, Hyman Bookbinder in 1966 made this assertion:"The poor can stop being poor if the rich are willing to become even richer at a slower rate."[5]

Dr. King summarize as follows:"A dream of equality of opportunity, of privilege and property widely distributed; a dream of a land where men will not take necessities from the many to give luxuries to the few."[6]

It is important that we re-examine the current system and ask some direct questions. (1) Who does capitalism benefit? (2) Who benefits from poverty? (3) Who influences both, capitalism and poverty? and (4) Does the evidence suggest that American economy features a principle of natural selection whereby firms must continue to maximize profits in order to continue to exist?

To answer the first question, Who does capitalism benefit? - We must admit that everybody benefits to some extent. However the owners benefit the most and the employees at lowest end of the scale, receive the least rewards, to the point that they can't meet the necessities of life.

The second question, Who benefits from poverty? An uninformed person would answer this question with a simple response like: no one benefits. However, that is not the correct answer because people do benefit from poverty. Herbert Gans, a sociologist, has some interesting insight about the benefits of poverty. Here is a summation of his observation:

(1) Poverty functions to provide a low-wage labor pool that is willing (or unable to be unwilling) to do society "dirty work". The middle and upper class are subsidized by the existence of economic activities that depend on the poor (low wages workers at hospitals, restaurants, and truck farms).

(2) The poor also serve as patients in research in hospitals or as guinea pigs. In addition they provide servants, gardeners, and house cleaners who make life easier for the well-to-do. This of course subsidizes economic activities for the affluent.

(3) Poverty creates jobs for a number of occupations and professions that serve the poor or protect the rest of society from them (penologists, social workers, police, pawn shop owners, numbers racketeers, and owners of liquor stores). Moreover, the presence of the poor also provides income for doctors, lawyers, teachers, and others who are too old, poorly trained, or incompetent to attract more affluent clients.

(4) The poor purchases seconds, dilapidated car, deteriorated housing, day-old bread, fruit, and vegetables. These activities subsidize merchants by purchasing these goods which otherwise would have little value.

(5) The poor serve as a group to be punished in order to uphold the legitimacy of conventional values.

(6) Poverty guarantees the status of those who are not poor. The poor provide a reliable and relatively permanent measuring rod for status comparison by occupying a position at the bottom of the status hierarchy.

(7) The poor aid the upward mobility of others. (A number of persons have entered the middle class by selling goods and providing services to people in the slums).

(8) The poor absorb the cost of change in society. They build the railroads, cities, and roads. They move from their homes to the buildings of the expressways, and parks. The poor are the last to be hired and the first to be fired. The poor are the ones who make the real sacrifice for the economy.

The next question, Who influences both, capitalism and poverty? Of course the affluent influences both and resist efforts to redistribute wealth to the disadvantaged.

Jack London said it this way: "affluence means influence".[7] Or better yet, the Medici family of sixteenth century Florence stated it best: "money to get power, power to protect the money."[8]

Eitzen states it as follows: "Decisions are made by the powerful, and these decisions tend to benefit the wealthy disproportionately. But the power elite is formally not organized. There is no conspiracy per se. The interests of the powerful (and the wealthy) are served, nevertheless, through the way in which society is structured. This bias occurs in three ways - by the elite's influence over elected and appointed government officials at all levels, by the structure of the system, and by ideological control of the masses." [9]

Ponder these thoughts as you review some of the benefits to the affluent and the cuts to the poor under Reagan's administration and a conservative Congress.

Benefits to the Affluent:

-   No inheritance taxes for Estates up to $600,000 (up from $175,000)
-   Children can receive up to $10,000 each from each parent (up from $3,000), so parents can avoid taxes
-   Persons working abroad can make up to $75,000 tax free.
-   The top tax rate was reduced from 70 percent to 50 percent.

Cuts to the poor:

- Aid to Families with Dependent Children (AFDC) will not go to families with more than $1,000 in assets (the old limit was $2,000)
-   The Community Services Administration was closed. This organization administered 900 locally run community action groups such as those dealing with jobs, legal services, Upward Bound, Head Start, and other programs for the benefit of the poor.

- Significant funds were cut from food stamps, CETA-funded public jobs, legal services, housing subsidies, Medicaid, and school lunches.

America is not aware of the great variety of government programs for the non-poor. This program includes price support, acreage allotments, low-interest loans, tax breaks and loopholes and government purchases. All of these programs subsidize the income of millions of non-poor.

In addition, individual, huge corporations are also subsidized. As cited in the work of Meltzer: "According to Citizens for Tax Justice, a private research group, 128 of the 250 most profitable corporations paid no taxes at all or received rebates in at least one of the first three years of President Reagan's administration. This happened despite these corporations' total profits of $56.7 billion. The five leading defense contractors - General Electric, Boeing, Dow Chemical, Tenneco, and Santa Fe/Southern Pacific - paid no income tax for three consecutive years in the early 1980's."[10]

Another interesting comparison made by Meltzer is that: "Social Security benefits were reduced by $100 billion between 1981 and 1985, while corporate tax subsidies in 1984 alone totaled an estimated $90 billion, excluding the defense budget."[11]

If the affluent are the political minority, why do they have so much power?

As Judge J. Skelly Wright observes, "Financial inequalities posed pervasive and growing threat to the principle of "one vote," and undermine the political proposition to which this nation is dedicated - that all men are created equal."[12]

Peter D. McClelland, professor of Economics at Cornell University in Ithaca, New York, and author of "The American Search For Economic Justice" has invested a lot of time investigating the subject of economic justice in America. Through his efforts, I had the opportunity to examine some of the philosophy of Economists Friedrich Hayek, Murray Rothbard, Milton Friedman, and Arhur Okun. After reviewing extreme views on the right and the extreme views on the left, I understand one of the reasons we have not obtained economic justice in the United States. We have failed to reach common ground because of personal greed. Personal greed is not common ground and it is not in the best interest of the country.

However, there has been much concern voiced about economic justice over the years. Below are some of the concerns voiced:

President Kennedy: "If a free society cannot help the many who are poor, it cannot save the few who are rich".[13]

Winston Churchill: "If we [carry] on in the happy-go-lucky way - the richer classes ever growing in wealth and in number, and the very poor remaining plunged or plunging ever deeper in helpless misery - then I think there is nothing before us but savage strife between class and class, with the increasing disorganization, with increasing waste of human strength and human virtue..."[14]

The cry of a Catholic bishop in support of the Full Employment Act in 1945 as he addressed congress: "A nation that is ill-housed, ill-fed, and ill-clothed in any considerable part is a fertile ground for the curse of totalitarianism."[15] In support of the same act, the voice of a rabbi resounded: "Where there is no bread there is no law."[16]

Congressman Estes Kefauver was also in support of the same act. He confronted his colleagues with the following commentary:

"Let me ask you, how can the Government assure freedom without seeing to it that every individual has the opportunity to earn a living? If a man has no job, how can he enjoy freedom of political participation, freedom of competition, freedom of health, education, recreation, and security, freedom of social and economic democracy, freedom to make the most of himself? How can a man on the dole exercise that initiative and self-reliance which is declared to be a major objective of this committee bill? Without the right to work, a man is not free."[17]

Here are some other concerns regarding factors pertaining to economic justice that have been made over the years:

President Johnson: "We want to offer the forgotten fifth of our people opportunity, not doles."[18]

Walter Reuther, President United Automobile Workers stated:

"This increasing imbalance in the distribution of wealth has been in part a consequence of the fact that those in our economy who possess a large measure of freedom to appropriate more than their fair share of the fruit of economic growth have been persistently abusing that freedom - particularly the major corporations which dominate whole industries, and which have use the power to set the prices of their products, and consequently their profits, at a level of their own choosing without being subjected to the pressure of competitive market forces. The abuse of power has been reflected in the fact that dividends, which go largely to a relatively few wealthy individuals, together with undistributed profit and depreciation allowances retained in corporate treasuries have increased in the past 10 years faster than the incomes of those who produces corporate wealth."[19]

There has been a number of Acts over the years for economic reasons and to address the genuine concerns for economic justice. These Acts include: Full Employment Act of 1946, The Manpower and Development and Training Act (1962), the Economic Opportunity Act (1964), the Comprehensive Employment and Training Act (1973), and the Job Training Partnership Act (1982).

All of these programs are designed to provide training primarily for the disadvantaged: minorities, welfare recipients, and low-income groups. The programs are to be facilitated through (a) classroom training and other institutional training, (b) on-the-job training programs that pay subsidy to employers for hiring disadvantaged workers. The impact of on-the-job program has been negligible, because the participation of employer has been negligible.

McClelland summarized the success of the programs as follow: "Even the staunch supporters usually conceded that no program has had startling success, and that each program even at its best has been made some difference to some of the participants some of the time. What is clear to supporters and critics alike is that the particular are far less tractable and less well understood than was originally believe when manpower training program were first initiated. What is also clear, although neither left nor right seems incline to emphasize the point, is that American public and their elected representatives have yet to take manpower training problems seriously. The limited nature of initiatives tried, their limited success, and the poverty of new proposals presently under serious review would all seem convincing proof of that." [20]

McClelland made a keen observation regarding the American public and their elected representatives not taking the manpower training problem seriously. Lessons learned have taught us, that concerns for minorities and the poor must be continuously pushed by special interest groups, if not the initiatives die. Oftentimes, the victims feel powerless because of the other pressures of daily survival. Therefore, they need the leadership of outside interest groups.

Do we have economic rights? Or have we allowed rationalization to protect the affluent and deny the poor and the workers to the necessities of life?

American history does not support the view that political freedom goes hand in hand with laissez-faire economics.

Since the 1930's the Supreme Court's approach to civil liberties and economic arrangements has drawn a sharp distinction between social and economic legislation and laws effecting civil liberties. This approach presumes that the legislature processes a greater institutional competence to set social and economic policy than do the courts, because legislatures express democratic will.

According to Dorsen, the distinction between economic legislation and fundamental rights has intuitive appeal. In practice, like the classical liberal concepts of natural right, it has also proven to be self-contradictory and class-biased. He cites several examples of his observations. Here are a couple of those observations:

(1) A law denying additional welfare payments to families of more than five people was upheld as mere "economic and social legislation," despite the obvious adverse impact on family autonomy and composition choice, which in other contexts the Court recognize as an aspect of constitutionally protected liberty.

(2) A law limiting campaign spending for Congressional elections violates the First Amendment because money is a form of speech, while a law excluding payment for medically necessary abortions from the otherwise comprehensive Medicaid program does not burden any fundamental right.

In 1971, the Supreme Court in the case, Goldberg v. Kelly, involved the claim that welfare recipients had the constitutional provision prohibition the state from taking life, liberty, or property without due process of law. This provision required that they be given notice and an opportunity for a hearing prior to the termination of aid.

As noted here, property may be in the form of land, wages, welfare, a license to practice law, or whatever society defines it to be.

Here is an excerpt of the Supreme Court ruling:

"From its founding the Nation's basic commitment has been to foster the dignity and well-being of all persons within its borders. We have the come to recognize that forces not within the control of the poor contribute to their poverty...Welfare, by meeting the basic demands of subsistence, can help bring within the reach of the poor the same opportunities that are available to others to participate meaningfully in the life of the community....Public assistance, then, is not mere charity, but a means to "promote the general Welfare, and secure Blessings of Liberty to ourselves and our Posterity."[21]

Civil libertarians now realize this ruling on welfare could also apply to work, "the material-accumulation functions of property." Nevertheless, the transforming potential has not been realized. In other words, under this ruling workers could be granted certain protections that are not currently being realized. For example: a hearing prior to termination. There are many of reasons why we have not realized the full impact of this ruling.

Here is a summation of reasons as expressed by Dorsen:

(1) Social movements that support this ruling have declined. We must remember that ideas in action shape constitutional doctrine more profoundly than ideas on paper - The Court would not have adopted the theory of Goldberg without the welfare rights movement of the late 1960's in which the poor people acted as if they had a right to subsistence and decent treatment.

(2) Lack of social movement - Significant Supreme Court actions protecting the political and economic rights of common people often come during periods of social struggle by those people.

(3) The death of important leaders (Martin Luther King, Jr., and Malcolm X) to the civil and welfare rights account for the decline in the movement.

(4) The war in Vietnam led many who were active in other social struggles to concentrate on the antiwar movement.

(5) The FBI harassed and destablized large numbers of groups and individuals working against the war and for civil rights and economics.

(6) The commercially-oriented and corporate-controlled mass media profoundly shape social movements, and contribute to their decline.

(7) The 1960s concept of economic relations and political liberty did not address the work and material-accumulation function of property. It could not sustain commitment to protecting individual interests in material support.

Dorsen concludes: "Economic justice and civil liberties are mutually reinforcing in many ways. Because individual material support is a prerequisite to the exercise of all rights. Civil libertarian value supports individual claims against the state for subsistence. Because work is a means of support and a central form of human self-actualization, commitment to civil libertarian values also demands concern that people have opportunity for work and for a voice in the control of work."[22]

We must truly reexamine our current economic system. Today we have 35 million to 50,000,000 people living in poverty. Many of those people are working people.

Economic justice will not come to us automatically. There must be a struggle for it. The affluent will not give up their positions for the ones less privileged without strong resistance. No it will not occur voluntarily. Bookbinder, described it best: "The poor can stop being poor if the rich are willing to become even richer at a slower rate."[23]

This is a black and white problem. However, it's also more than black and white. It is a black and white problem because it impacts upon Blacks disproportionally than more any other group. And it's more, because this problem affects the poor white, Hispanic, Native Americans and all other minorities. If we fail to address this problem, there will be more social chaos. Our streets will not become safer. We can't build enough jails, we can't buy enough guns, we can't move any farther away from the inner-cities. Moreover, we will find trouble on every front.

We always can rationalize our positions. However, our rationalization to keep the system as it is, is not in the best interest of the country. Rationalization is key to discrimination, which supports our current economic system. However, rationalization will not stop the realization that what affects the poor indirectly affects the affluent. The United States is too small to find a safety zone for anyone if we fail to correct this destructive condition.

We have learned many lessons from the past, we know what we must do here. We must educate America, on what's going on. Martin Luther King, Jr., tried, however, America didn't listen. So, why should you listen to me? I ask that you not listen to me, but listen to the facts. Listen to sound reasoning. Listen to the history of lessons learned, and to wisdom.

Our elected leadership is failing us in America in short term and long term planning. We the people must guide them and develop them or else these ineffective leaders will destroy what our foreparents worked so hard for.

I agree with the current trend of thought that we need welfare reforms. However, more than Aid to Families with Dependent Children (AFDC) needs reforming. AFDC has become the center of debates, however, of all welfare problems this one is costing us the least amount of money. "The annual federal expenditure for family support payments, primarily in the form of AFDC, but also including child support collection programs, was budgeted at $11.2 billion in fiscal year 1990. This amount is only 9.0 percent of the poor welfare state and only 1.4 percent of the grand welfare state. On a side note: "...federal tax expenditures for home-mortgage tax deductions alone are more than twice the federal expenditures for AFDC.

The ACLU made the following comparison with SSI and AFDC:

"Experience in the past decade with the Supplemental Security Income (SSI) program for the aged, blind, and disabled, and the AFDC program for needy women and children is illustrative. Since 1974 the SSI program has been financed through general federal revenues, while the AFDC program depends in significant part upon more regressive state and local taxes. Today SSI benefits exceed AFDC benefits for families of comparable size in every state. In twenty-two states, SSI benefits exceed benefits for needy women and children by more than 100 percent. In six states SSI benefits exceed AFDC benefits by more than 400 percent.[24] AFDC is the only major subsistence program that is not indexed for inflation. In the past decade the real value of already meager AFDC grants has declined by 56 percent. The federal government is not inherently more humane toward the poor than the states. But the federal government does have a greater power to tax progressively to raise funds to provide the material support that is the necessity of liberty."[25]

People need jobs and not AFDC. However, they must earn enough on the jobs to at least live a decent lifestyle. This observation made by Sherraden must be really considered when making reforms to AFDC:

"It may be surprising to some, but most single mothers are not on welfare, and a very large number hold full-time jobs. Some 55 percent to 60 percent of single mothers worked outside the home. But in 1986, almost half of these 6.3 million single mothers earned less than ten thousand dollars per year. Although there has been extensive interest in welfare-to-work programs in the United States, it is clear that there are not enough well-paying jobs. People can work full time and still be in poverty."[26]

Other evidence makes it abundantly clear: that the majority of those who receive this type of welfare in America are poor for only a brief period, usually two years or less. However, there is a subset of welfare recipients with a much different record. Roughly one-sixth of those who are poor remain poor for eight years or more, and for many of these, receiving welfare has become a way of life.

The problem with economics in this country is much larger than AFDC. However, some politicians have resolved to toy with America. Consequently, in the short term the politicians win, but in the end, America will lose because of this ineffective leadership. World War II taught us that an informed America, and a threatened America will work together and will make personal sacrifices. Strong leadership will realize that America is threatened from within and the people of America need to be informed.

Every right of the affluent should be protected because for the most part they have earned those rights. Nevertheless, on this issue we must find common ground. Poverty has no place in America, especially when about 40% of the people who live in poverty are children. One may continue to frown on helping the disadvantaged adults, however, if we closely examine their problem we find that it interconnected with their childhood.

McClelland phrased it as follows: "If the problems of disadvantaged adults are not unrelated to problems they encountered before becoming adults, then policies need to be designed not only to remedy skill and attitudinal deficiencies among the present generation, but also to reduce the flow from childhood into adulthood of those similar disadvantaged in the next generation."[27]

Regardless, whether we are rich or poor, most of us would agree that all children should have a fair chance to attain whatever respect, riches, and rewards our society has to offer. However, to date equal opportunity has been a myth in America. In the work of Keniston and the Carnegie Council on Children the question of the myth of equal opportunity was addressed. Prior to closing this discussion on economics, we must explore their observations:

"Why have we so consistently built program after program, through a long lineage of charity and reform, on an inaccurate assumption? To answer this question, it is necessary to examine another American myth -the myth of equal opportunity. The United States, we have long believed, is a society fundamentally open to success through hard work and talent; personal qualities largely determined the position of respect, power, and wealth any individual ultimately achieves in his or her lifetime. The myth denies that the circumstances of birth - and in particular the social and economic position into which a child is born - have much effect in determining where the individual ends up in life. Parental wealth, power, status, and race are seen as irrelevant to one's final status. The poor can rise from rags to riches, while those born to wealth will fall to poverty if they lack talent and industry. According to this view, the social level at which any individual is found directly reflects his or her effort and abilities."[28]

This myth of equal opportunity flowered in the first half of the nineteenth century. However, by the end of the nineteenth century, more Americans began to realize, however dimly, that economic wealth conveyed political power even in a democracy, for the rich gained access to political decision makers and exercised influence on local, state, and federal policies which people of lesser means could not have.

Today, studies support that many Americans have been able to live the reality that offspring of the poor had a way, more than not, of ending up poor. Today most Americans realize that the stories of "rags to riches" are the exception and not the rule. Nevertheless, unfortunately even today some still hold firm and try to address the problems of poverty and deprivation as equal opportunity problems. However, these are problems of distribution.

Keniston and the Carnegie Council on Children view it as follows: "Distribution of the rewards - as distinct from the opportunity to compete for the rewards - is far more unequal than our national self-image seems to imply."[29]

According to Sherraden:

"In general, the pattern of asset distribution is related to the pattern of income distribution; that is, those in low incomes tend to have few assets and those with high incomes tend to have many assets. However, asset distribution is much more unequal than is income distribution. **To summarize very simply, the richest 5 percent of Americans receive about the same income as the bottom 40 percent, but the richest one percent own more assets than the bottom 80 percent.**"[30]

Helping the unfortunate by ensuring economic justice will take personal sacrifices. Some people will have to make more sacrifices than others. Nevertheless, it is always best when you decide on the course that you going are to take. The United States and the world are full of tension and problems all around us. There is far too much suffering in this land of plenty. We are too rich to be so poor in spirit.

To the affluent, as we work on this Point, let us weigh each factor. Talk to your peers and business partners. Help develop an approach that will do both, protect your interest and uplift humanity.

To the poor, workers, civil rights and community-based organizations, accept this task like concerned Americans did during the 1960s. Use the nonviolent approach. Share what you have with one another. Enter this effort not to defeat or to humiliate the affluent, but to win his or her friendship and understanding.

However, as Dr. King pointed out: regardless of how we act, this struggle will not be free of violence initiated by enemies. History bears witness to this. It took Dr. King's life and prior to that it took the life of Huey Pierce Long in 1935, the first major southern politician to put aside racism and seek to help the poor. We need ample courage and willingness to sacrifice to defeat this manifestation of violence. Once we start protesting, we must keep protesting daily and weekly.

Now is the time for economic justice. It is okay to be conservatives in our views, but let's not be conservatives in our reasoning as we review these facts. Moreover, it is alright to be on the left. However, let's not be too far left and forget that the affluent have rights too. Many have earned what they have and deserve the protection of the law to that end. The bottom line, we must discover common ground - the future of this country is at hand. Here, President Kennedy's comment is quite fitting: "If a free society cannot help the many who are poor, it cannot save the few who are rich."[31]

America needs to be informed. An informed America is a strong America, a willing America, a cooperative America, a concerned America, a prospering America, a working America, a stable America and a lasting America, that's second to none.

POINT 55 - ACHIEVING PARITY IN RECEIVING BANK LOANS FOR BLACKS AND HISPANICS

During the Los Angeles riot/rebellion, Rodney King made a statement to the media which was played throughout the nation: "Can we just get along?" A few months later, I observed a black individual protesting in front of a bank in South Central Los Angeles holding a sign that read: "Can we just get a loan." This is a true statement and I thought that it was good for a chuckle, or two. However, this is not a "joking matter" regarding the gross economic injustice of issuing loans to blacks and hispanics from banks.

There is a great imbalance in the issuing business and home bank loans to African Americans and Hispanic. The root cause of this disparity in lending by the banks in America must be addressed. The Third Annual Greenlining Report on Home Lending By California Banks, December 7, 1993, clearly points out a serious problem in this area. Here is an example of its findings:

"In summary, the eighth largest California banks (responsible for over 95 percent of home purchase loans made by commercial banks), failed to make home purchase loans to the public, and, in particular, minorities. The Bank of America was the only exception.

.....In 1992 no bank made even one home purchase loan per branch to African-Americans. And, with the exception of Bank of America, no bank made more than one home purchase loan per branch to California's 8.3 million Latinos....."

Equal disturbing, no bank, with the exception of Bank of America, made more than one home purchase loan per billion dollar in asset to California's 2.5 million African-Americans. Similarly, no bank, with the exception of Bank of America, no bank made more than one home purchase loan per branch to California's 8.3 million Latinos..." [32]

Though California may not be a mirror reflection of other states, these findings clearly show there is a serious problem in this area that we need to address.

Banks must improve their marketing programs for Blacks and Latinos.

It is very unfortunate that we have not listened closely to what Dr. King said on April 3, 1968, the day before he was killed in Memphis. Some people only recall Dr. King saying on that night "I have seen the promised land." Listen carefully because Dr. King said much more than that. In fact, he told us how we should address this situation with the banks. Here is an excerpt of Dr. King's last sermon:

"We don't have to argue with anybody. We don't have to curse and go around acting bad with our words. We don't need any bricks and bottles, we don't need any Molotov cocktails, we just need to go around to these stores, and to these massive industries in our country, and say, "God sent us by here, to say to you that you're not treating his children right. And we've come by here to ask you to make the first item on your agenda - fair treatment, where God's children are concerned. Now, if you are not prepared to do that, we do have an agenda that we must follow. And our agenda calls for withdrawing economic support from you." [33]

King further stated:

And so, as a result of this, we are asking you tonight, to go out and tell your neighbors not to buy Coca-Cola in Memphis. Go by and tell them not to buy Sealtest milk. Tell them not to buy-what is the other bread?-Wonder Bread. And what is the other bread company, Jesse? Tell them not to buy Hart's bread. As Jesse Jackson has said, up to now, only the garbage men have been feeling pain; now we must kind of redistribute the pain. We are choosing these companies because they haven't been fair in their hiring policies; and we are choosing them because they can begin the process of saying, they are going to support the needs and the rights of these men who are on strike. And then they can move on downtown and tell Mayor Loeb to do what is right.

But not only that, we've got to strengthen black institutions. I call upon you to take your money out of the banks

downtown and deposit your money in Tri-State Bank-we
want a "bank-in" movement in Memphis."[34]

African Americans and Hispanics must discover their banking lending
policies and practices. My initial thought is that we may need to have
a "bank-in" throughout the state of California and throughout the nation
if the findings in California is a reflection of what's going on in other
states. Take actions to monitor and ensure that people are given fair and
equal consideration when borrowing money from these lending
institutions. Develop coalitions or groups to monitor, conduct "bank-ins"
and take legal action against these banks, when appropriate.

However, we must not charge full speed ahead without organizing.
We address organizing in Chapter VIII of this book. You are also
cautioned, not to "sell-out", if you are offered a sum of money. It is
imperative that the boycott, sit-in, or "bank-in" continue until the goal is
accomplished.

We have a lot of work to do. America, your African Americans and
Hispanics will receive social and economic justice because we are
preparing our agenda.

POINT 56 - IMPROVING BUSINESS OPPORTUNITIES

We must take action to improve business opportunities for African
Americans. Data released from a Survey of Minority-Owned Businesses
shows black business ownership in 1987 was 19.8 percent of the total
per capita firm ownership (Black owned 424,000 of a total of
17,526,000). The total overall receipt week was 10.8 trillion dollars,
however, black owned business generated receipts of only 2.6 billion.
In other words, the contributions of black business per black person
were only 1.6 of the per capita contributions of all American business.

Like small dollar contributions, the contribution to the labor pool is
also small. Accordingly, the total employment of all Black businesses in
1982 was only 165,765 people, as compared to a total private sector
employment of over 70 million and total Black employment of 9.2 million
persons.

In the work of Dr. David H. Swinton entitled: "The Economic
Status of African Americans During the Reagan-Bush Era: Withered
Opportunities, Limited Outcomes, and Uncertain Outlook" he clearly
points out Black America Business status. Here is a few of his
observations:

- The small size of black-owned businesses is indicated by the
fact that all of them together generated receipts of only $22.8 billion
compared to receipts of $11,893 billion for all businesses.

- Black business accounted for only 0.19 percent of total receipts.

- In the aggregate, business ownership inequality was very large. The gap in number of firms owned in 1987 was over 1.7 trillion enterprises. The receipts gap was a startling $1.4 billion.[35]

Another disturbing fact: In most communities, money circulate at least seven times. But, within the black community it only circulates once.

Here are some observations that I have made: (1) Most black businesses provide services of retail goods and very few manufactured products. (2) Often there are poor relationships between some black businesses and patrons. (3) Concerns are voiced about the quality of services. (4) Moreover, there is not much working capital within the black business network. (5) There appears to be a lack of trust among Blacks.

If we address these observations, we could increase the number of times that money circulates within the black community and improve black businesses opportunities.

Based on the complexity of each subject, I decided to address each observation as a Point:

Observation (1) is addressed at Point 57: Increasing the Market for Black Businesses

Observation (2) is addressed at Point 58: Enhancing Black on Black Business Relationships.

Observation (3) is addressed at Point 59: Ensuring the Highest Quality of Services by Black Businesses to Their Customers.

Observation (4) is addressed at Point 60: Establishing Financial Investment Groups (FIG).

Observation (5) is addressed at Point 61: Building Trust Among African Americans.

POINT 57 - INCREASING THE MARKET FOR BLACK BUSINESSES

There is a one-quarter trillion-dollar black consumer base, however, the black business base is only 19.7 billions. African Americans must become more business minded and create business that meet the needs of the consumers. According to various sources, African

Americans spend from 175 billion to more than $284 billion annually. The Joint Center for Political and Economic Studies reports that African Americans represent over $350 billion in household income annually. This is equivalent to the ninth wealthiest country and is bigger than Canada's or Australia's GNP. (The Gross National Product (GNP) is the sum of all the goods and services produced in a specific period (usually one year), showing them in terms of their total dollar value.)

Nevertheless, the black business base is only 19.7 billion dollars. For black business owners to get a larger share of this income the following finding must be considered:

(1) Only one in four black shoppers said that African American ownership of a business was an important factor in deciding where to shop. (Burrell/Yankelovich African-American MONITOR).

(2) African Americans place strong emphasis on reasonable prices when deciding where to shop.

(3) African Americans are brand loyal at all age levels and quality and status conscious.

(4) Fair treatment is the most important factor of all according to a recent nationwide study. (Alexis and Henderson)

"The State of Black America," 1994, Marcus Alexis, Ph.D. and Geraldine R. Henderson have an outstanding article entitled: "The Economic Base of African-American Communities:A Study of Consumption Patterns". Reading of this writing is highly recommended for every black business owner and black consumer.

Here are several important findings in their report:

African Americans spend 20 percent of their income on food to be eaten at home.

One fifth of all portable televisions are purchased by African Americans.

African Americans only makes up about 12 percent of the nation's population, however, they purchase about 50% of the movie tickets.

African American consumers buy 36 percent of all hair care conditioners and 25 to 35 percent of all detergent and toothpaste.

African American women makeup 6 percent of the United States population, however, they consume 15 percent of the $4 billion cosmetic industry and 26 percent more on perfume than any other group.

Black business owners must study these findings and become more competitive to meet the needs of the African American consumers. For this to occur, it may require pooling resources, partnerships, joint ventures, forming co-ops, and business alliances. Moreover, the type of services offered must become broader.

If we look closely at the findings, we notice that 20 percent of the black income are spent on groceries. However, I ask you, how many large grocery stores are owned by blacks in your community, that can sell products at a competitive price? In Los Angeles, I personally have not discovered any - no, not one. This problem can be quickly addressed by black entertainers, sports figures and others by pooling their resources and buying a chain of large grocery stores. This will also create jobs and other opportunities for distributors, cattle ranchers, etc.

If 50 percent of the movie tickets are purchased by African Americans, should owning movie theaters be profitable for African American? Does this sound like a good business to own? Again, this will call for pooling resources. However, I must caution you here, these theaters must be first class.

Often black businesses are started without proper working capital, lack of business knowledge, and working in the environment with other business owners with "inflated egos". These inflated egos destroy the much needed support system. To meet the demand of the 21st century, we must be willing to share and show others how to access the system.

In addition to reaching the African American consumers, black business owners must take aggressive action to reach the larger population. For this to occur, the services must be expanded to include: construction, financial services, transportation, insurance, VCR and Television Repair shops, and mail order businesses.

Being an entrepreneurship is risky business. Fifty percent (50%) survive through the first year and 80 to 90 percent fail within ten years. As we work to gain more control of the market it is also imperative that we heed to some advice from experts to avoid ten small business owner pitfalls:

(1) Fail to make self-examination. Am I prepared to work long hours? Do I have management ability? Am I experienced enough? Am I self-disciplined? Are my goals realistic and attainable?

(2) Lack of a good business plan. Without a business plan the entrepreneur is more subject to these pitfalls. Remember, a business plan is your road map to success. Without one, it will be quite difficult for you to get there.

(3) Inadequate Financing

(4) Incomplete Records. A comprehensive and understandable bookkeeping system is one of the most basic requirements. Without it entrepreneurs find themselves making decisions in the dark.

(5) Lack of a Market Strategy. There must be a plan to build both new and repeat business.

(6) Choosing a Bad Location.

(7) Not Practicing Good Management. According to the U.S. Small Business Administration, poor management is the greatest single cause of small business failure. Common mistakes include: inadequate employee training, hiring weak personnel, trying to do too much and misuse of time.

(8) Hiring the Wrong People

(9) Poor Customer Service. To succeed, you must give your customers what they want, not what you think they want. Give your customers the level of service you would like to receive.

(10) Being Afraid to Ask for Help. It is important to know what kind of help you need, and then getting it early enough.

African American business owners must obtain a greater share of the consumer market. We must work together to accomplish this. Our plan must be clearly stated. The community must become aware of our intention. The black business owners must unite and support one another, buy from one another, share lessons learned, information and referrals. The consumers must become aware of this resolve.

POINT 58 - ENHANCING BLACK ON BLACK BUSINESS RELATIONSHIPS

Like any other American, when African Americans buy goods or pay for services they want the best possible service for their money. A complaint often heard when talking to some African Americans business owners is that they are not receiving the support of the African American community. On the other hand, when talking to some African American consumers, their complaints are: they don't receive the quality of service they deserve, African Americans businesses charge too much, they don't complete their work on schedule, and the list goes on.

To improve the relationships between African American businesses and the African American consumers, we must confront these issues head on. In order to "buy black" or "recycle black dollars" there must be quality products, and quality and timely services in the black community. This will also cause for better communication within the community.

I had the opportunity to research and study a black construction contractor's record. I discovered that he would under bid on jobs in order to get money to complete another job. I also observed: (1) He was always in the red, (2) some jobs he never completed, however, (3) when he did complete one, his work was first class. After carefully reviewing his operation it became apparent to me that some people wanted top services, but, they didn't pay him for it. And in most cases they were not willing to pay him a higher bid. In every case, I observed the following two problems with his relationships with his customers.

(1) He made promises that he could not keep, primarily because he under-bid and had a history of incomplete work due to this practice.

(2) The customer hired him because they observed the quality of his work and his bid was probably the lowest bid they had received. Nevertheless, even though his bid would already be too low to do the work, the customers were able to get him to make an even lower bid. Once the contractor received the contracts and deposits, he had no intention to use the money to commence the job.

Consequently, in some cases the contractor defaulted. In these agreements, who was at fault, the consumers or the contractor? Most people would say that it's the contractor's fault. However, I believe that both the consumer and contractor contributed to a bad deal. Lets look at this in another way. It would be hard to purchase a new car off a new car lot for half price, wouldn't it? Nevertheless, consumers would hire this contractor to do work for less that half of the value of the jobs. He would accept the bid because he needed the money.

Of course, when the contractor defaulted, the consumers become angry and spread the word: Don't hire these **Black Contractors** because they will not complete the work.

Now the consumers are at fault because the consumers spread unfavorable information on all other **Black Contractors**. They have failed to admit how they, the consumers, contributed to the making of a bad deal in their attempt to get something for nothing. This process repeats itself over and over. This observation helps to explain the fact that the average black construction firm had revenues of only $70,270 compared to $1,100,000 for the average construction firm in general.[36] We must end this cycle by confronting these issues head on.

Over-Charging for Goods. A general complaint: Things are too expensive at these black stores, so go to a swapmeet or department store. What is the problem, here?

When small shops do not buy in bulk, the shop owners pay more for the goods and then pass the cost on to the consumers.

The solution to this one is simple. Similar black businesses should establish alliances and purchase in bulk. This will allow them to sell goods at lower prices and consequently, it will make black businesses more competitive.

Poor Service By Waiters and Waitresses - This is a common complaint about small black restaurants.

The answer to this is also simple. Establish training schools within the community that provide training in this field through a black business alliance group. Some restaurant owners may frown on this expenditure. However, if these owners fail to invest in their employee's training, their will be many other days for them to frown because they may have a difficult time keeping satisfied customers.

To improve the relations there must be more communication between the black business owners and the patrons. Non-profit organizations could be established to help bridge the gap. These organizations could receive and process complaints and concerns of the patrons directly to the black business owners within the neighborhood. The purpose of these groups will be to improve relationships and not to destroy businesses. This group's functions would me more personal than that of the better business bureaus or consumer affairs offices.

There is a need for effecting this type of organizations It is not enough to just complain among ourselves, we must organize and address these issues. Addressing these issues is a must in order to recycle "black dollars" or to "buy black".

POINT 59 - ENSURING THE HIGHEST QUALITY OF SERVICES BY BLACK BUSINESSES TO THEIR CUSTOMERS

Refer to Point 58: we must develop measures that ensure services by black business owners to their patrons are of the highest quality.

Each African American business owner should ask and answer these questions: If there were no White people, what would I do? Where would I buy my beef, can goods, dairy products, shoes, nails for building, etc. How can Blacks recycle dollars within the community when we don't produce products or provide much needed services? How can we as African American businesses ensure that our patrons are given the best possible services and given the utmost respect, when we fail to give our employees adequate customer relations training? Are we hiring the best qualified to do the job?

Recommend that business seminars and workshops be conducted to address these points and initiatives be developed to ensure that Black Americans become producers of more products. Black Americans have the knowledge and expertise to produce a broader range of products. However, in the past our chief complaint was, "If I had the money, I would do this or I would do that. Today money is not the real problem, because Black America has enough money to make a big difference. At Point 60, we will explore ways designed to make our money work for us.

POINT 60 - ESTABLISHING FINANCIAL INVESTMENT GROUPS (FIG)

All major cultures except African Americans have a collective economics system which allows them to pool their money in order to financially empower their members. These systems are usually quite informal, depending a great deal on **TRUST** for all involved. The Chinese have the HUI which they have consistently utilized to construct a "Chinatown" in every major city in the U.S. The Japanese call theirs "Tanomoshi". The Koreans have the "KEI" pronounced "Key" and they are using it as a real **Key** to business establishment throughout African American communities coast to coast! The Vietnamese use the "HOI" (Hoy) and are buying properties throughout Orange County in California. The Mexicans utilize the "Cundina" for acquiring both residential and commercial property throughout Los Angeles County and beyond. The Jews have utilized the powerful "Kibbutz" system for decades. Living and working together in their own communities has enabled them to amass more than 1/3 of the world's wealth.

The Joint Center for Political and Economic Studies reports that African Americans represent over $350 billion in household income annually. This is equivalent to the ninth wealthiest country and is bigger than Canada's or Australia's GNP. African Americans should be able to develop a collective economics system for the African American communities to make it possible for us to collectively and continuously build businesses and wealth in our own communities.

In Los Angeles, there is such a group that has formed that is designed to create a program nationally that will meet this challenge. This group is called Financial Investment Group (F.I.G.). Under the FIG concept Black Americans can pool their money together and purchase businesses throughout the United States.

In regard to money in the African American community, this is not a new factor. In 1967, African Americans annual income was 19 billion dollars and at that time, it was equal to the ninth wealthiest country in the world. Until we resolve the trust factor, we can't recycle black dollars, and we can't create more jobs. In fact, we are working against ourselves.

Another concept of making money work for you was designed by Lou Brooks, a former member of the Apollo Luna Mission Team. Mr. Brooks founded International Business Specialists, Inc. to enable others to share in the wealth of America. As mentioned at Point 54, the richest one percent own more assets than the bottom 80 percent. This is no accident. This occurs by our economic system design. IBS provides an opportunity that help counter the unequal distribution of wealth. Under this concept, consumers are able to benefit from all the profits that would normally go to the retailers, wholesalers, merchants, and advertising cost.

Though the company has been in existence for less than two years, it is creating a lot of excitement for its members because they realize that the dollar can be recycled through the "multi-plier effect", thus creating an economy within itself. Under IBS when its members share this opportunity with others and they do the same, this activity will induce the **"Multiplier Effect"** which is the key to generating wealth. Let's examine the **"Multiplier Effect"** and see how it works.

What Is It. Basically, the "Multiplier Effect" occurs when the same money circulates over and over again, within the same general area, such as in a community or a country. Under IBS, money circulates among its members.

The Multiplier Effect Is Nothing New. It was always with us, just as electricity has always been with us. But, until Benjamin Franklin tapped into electricity and learned how to harness its energy and control it; man did not know how to utilize its power.

What happens when you control the circulation of Money? When you control how many times the same money circulates (multiplies) itself within a given environment, such as a business, you then have a wealth generating system.

How does this apply to IBS? IBS has created a unique way for its members to buy quality products, with the same money, simply by using the multiplier effect. Moreover, through this process, they can make money from buying products and services from other business owners who are members of IBS. Members are paid through bonus incomes from their purchases and the purchases of others.

IBS' goal is to rapidly spread this concept throughout the United States to enable more people to share the wealth of this country. For information on IBS write: IBS, 400 S. Burnside Street, Suite 2K, Los Angeles, CA 90036.

POINT 61 - BUILDING TRUST AMONG AFRICAN AMERICANS

Before economic justice can be realized in Black America we must build trust among African Americans. This old "lack of trust factor" keeps us down and it must be eliminated. We know that one of the major ingredients necessary to make a financial investment system work is trust among the investors and the other people involved. Below is a reprint of an article I read in a community newspaper in Los Angeles. Here is a thought to ponder.

Why Don't Blacks Trust Each Other?

"......To shed some light on this very question we have used our Community Circle Time Capsule to travel back to the year 1712 to witness one very significant speech being given to hundreds of plantation owners by a certain Mr. Willie Lynch.

Gentlemen:

I greet you here on the bank of the James River in the year of our Lord one thousand seven hundred and twelve. First, I shall thank you the Gentlemen of the colony of Virginia for bringing me here. I am here to help you solve some of your problems with slaves. Ancient Rome would envy us if my program is implemented. As our boat sailed south on the James river, named for our illustrious King, whose version of the Bible we cherish, I saw enough to know that your problem is not unique. While Rome used cords of wood crosses for standing human bodies along its old highways in great numbers you are here using the tree and the rope on occasion.

I caught whiff of a dead slave hanging from a tree a couple of miles back. You are not only losing valuable stock by hanging, you are having uprisings, slaves are running away, your crops are sometimes left in the field too long for minimum profit, you suffer occasional fires, and your animals are killed. Gentlemen, you know what your problems are; I do not need to elaborate. I am not here to enumerate your problems. I am here to introduce you to a method of solving problems.

In my bag here, I have a fool proof method for controlling our Black Slaves. I guarantee everyone of you that if installed correctly, it will control the slaves for at least **300** years. My method is simple, any member of your family or any Overseer can use it.

I have outlined a number of differences among slaves; and I take these differences and make them bigger. I use fear, distrust, and envy for control purposes. These methods have worked on my modest planation in the West Indies and it will work throughout the South. Take this simple little list of differences, and think about them. On the top of my list is "Age" but it is there only because it starts with an "A"; The second is "Color" or shade. Then there is intelligence, size, sex, size of plantation, status of plantation, attitude of owners, whether slave live in the valley, on a hill, East, West, North, South, has fine coarse hair, or is tall or short. Now that you have a list of differences, I shall give an outline of action - but before that I shall assure you that distrust is stronger than trust, and envy is stronger than adulation, respect or admiration.

Black slave after receiving this indoctrination shall carry on and will become self re-fueling and self generating for hundreds of years, maybe thousands!

Don't forget you must pitch the old black v. the young black male, and the young black male against the old black male. You must use the dark skin slave v. light skin slave and the light skin slaves v. the dark skin slaves. You must use the female v. male, and the male v. the female. You must also have your White servant overseer distrust all Blacks, but it is necessary that your slaves trust and depend on us. They must love, respect, and trust only us.!

Gentlemen these kits are your key to **control**, use them. Have your wives and children use them. Never miss an opportunity.

My plan is guaranteed, and the good thing about this plan is that if used intensely for one year, the slaves themselves will remain **perpetually distrustful**."

There you have it! The seed of distrust was consciously implanted hundreds of years ago during slavery. Now the question is "How do we up-root this seminally perpetual seed of distrust that has been implanted in our culture? The only solution to this problem is for each one of us to start actually practicing love, respect, and trust towards one another and become the type of person that commands the best expectations from others. So in fact, the answer to the question rests within each one of us."[37]

This is quite a bit to ponder, however, if we fail to meditate on the lack of trust factor, we will fail as a people to develop to our full potential. Before addressing how we must resolve this problem. Let's look at another historical record that impacted upon our trust factor.

In 1865 the Freedmen's Bureau, a branch of the U.S. War Department was established to help Southern Blacks adjust to freedom after the Civil War. From 1865 through 1872, the bureau established schools, hospitals, charities, and employment agencies to promote black social welfare and, supposedly, land ownership. However, whites in the South systematically denied blacks opportunity to purchase land and banks denied blacks the right to make deposits. Of course, if blacks couldn't make deposits, they couldn't obtain home loans. However, there was one major institution, the Freedman's Bank that encouraged blacks to save and facilitate land and home purchases.

Blacks were able to increase their savings and purchases of both agricultural and residential property through the Freedman's Bank. However, there was a pattern of racism of the bank practices, to include a board of directors that was controlled by whites and highly questionable no-interest loans from the bank to white companies. The Freedman's Bank did not withstand the economic panic of 1873 and it failed in 1874. Consequently, thousands of blacks lost their small savings and were never repaid. This was a big loss for many blacks. As noted by Du Bois:"...all the faith in saving went too, and much of the faith in men..."[38]

Booker T. Washington, later made this observation about the Freedman's Bank:

"When they found that they had lost, or been swindled out of all their little savings, they lost faith in savings banks, and it was a long time after this before it was possible to mention a saving bank for Negroes without some reference being made to the disaster of the Freedman's Bank. The effect of this disaster was the more far-reaching because of the wide extent of territory which the Freedman's Bank covered through its agencies."[39]

Over the years there probably were many stories regarding the fall of the Freedman's Bank, its ownership and who controlled it.

We must work together and develop a system that will counter a programming that has been ingrained into our socialization process. Deprogramming can't occur overnight, it will take time. However, we must work now to deprogram this reality.

In order to deprogram you must examine your current beliefs and determine if you have some myths/stereotypes that you need to dispel.

First we suggest you list your myths and stereotypes about African Americans not being trustworthy over the years. List the first thoughts that come to your mind.

I have heard that you shouldn't trust black because?

Reason #1. _____
Reason #2. _____
Reason #3. _____
Reason #4. _____
Reason #5. _____
Reason #6. _____
Reason #7. _____
Reason #8. _____
Reason #9. _____
Reason #10. _____

After you have completed your list, you are now asked to openly challenge each reason and make the following determination.

- Decide if it is myth or the truth

- Determine what your decision is based on

- State how you've reached these conclusions

- Determine if the statement is all inclusive of if there are exceptions

- Decide if you are going to continue to support this myth or if you are going to discard it

If you go through this process you can bring these thoughts to the conscious mind; at that point you can begin to deal with them.

- Modify negative behavior

- Ask yourself why should you trust a "non African American" more than an African American?

Going through this exercise is a good starting point. Now you must work to replace old habits when you shop, bank, order services, and invest.

In respect to investment, you may wish to start an investment group under the Financial Investment Group (FIG) concept with 35 of your friends. You can write to: FIG, P.O. Box 43971, Los Angeles, California 90043 for more details.

Nevertheless, to address this lack of trust factor will require work on all of our parts. We must become creative and develop a check and balance program. Programs could be established relating to the black business community that provides a type of liability check, like a five star rating system. There are a number of activities that can assist us in improving the trust factor among African Americans. We first must have the resolve to work to that end. Once we have the resolve, everything else will follow.

POINT 62 - PROMOTING BLACK-OWNED BUSINESS

In order to promote tomorrow's Black-owned businesses, now, we must work through our youth, today. We must establish training grounds for youth to build trust and support for one another. By working with our youth, it will serve as therapy for the older adults who have made up their minds and are determined that you can't trust Blacks.

Recommend that we create Black businesses for tomorrow by investing in our youth, today. Establish business training schools like we did when we established black colleges. Lets train our youth now on what it takes to operate effective businesses.

We must teach these young minds about our economy and how it works. We also must teach them about the free market system. They must learn that they have the right to fail, the need of sacrifice, and their individual responsibility. These subjects aren't taught in school, therefore, we must teach them to our young people through seminars, workshops, and provide for them on-the-job training, running their own businesses. Moreover, training of this type should also be afforded to current business owners. This is an excellent initiative for a business for profit or a non profit organization to undertake.

Through this effort we can effectively promote black-owned grocery stores and businesses throughout the black community. This will help us to create a more broader business base. This development effort should also include a program that (1) provides locations for "at risk" youth to operate on-site entrepreneurial businesses; (2) coaching and support in effecting home base businesses; (3) creating a business network that ingrains high business ethics throughout the course curriculum; (4) allow "at risk" youth to effect employment opportunities for other at risk youth thereby, building and restoring the moral fiber throughout the community; and (5) develop communities outreach that encourages and restores community support, a sense of pride, a spirit of togetherness, and hope.

Let's not wait for funding prior to starting this very important program. Let's pool our resources and then seek funding to enhance our efforts.

POINT 63 - ENHANCING YOUR PERSONAL CREDIT WORTHINESS

Enhancing personal credit worthiness is very important and for too many of us has been a learning experience by trial and error. Like shopping to buy a car - you should shop for the credit and use it wisely. Many young people make mistakes and borrow from finance companies because this method of borrowing was passed on to them by their parents. A finance company is the last place you should borrow from because of the high rate of interest on loans. Your child should be taught how to establish credit and from whom to borrow from at an early age. In addition, it is also important that you know how to maintain an actual credit history and your children should be taught the same.

Nevertheless, no working American should be treated like a second class citizen due to erroneous data in their credit profile. Sometimes, erroneous data are entered into our files and we remain unaware of it until we are denied credit. Unfortunately, some people never check their credit profile even after they are refused credit. Some just throw these letters away.

You should never just throw away a letter that refuses you credit. Suggest you always follow-up and determine the nature of the adverse information being maintained on you.

The Fair Credit Reporting Act and You.

The Fair Credit Reporting Act became law on April 25, 1971. This act was passed by Congress to protect consumers against the circulation of inaccurate or obsolete information and to ensure that Consumer Reporting Agencies adopt fair and equitable procedures for obtaining, maintaining and releasing information about consumers.

Under this law you can take steps to protect yourself if you have been denied credit, insurance or employment, or if you believe you have had difficulties because of an inaccurate or an unfair Consumer Report.

Your Rights As a Consumer.

(1) To be told the name and address of the Consumer Reporting Agency responsible for preparing a Consumer Report used to deny you credit, insurance or employment or to increase the cost of credit insurance.

(2) To be told by a Consumer Reporting Agency the nature, substance, and sources (except investigative-type sources) of the information (except medical) collected about you.

(3) To take a guest of your choice with you when you visit the Consumer Reporting Agency to check on your file.

(4) To obtain, free of charge, all information to which you are entitled if your request is made within 30 days after receipt of notification that you have been denied credit, insurance, or employment due to information contained in a Consumer Report. Otherwise, the Consumer Reporting Agency is permitted to charge reasonable fee for giving you the information.

(5) To be told who has received a Consumer Report on you within the preceding 6 months (or within the preceding 2 years if the report was furnished for employment purposes).

(6) To have incomplete or incorrect information reinvestigated unless the Consumer Reporting Agency has reasonable grounds to believe the dispute is frivolous or irrelevant. If the information is investigated and found to be inaccurate or if the information cannot be verified, you have the right to have such information removed from your file.

(7) To have the Agency notify those companies you name (at no cost to you), who have previously received the incorrect or incomplete information that this information has been deleted from your file.

(8) When a dispute between you and the Reporting Agency about information in your file cannot be resolved, you have the right to have your version of such dispute placed in the file and included in further Consumer Reports.

(9) To request the Reporting Agency to send your version of the dispute to certain businesses without charge, if requested within 30 days of the adverse action.

(10) To have a Consumer Report withheld from anyone who, under the law, does not have a legitimate business need for the information.

(11) To sue a Reporting Agency for damages if the Agency willfully or negligently violates the law and, if you are successful, to collect attorney's fees and court costs.

(12) To have adverse information deleted after 7 years. One major exception is bankruptcy, which may be reported for 10 years.

(13) To be notified by a business that it is seeking information about you which would constitute an Investigative Consumer Report.

(14) To request from the business that ordered an Investigative Consumer Report more information about the nature and scope of the investigation.

(15) To discover the nature and substance (but not the sources) of the information that was collected for an Investigative Consumer Report.

Recommend that you share this information with the young people in your community. In addition programs should be developed that increase awareness on how to manage financial affairs and enhance credit worthiness through workshops, seminars, and etc.

The AFSA Consumer Credit Education Foundation[40] has developed a very helpful "Credit-Ability Scorecard". Thanks to them, I'm able to share this information with you. Hopefully, you will share it with others.

CREDIT-ABILITY SCORECARD

Test your credit I.Q. For each question, circle the letter that best describes your credit habits.

1. I pay my bills when they are due.

    (A) Always   (B) Almost Always   (C) Sometimes

2. After paying my regular bill each month, I have money left from my income.

    (A) Yes   (B) Sometimes   (C) Never

3. I know how much I owe on my credit cards each month before I receive my bills.

    (A) Yes   (B) Sometimes   (C) No

4. When I get behind in my payments, I ignore the past due notices.

    (A) Never or Not Applicable   (B) Sometimes   (C) Always

5. When I need more money for my regular living expenses, I take out a loan or use my line of credit on my credit card or checking account.

    (A) Never   (B) Sometimes   (C) Often

6. If I want to see a copy of my credit report, I would contact...

    (A) A credit reporting agency   (B) My lenders   (C) My Lawyer

7. My credit record shows that I am current on all my loans and charge accounts.

    (A) Yes   (B) Don't Know   (C) No

8. I pay more than the minimum balance due on my credit card accounts.

    (A) Always   (B) Sometimes   (C) Never

9. To pay off my current credit and charge card accounts, it would take me....

    (A) 4 months or less   (B) 5 to 8 months   (C) Over 8 months

10. My consumer loans (including auto loans, but not mortgage payment) and credit card bills each month average more than 20% of my take home pay.

   (A) No   (B) Sometimes   (C) Always

11. If I had serious problems, I would contact my creditors to explain the problem.

   (A) Yes   (B) Probably   (C) No

12. If I default (don't repay) on a loan, that fact can stay on my credit report for ....

   (A) 7 years   (B) 3 years   (C) 1 year

Assign a score of 3 for each "A" answer, 2 for each "B" answer; and 1 for each "C" response. Total the score.

If you scored:

31 - 36 You have an excellent knowledge of credit and its responsible use.

24 - 30 You should take steps toward a better understanding of your personal finances and of the credit process.

18 - 23 You probably need to take a serious look at your personal finances; consider controlling your spending and keeping on a tight budget.

12 - 17 You may be heading for serious trouble; consider seeking help, such as non-profit consumer credit counseling services.

Chapter IV Notes

1 Dorsen, Norman (1984) Our Endangered Rights: The ACLU Report On Civil Liberties Today, p. 151

2 Ibid. p. 143

3 Eitzen, Stanley D. (1983), Social Problems, p. 75

4 Robertson, Ian (1981) Sociology, 2ed, p. 271. quoted by Eitzen in Social Problems, p. 75

5 Washington, James M., (1986) A Testament Of Hope:The Essential Writings Of Martin Luther King, Jr. p.

6 Ibid. p.151

7 McClelland, Peter D. (1990), The American Search For Economic Justice, p. 139

8 Ibid. p. 139

9 Eitzen, D. Stanley, (1983) Social Problems, p.44

10 Melzer, Milton (1986), Poverty In America, pp. 97,98

11 Ibid. p. 98

12 Wright, Skelly J., Money And Pollution Of Politics:Is The First Amendment An Obstacle To Political Equality? 82 Columbia Law Review p. 609, 610 (1982). Quoted by Dorsen in Our Endangered Rights:The ACLU Report On Liberties Today

13 McClelland, Peter D. (1990), The American Search For Economic Justice, p. 130

14 Ibid. p. 130

15 Testimony of Bernard J. Sheil, Auxiliary Bishop of Chicago, In U.S. Congress, Senate, Subcommittee of the Committee On Banking and Currency, hearings, Full Employment Act of 1945, 79th Cong., 1st Sess., 1945, p.839, quoted by McClelland in The American Search For Economic Justice, (1990), p. 143

16 Ibid. p.1016

17 U.S. Congress House, S. 380 Debated in House, 79th Cong., 1st Sess., December 13, 1945, Congressional Record, 91, 12015. quoted by McClelland, The American Search For Economic Justice (1990) p.111

18 "Office Of Economic Opportunity during the Administration of President Lyndon B. Johnson, Nov. 1973 - Jan. 1969: An Administrative History," Vol. I, p. 33, Lyndon Johnson Library, Austin, Tx; quoted in Patterson, America's Struggle Against poverty, p. 135. and quoted in McClelland, The American Search For Economic Justice, p. 149

19 U.S. Congress, House Subcommittee on the War of Poverty Program of he Committee on Education and Labor, Hearings, Economic Opportunity Act of 1964, 88th Cong., 2nd Sess., 1964, p. 438. quoted in McClelland, The American Search For Economic Justice, (1990), pp. 132,133

20 McClelland, Peter D. (1990), The American Search For Economic Justice, p.128

21 Goldberg v. Kelly, 397 U.S. at 264 (1970), quoted by Dorsen, Our Endangered Rights: The ACLU Report On Civil Liberties Today (1984), p.141

22 Dorsen, Norman (1984) Our Endangered Rights:The ACLU Report On Civil Liberties Today, pp. 154, 155

23 Washington, James M., (1986),A Testament Of Hope: The Essential Writings Of Martin Luther King, Jr., p. 558

24 Dorsen, Norman (1984), Our Endangered Rights: The ACLU Report On Civil Liberties Today, p. 151. Background Material and Data on Major Programs within the committee on ways and means, Committee On Ways and Means, 98th Cong., 1st Sess. (1983), AFDC data, table 5 at 259; SSI data, table 16 at 330.

25 Dorsen, Norman (1984), Our Endangered Rights: The ACLU Report On Civil Liberties Today, p. 151

26 Sherraden, Michael, (1991), Assets And The Poor: A New American Welfare Policy, p. 254

27 McClelland, Peter D., (1990), The American Search For Economic Justice, p. 313

28 Keniston, Kenneth & The Carnegie Council On Children (1977), All Our Children, p. 39

29 Ibid. p. 44

30 Sherraden, Michael (1991), Assets And The Poor:A New American Welfare Policy, p. 109

31 Kennedy, John F. "Inaugural Address, January 20, 1961," The Inaugural Addresses Of The American Presidents, ed. Davis Newton Lott (New York: Holt, Rinehart & Winston, 1961), p. 270. quoted by McClelland in "The American Search For Economic Justice (1990) p. 334

32 The Third Annual Greenlining Report On Home Lending by California Banks, December 7, 1993.

33 Washington, James M., (1986), A Testament Of Hope:The Essential Writings Of Martin Luther King, Jr., p. 283. Excerpts from

Dr. King's last sermon, on the eve of his assassination, at [the Bishop Charles] Mason Temple in Memphis, Tennessee, on April 3, 1968.

34 Ibid p. 283

35 Dewart, Janet (1993), The State of Black America, p. 142, "The Economic Status of African Americans During the Reagan-Bush Era: Withered Opportunities, Limited Outcomes, and Uncertain Outlook, By: David H. Swinton, Ph.D.

36 Dewart, Janet (1993), "The State of Black America", p. 142, National Urban League, "The Economic Status of African Americans During the Reagan-Bush Era: Withered Opportunities, Limited Outcomes, and Uncertain Outlook, by; David H. Swinton, Ph.D.

37 Why Don't Blacks Trust Each Other?, published in Los Angeles Community Clipper, April 15 - 30. 1994

38 Du Bois, W.E.B., The Souls of Black Folk, Greenwich, CT: Fawcett Publications, 1970 (Originally published in 1903), 39. Quoted by Sherraden in Assets And The Poor: A New American Welfare Policy (1991), p.134

39 Washington, Booker T., The Story Of The Negro, (1909) New York; Doubleday, Page & Co., vol. 2, p. 214, quoted by Sherraden in Assets And The Poor: A New American Welfare Policy, (1991) p. 134

40 AFSA Consumer Credit Education Foundation, 919 Eighteenth St. N.W., Washington, D. C. 20006

CHAPTER V

EQUAL EMPLOYMENT OPPORTUNITY

In this chapter, we examine how we can increase our opportunities to work in the job market throughout our job life cycle. We also suggest ways to adjust to the job market and recommend actions that should be taken to increase opportunities for employment for our youth and individuals with felony convictions.

POINT 64 - CREATING A MORE EFFECTIVE EEOC

We must improve the effectiveness of the Equal Employment Opportunity Commission (EEOC). It takes far too long to process complaints and the standard to prove discrimination in the work place must be reduced.

Discrimination occurs in the work place at different levels, however, some of these acts of discrimination would not be substantiated in a court of law. Especially, in light of many of the Supreme Court rulings between 1988 and 1989. Yet, the acts of discrimination have severe impacts upon its victims. To end discrimination in the work place, action must be taken at the early stages of discrimination, to include subtle acts, discrimination by inference, avoidance, covert and overt acts, intentional, unintentional discrimination and discrimination by inaction.

At Point 67, I have included a mini human relations lesson on discrimination because often the victim of discrimination does not recognize when he or she is being discriminated against. At times the violator doesn't know when he or she has committed an act of discrimination. Moreover, it appears that the legislators don't realize the impact of discrimination to include the subtle acts on its victims at the early stages of the job discriminatory process.

A person should not have to suffer discrimination over a long period of time and build a diary of the acts of discrimination. Granted, it makes good for a court settlement, however, ending discrimination in the work place is not about good court settlements. It is about giving individuals opportunities to work in environments free from discrimination throughout their job life cycle.

To counter discrimination practices, it will take a well-thought out plan to cover all facets of an employee's or potential employee's life cycle.

First, an individual must have an opportunity to apply for employment; therefore, an individual should be fully aware of the jobs available. Recruitment efforts must be broad enough to reach all segments of the eligible population.

Second, once an individual is hired, the individual must have an opportunity to become educated and trained without discrimination.

Third, once educated and trained, the individual must be utilized in a position commensurate with their pay grade, status, skills and abilities.

Fourth, the person must be sustained by ensuring promotion opportunities, recognition, status, and fringe benefits.

Lastly, the individual must be given the opportunity to retire or separate without discrimination.

Our current EEOC's efforts and enforcement of the Law of 1866, 1964 and 1991 does not ensure that these conditions described above take place. We must rethink our approach to addressing discrimination in the work place because our current efforts are failing. The Act of 1964 was designed to provide remedies for past discrimination, and to prevent future discrimination. Of course, initially the courts interpreted the statute liberally with respect to procedures for filing claim, defining what constituted a violation of the law and determining adequate remedies (An extensive commentary on this area is at Point 80.). However, today this is not the case.

The law is not designed for the lawyers to go into courts, years after a person has suffered discrimination for months and even for years. One act of discrimination is enough for a person to take action to end the discriminatory act. If current legislation doesn't ensure a person is afforded equal opportunity throughout their job life cycle, we must write new laws, pass them and then enforce these new laws.

I have processed equal employment opportunity concerns for over 20 years and I believe the law was designed to end discrimination in the work place and not to allow situations like the case described below to go unresolved. Here is my account of a complaint that I processed:

"I can recall one case whereby a young woman filed a complaint - she said that she was being discriminated against because she was black, and because she was a woman. The woman also claimed she was being sexually harassed.

As I began to process her complaint. I discovered that the young woman had two ninety-minute tapes that she had recorded over a six-month period. These tapes contained records of encounters which she experienced on the job.

I had the opportunity to listen to those tapes. I was amazed because I discovered that she was using her tape recorder as a sounding board. She would talk from five to fifteen minutes each day when she experienced negative encounters on the job. She made comments such as "I don't know about this person, he said that he was not going to say that again - He told me he was going to treat me fair - I just don't know because it seems as if I'm getting all of the dirty jobs ", "Today they laughed at me and made fun of me. No one else is being treated like this, but me - I'm tired of his Bull... - I'm not going to take this any more - They think I'm a play thing. He actually put his hand on me and told me that I would be cute if I wasn't so evil - This... has gone too far now - Everybody thinks they can touch my behind and get away with it. They just don't know who they are messing with".

Sometimes she was up and sometimes she was down...it went on and on...It was two ninety minutes tapes of these encounters which had happened to her on the job over a six-month period.

This person was having all kinds of problems on the job and at home. It seemed as if no one could get along with her - to include her supervisor, co-workers, husband and even her children were victims of this now hostile person.

She then became ill. I am not suggesting that the discrimination made her ill, but, she didn't have a history of passing out. She began to pass out while driving. I recall the conversation I had with her husband. He said: "She had never passed out before, she once was a very sweet and loving wife until she began to work in that department - now it has become very difficult to live with her."

The EEOC and law makers must understand that civil rights laws were passed to end discrimination in the work place, not to allow conditions to be built to create large court settlements. A person who is a victim of discrimination needs immediate relief.

Here are some other impacts of discrimination on its victims:

- Individuals can't perform to their maximum if they are victims of discrimination. We must be mindful of the real effect of discrimination on its victims. It has tremendous impact.

- Sometimes victims may loose respect for others and respect for themselves.

- They may even disrespect authority because of the way they are being treated.

- Individuals may even use mood altering substances because of the way that they are being treated.

- Some may become highly frustrated, and unable to effectively do the job.

- Some will become hostile or become ill.

- Some will break down in tears and even threaten to kill or eventually kill.

Recommend action be taken to establish a more effective EEOC. Take measures to improve the processing time. Recommend Congress review the overall effectiveness of our current legislation to end discrimination in the work place. However, prior to the review, every member of Congress should receive an education in human relations to ensure that every elected official understand the severity of today's problems and the impact of discrimination on its victims and the nation.

Recommend that Clinton's administration and future administrations articulate a new resolve to end discrimination in the work place and ensure that laws are enforced that adequately address this real problem.

Recommend that the Department of Labor take measures to create a more cooperative approach when addressing discrimination between labor and management. The key to ending discrimination is not large court settlements, though these large settlements help deter. Nevertheless, action must be taken at a much lower level in a more timely fashion. At Point 66, I discussed the "Destructive Perception of Discrimination Cycle", every worker, manager, and supervisor must become familiar with this concept.

POINT 65 - REDUCING THE PROCESSING TIME OF COMPLAINTS FILED WITH THE EEOC

In 1866, a Civil Rights Act became law and section 1981 of the Act prohibits race discrimination in the making and enforcement of contracts. In 1964, another Civil Rights Act was enacted and Title VII prohibits discrimination in the work place. In 1972 Congress passed amendments to Title VII of the Civil Rights Act of 1964 that took the authority to institute discrimination suits against private employers away from the Department of Justice. The 1972 amendments gave power and responsibility to the Equal Employment Opportunity Commission to investigation complaints of discrimination by individuals.

The Equal Employment Opportunity Commission has a history of processing complaints of alleged employment discrimination in an untimely manner. For example, in 1977, the backlog was over 100,000 charges. In 1991, there a backlog of thirteen thousand age discrimination cases, alone.

In addition to the EEOC's slow processing time, there is no prompt judicial response to suits filed under Title VII. In fact, it is now common for Title VII cases to be delayed for five to ten years, during which the challenged practices continue.

To address systemic discrimination prompt action is required on each case. The current process is ineffective. In fact, it is intolerable and will not rid discrimination from the work place.

Immediate reforms are needed to make the process more effective. In 1991, another Civil Rights Act was passed however, it still was not enough to create work places in America free of discrimination. New legislation is needed to combine laws and to facilitate the early resolution of complaints of employment discrimination. Moreover, the EEOC must be better staffed to investigate complaints in a timely manner. In addition, the courts should be required to take swift action on equal employment opportunity cases.

Recommendations have now been made, but, where do we go from here. We can't depend on the government to correct this problem without pressure from us, the people. We must organize and apply the needed pressure to ensure that equal employment opportunity become a reality in the work place.

Through African Americans' support of the Power Pack, eventually it will become as simple as making a call to the NAACP and requesting that we take action on Point 65. We must organize and give better support to these organizations that are designed to work in our interests to make social and economic justice become a reality.

POINT 66 - EDUCATING EMPLOYERS AND EMPLOYEES ON THE "DESTRUCTIVE PERCEPTION OF DISCRIMINATION CYCLE"

Employers and employees must become educated on the damaging impact of the "Destructive Perception of Discrimination Cycle". Dr. Michael D. Woodard and Elmore Richmond Jr. developed a principle that unlocks the mystery of what makes law ineffective against discrimination in the work place. They call this principle the "Destructive Perception of Discrimination Cycle." They concluded that perception becomes an individual's reality unless action is taken to clarify the perception.

This is true for the perceptions of discrimination. When an individual perceives, correctly or incorrectly, that he or she is being discriminated against, the person will react in the same way. If an employee perceives that he/she is the victim of discrimination, then that employee cannot perform up to his/her full potential.

Here is the background of "The Destructive Perception of Discrimination Cycle"

An employee's failure to get clarification of management's action can lead to a counterproductive cycle of events referred to as the **"Destructive Perception of Discrimination Cycle."** The cycle consists of the following elements: (1) First, there is an action by the supervisor/manager; (2) that action is perceived by the employee as discrimination; (3) the employee fails to get clarification of his/her perception; and (4) there is a drop in the employee's performance usually accompanied by a negative attitude.

The Cycle repeats itself until action is taken to clarify the perception, or until one of the parties is removed from the work unit, or there is a change in management action.

To achieve and maintain maximum production, management must become aware of the perception of their subordinates and take steps to address those perceptions. Failure by management to forthrightly address correct or incorrect employees perception will result in reduced productivity, a hostile human relations environment, and perhaps irreparable damages to the career of the employee.

African Americans, Hispanics and other minorities must understand that if they perceive themselves to be victims of discrimination, it becomes their reality and they begin to act as if they were actually being discriminated against. If people perceive they are victims of discrimination, they cannot perform up to their full potential. It is possible that, at one time, employees who feel aggrieved may have been high achievers, but this perception of discrimination keeps them from performing at their best.

Their performance, under these circumstances, may not measure up to their co-workers. As a consequence, an employee may not be able to take advantage of opportunities that are afforded to high achievers. When this occurs, claims of discrimination are sometimes filed. The claim is based on perception and not actual discrimination by the supervisor. To avoid this destructive series of events, employees should be encouraged to take steps to clarify their perceptions.

Often individuals fail to clarify their perceptions because of (1) awaiting a performance report, (2) pending decision regarding a pay raise and (3) fear of being labeled as a trouble maker. It is imperative that African Americans, women and Hispanics become familiar with this concept and take measures to clarify their perceptions of discrimination as soon as possible after the perceived act of discrimination.

Training must be afforded to both management and employees to help address these perceptions of discrimination in a non-confrontational manner.

POINT 67 - MAKING HUMAN RELATIONS TRAINING MANDATORY FOR THE WORK PLACE

After twenty years of training thousands of individuals in various aspects of human relations, I realize there is a continual need for this type of training, to create positive human relations and to help combat personal discrimination. Moreover, it is important for employees, managers and supervisors to understand the concepts of discrimination in order to effectively deal with it.

Here is a Mini Human Relations Lesson on Discrimination, at a minimum every individual who works with people needs to know this information.

Mini Human Relations Lesson on Discrimination

To understand discrimination, you must understand prejudice, which can be defined as "an unfavorable opinion or feeling formed beforehand or without knowledge, thought or reason, or a prejudgment without just cause." Prejudice is an attitude. Some of the prejudicial attitudes you should be concerned with are racism, sexism, ageism, anti-Semitism, and stereotyping. Below are the definitions as defined by Webster's New Universal Unabridged Dictionary for the forementioned dispositions and sexual harassment as defined by the law.

Racism - "Program or practice of racial discrimination, segregation, persecution, and domination based on racialism."

Sexism - "The economic exploitation and social domination of members of one sex by the other."

Ageism - "Discrimination against people on the basis of age: specifically, discrimination against, and prejudicial stereotyping of, older people."

Anti-Semitism - "1. Prejudice against Jews; dislike or fear of Jews and Jewish things. 2. Discrimination against or persecution of Jews."

Sexual Harassment - Sexual Harassment is a subcategory of Sex discrimination. Sexual Harassment is defined as follows:

"Unwelcome sexual advances, request for sexual favors, and other verbal or physical conduct of a sexual nature constitutes sexual harassment when:

1. submission to such conduct is made either explicitly or implicitly a term or condition of an individual's employment; **OR**

2. submission to or rejection of such conduct by an individual is used as the basis for employment decisions affecting such individual; **OR**

3. such conduct has the purpose or effect of unreasonably interfering with an individual's work performance or creating an intimidating, hostile, or offensive working environment.

Stereotype - "An unvarying form or pattern; fixed or conventional expression, notion, character, mental pattern, etc., having no individuality, as though cast from a mold..."

Often these attitudes, practices, or dispositions are learned from overbearing parents, parent's stereotypes, the news media, or even early childhood fears. However, when these attitudes are mixed with power, control or influence, the by-product is discrimination.

Discrimination is the acting out of these prejudgments. Individuals are actually denied, or deprived of something due to their sex, color, race, age, religion, national origin, or physical or mental impairment. Discrimination can occur overtly, covertly, intentionally, or unintentionally. In addition, it can be personal or institutional. Moreover, it can be either by action, inaction, or inference.

Now let's explore discrimination by looking at each type we just mentioned.

Overt Discrimination - Overt discrimination is obvious, because it is in plain view. For example, "Sue, I didn't hire you because you are a woman, and I don't think women should work in this department."

Covert Discrimination - An example of covert discrimination is as follows:

"A supervisor wrote five appraisal reports and all but one of the recipients were majority members. The majority members received outstanding reports, and the minority member received less than a satisfactory report. However, the minority member had met all standards well above average and his/her peers depended on him/her for advice. The supervisor is well aware of these facts. The minority's file contains no derogatory information. When the supervisor was questioned, the supervisor replied "he/she (the minority member) just didn't perform like his/her peers."

Intentional Discrimination - Intentional discrimination occurs when there is conscious intent to discriminate.

Unintentional Discrimination - Unintentional discrimination is when there is no conscience thought regarding the action. An example of unintentional discrimination is as follows:

"A male supervisor approached Mary (a computer technician) while she was repairing a computer. The supervisor asked her how long she had been working on the computer. Mary replied, "About two hours." The supervisor then told Mary to move over and let him take care of the task.

Later, the supervisor approached Bob, who is a male technician. He was repairing a computer also. Bob's progression repairing the computer was at the same stage of repair as Mary's when she was approached by the supervisor. The supervisor asked Bob how long he had been working on the computer. Bob replied, "About two hours." The supervisor then told Bob, "You are doing an outstanding job, now let me show you how to complete this difficult task."

In this example Mary was discriminated against because she was not given the same type of encouragement and was not afforded the same opportunity to complete the task as Bob.

The question now is whether the discrimination was intentional or unintentional. There is a good possibility the discrimination was unintentional. The point here is that the supervisor may believe females shouldn't really work on computers. He also may believe that females should be a home when their husbands get home, raising the kids and cooking their husbands' dinners. The bottom line is, he may not have thought about his action.

It can be debated whether or no he was consciously aware of this act of discrimination. Often, when unintentional discrimination occurs, the discriminators say they were not aware they were causing a problem, or they were not trying to discriminate.

Discrimination By Act - Discrimination by act is self explanatory.

Discrimination By Inference - The following short explanation will help clarify his point.

The word inference means the act of implying. Here are several examples of discrimination by inference. (1) The use of racial slurs or racial jokes, (2) a sexually degrading remark, (3) A comment such as "Don't send me any more women in my department; I have my quota."

Discrimination By Inaction - In addition to discrimination by act or inference, a supervisor may also become involved in a discrimination process by inaction. Discrimination by inaction occurs when a supervisor becomes aware of an act of discrimination, and is in position to correct it, however, fails to act. Although, the supervisor didn't actually commit the act, he/she become involved in the process by his/her inaction. This often occurs when supervisors fail to correct an employee after hearing employees make racial jokes, sexually degrading remarks or anti-Semitic comments.

Understanding the concepts of discrimination is key to creating a non-discrimination climate and ensuring that you are given equal opportunity, treatment, selection, and representation, and equal consideration throughout your job life cycle. This job life cycle includes being procured, educated, trained and used in a position commensurate with their pay grade and skill level, and given an opportunity to retire or separate without discrimination.

POINT 68 - ADJUSTING TO THE JOB MARKET

To some people, adjusting to the job market is not a difficult task, especially if they have several degrees and the skills that needed by the new market. However, for some it is quite difficult. In the book, "Let's Put America Back To Work" Senator Paul Simon made the following observation:

"President Reagan is known to occasionally hold up the "Help Wanted" classified advertisements from the Sunday Washington Post and assure his listeners that anyone who really wants a job can get one. I've looked at those ads. I like to believe I'm a reasonably talented person, but I am not qualified for perhaps 95 percent of the jobs listed. I am not a computer operator or a beautician; I can type, but no one would want to hire me as a secretary; I'm not an engineer or a chef. And what chance does someone have for one of those jobs who can't read or write? What if you can't speak English well? Or at all? What if you have a prison record? What if you have an obvious physical handicap? What if you're a person who is not mentally retarded but close to it? What if you are nervous and you don't make a good impression in an interview? What if you are black or Hispanic or a woman and the employer discriminates, but you can't prove it? I do not suggest that everyone facing unemployment has these handicaps. Most people unemployed are not dramatically different in background from most people who are employed...."[1]

Senator Simon made some very good points in his observation. In fact in his work, he also offers America an outstanding approach on how to put America back to work. I've include a few of his thoughts at Point 82.

As we move into this new information era, it will require much to obtain new skills to keep pace. We must also ensure that we acquire the needed skills to keep pace with the technology that inundates the market daily. However, in addition to this problem, there is even a bigger problem. There are millions of Americans who have never been in the job market, unskilled and can't read. And this number is increasing.

For too long America has invested much of its research in defense instead of civilian research, like Japan and West Germany. Today, with the ending of the cold war, we are shifting our strategy to become more competitive in modern technology. Consequently, this will cause more engineers and more technical people to operate the new products.

Though the North Atlantic Free Trade Alliance was recently approved, America must be careful and ensure that its workers are protected from this act. It is true that private industries can lower the cost of production by acquiring cheaper labor in foreign countries, however, on the other hand there are a number of people in America who may become unemployed as a result of these actions. Again, I must point out, unfortunately, we can't depend on our government to protect the American workers without pressure. Therefore, we must monitor this alliance carefully and apply pressure as appropriate.

Like Simon pointed out: "While I am pleased to have good financial data, improved health care and other results of a service-oriented society, I also recognized that I cannot eat information, I cannot sit on service, I cannot drive in it either. To maintain a quality standard of living, and to improve it, we have to produce things that people consume. Our tax laws should encourage that. That also creates jobs."[2]

In order for Black America to prepare for this market, we must assess where we are and establish community based programs to increase awareness and to educate the people across the United States of America on the State of Black America. We must work together and effect every Point in Power Pack.

In order to adjust for the job market, there must be more jobs. This is not only a problem for Black America, but this is a problem for America in general. Therefore, all Americans must apply continued pressure on the politicians to ensure that every measure passed is in the best interest of America and its workers, and not just for the big business owners.

POINT 69 - EFFECTING JOB READINESS TRAINING

The evident is overwhelming that millions of Americans can't read, therefore they can't complete job applications. The Committee on Economic Development report in 1985 made the following comment: "Employers in both large and small businesses decry the lack of preparation for work among the nation's high school graduates. Too many students lack reading, writing, and mathematical skills, positive attitudes toward work, and appropriate behavior on the job. Nor have they learned how to learn, how to solve problems, make decisions, or set priorities. Many high school graduates are virtually unemployable, even at today's minimum wage."[3]

Moreover, black young men and women dropped out of school and have never entered the formal job market and they too are underdeveloped. In order to prepare this group for the job market, it will require the involvement of many Americans. Along with federal, state and local government actions, there must be a large volunteer action to master this problem as we prepare individuals for the job market.

As mentioned at Point 51, the federal government's program, Job Training Partnership Act (JTPA) can make a difference and there are many success stories. However, the program is only reaching a small percentage of the people who need this training. Therefore, action is needed on two additional fronts. The first front is prevention by assuring that our system make the required adjustments to better prepare young people for the job market. The second front calls for us to work together as in communities throughout the United States, assessing the problem and establishing and staffing job readiness centers to correct the problem. We must look at this as a crisis and one of the root causes of crime, senseless killings, and gang violence.

Moreover, this is not only a problem with our youth, but a problem with millions of other Americans who find themselves unemployed, with low self-esteem, unable to read, and in need of help, but afraid to ask. Many feel so alone and worse of all, they think that no one cares.

Here, another seed is planted. You know what we must do to correct this problem. You know your resources, i.e organizations, churches, sororities, fraternities and personal assets. This problem will not go away on its own, but it will grow and become even more destructive and costly to correct later on. In addition, private foundations should allocate more money to fund this initiative.

POINT 70 - CREATING A MARKET FOR INDIVIDUALS WITH FELONY CONVICTIONS

It is extremely difficult for individuals with felony convictions to obtain jobs, especially meaningful jobs to earn a living. Why should they be penalized for the rest of their lives by denying them an opportunity to earn a living?

Have you every talked to someone who has just come out of prison, an ex-convict who doesn't wish to go back? One who is looking for employment but no one will hire him or her. A good place to meet such a person is at the service station. You'll find this person trying to earn some money by pumping gas or along the entry ramp of freeways with old newspapers trying to clean the windshield of your car for your lose coins.

Have you every talked to a prostitute to find out why she/he decided to live the life of a as prostitute? A life where they find themselves in and out of prisons? Many of the their stories are very common. I needed to work; I lost my job; I have to make a living some how, my welfare check is not enough to take care of all my children. Of course, some of them are on drugs, and they need to support their drug habits. However, if you probe a little farther you may find that their drug problems often are the result of being undeveloped and without the skills needed to earn a living in the traditional job market.

In order to stop recycling prisoners, we must create opportunities for them to become employed and to become productive citizens. Though this is only one of our many problems, it is a serious problem that must be corrected. I don't believe people in America are bad, but, we have created an unfair society in America. A society, that create criminals and a number of social ills. We must address each of these social ills. But most importantly, we must address the structure.

Our current system is unfair to individuals who are in prison, however, once they are set free, they don't have a fair chance to become gainfully employed. There are a few success stories that show how ex-convicts have been able to become involved in their own businesses or to be hired after completion of various community-base training programs. However, there are not enough of these success stories.

Our current approach is to build more prisons to deal with the anticipated increased prisoners population. America, must rise up and oppose this option because it does not address problem. Instead of constructing more prisons, a more affirmative approach should be adopted. Many of the prisoners can't read, dropped out of high school, never been in the formal job market. Currently, we have over 900,000 people in our state and federal prisons. It costs us about $20,000 annually to house each prisoner.

Recommend that the federal and state government take the lead to address this problem. Solicit solutions from throughout the United States. Look for model programs that are cost effective. Shift the emphasis from building more institutions to building conditions that offer alternatives to a life of crime or the life behind four walls.

POINT 71 - INCREASING EMPLOYMENT OPPORTUNITIES FOR YOUTH

Like their parents, the unemployment rate for African Americans and Hispanic is much higher than that of the whites. On the average for Black teens it is greater than 40 percent and for Hispanic's it is about 24 percent.

Again, the federal and state government must take the lead. Initiatives must be passed and funded to address this real problem. If you don't address it directly, taxpayers still pay for it indirectly by taking action against juvenile crime offenders. Jobs for youth help build self esteem and consequently, it will have a big impact on reducing crime and preparing our young people for the future.

Simon commented on the following initiative:

> "Congressman John Seiberling of Ohio pioneered an effort to establish an American Conservation Corps, a program designed to help the nation's parks and forests and to give young people a chance to contribute at a modest wage, similar to the Civilian Conservation Corps (CCC) of the 1930's. For less than $200 million a year, 85,000 young people could be given that opportunity. The entire nation would benefit. Educational enrichment should be part of this."[4]

Initiatives like this one need to be passed and funded.

The Drug Free School Zone Project is another initiative that is currently in effect that provides employment opportunities for youth at risk. However, this program does not reach enough young people. We must increase funding to make the programs more far reaching.

It appears that our current approach to these problems is reactionary and not proactive. More proactive measures could propel us to new realities, and a healthy and prosperous America.

Although, the bulk of the money to fund these programs should come from federal, state and local government, the private and corporate communities have a big and important part in creating more opportunities for our young people.

Recommend that cities across the United States establish programs that have the following mandates: (1) Determine the eligible population (2) Establish a Youth Jobs Clearing House (3) Obtain Corporate America participation in hiring youth (4) Establish training programs (5) Establish Recognition Programs (6) Establish a three to five year plan to hire all youth who would like to work.

The bottom line, if we fail to plan, it will not improve on its own merits. Much consideration should be given to effect youth jobs programs. Initiatives of this type will have a positive impact on America's future.

Chapter V Notes

1 Simon, Paul, <u>Let's Put America Back To Work</u>, p.10

2 Ibid. p.96

3 Ibid. p. 104

4 Ibid. p. 152

CHAPTER VI

CRIMINAL

In this chapter we'll take a look at the criminal justice system from several perspective, offer ways to reduce crime and gang violence in our community. Moreover, we discuss the need for ensuring the due process for juveniles offenders and means of reducing the prisoners population. Furthermore, a formula is shared for developing a more effective police force, a police force that truly protect and serve. Consequently, by following the process described herein, an empowered community against crime can be realized.

POINT 72 - REDUCING CRIME IN OUR COMMUNITY

The sell of drugs, carjacking, robbery, burglaries, and prostitution are common in many communities throughout the country. If African Americans work together we can reduce these type of incidents. Many of these crimes are related to the sell and demand for drugs, unemployment or underemployment.

At Points 9 and 10, we covered the drugs and the demand for drugs. At Point 71, we discussed how to prepare and provide more employment opportunities. At Point 73, we suggest developing transitional programs for people coming out of prisons. Here as we discuss reducing crime, it is imperative that we address changing behaviors.

We can create communities that are less conducive to commit crime, by ensuring proper lighting, positive interaction among neighbors, effective neighborhood watch programs, and engraving of properties. All of these measures are good means to deter crime. In addition to these measures there are some other thoughts to consider.

We must make it more difficult for individuals to sell stolen goods to pawn shops and to others.

As a community we must discover ways to deter and get people to alter their behaviors. For example: Prostitution, these ladies and men are on the streets to make money, though its a very dangerous life style. Do they really want to be out there? What are their needs? Who are their customers? How much money are they making? Do they want to change their life style? Do they have drug problems? Can they be approached? Are there people in the community willing to give them a chance to do something different?

Like we posed questions about the prostitutes, we can look at the common thief, the drug pusher, and mugger, etc. in the same way and provide alternatives. Once we begin to ask questions, we will discover solutions and ways to alter behaviors. We must address the offenses as they are committed, however, we must go far beyond that. Our law enforcers are geared to address offenses as they occur. However, it will take the people in the community to coach individuals in changing their behaviors.

Recommend community groups organize to address each of the problems related to crime. Look for real answers. At the next Point, you will discover that punishing the offenders is only a temporary fix. It is not the answer. We must work to alter behaviors.

POINT 73 - REDUCING THE NUMBER OF PRISONERS

The current thinking of the government will lead to increasing the prisoner population with measures like "Three Strikes You Are Out". Let's remember, there is a disproportionate number of African Americans in these institutions who were undeveloped youth when they first became involved in crime. These institutions are not designed to rehabilitate, but dehumanize and most come out worse for being in. Below you will find several dispositions that clearly show that we need to address this problem from a new approach.

Here is a short excerpt from the novel "Walden Two" the eminent behaviorist B. F. Skinner depicts a utopian community constructed according to the principles of "behavioral engineering." Skinner and his followers developed this principle in the learning laboratory. The principles rely heavily on the concept of reinforcement-the arrangement of circumstances so that desired or acceptable behavior is rewarded ("reinforced"). The desired outcome is to create conditions to made the behavior to recur in a similar situation. In this excerpt Frazier and Castle discuss the effect of punishment.

"I shall have to be technical," said Frazier. "But only for a moment. It's what the scene of behavior calls "reinforcement theory." The things that can happen to us fall into three classes. To some things we are indifferent. Other things we like-we want them to happen, and we take steps to make them happen again. Still other things we don't like-we don't want them to happen, and we take steps to get rid of them or keep them from happening again.

"Now," Frazier continues earnestly, "if it's in our power to create any of the situations which a person likes or to remove any situation he doesn't like, we can control his behavior. When he behaves as we want him to behave, we simply create a situation he likes, or remove one he doesn't like. As a result, the probability that he will behave that way again goes up, which is what we want. Technically it's called "positive reinforcement".

"The old school made the amazing mistake of supposing that the reverse was true, that by removing a situation a person likes or setting up one he doesn't like-in other words by punishing him-it was possible to reduce the probability that he would behave in a given way again. That simply doesn't hold. It has been established beyond question. What is emerging at this critical stage in the evolution of society is a behavioral and cultural technology based on positive reinforcement alone. We are gradually discovering-at an untold cost in human suffering-that in the long run punishment doesn't reduce the probability that an act will occur. We have been so preoccupied with the contrary that we always take force to mean punishment. We don't say we're using force when we send shiploads of food into a starving country, though we're displaying quite as much power as if we were sending troops and guns."

"I'm certainly not an advocate of force," said Castle. "But I can't agree that it's not effective."

"It's temporarily effective, that's the worst of it. That explains several thousands years of bloodshed. Even nature has been fooled. We "instinctively" punish a person who doesn't behave as we like. We spank him if he's a child or strike him if he's a man. A nice distinction! The immediate effect of the bow teaches us to strike again. Retribution and revenge are the most natural things on earth. But in the long run the man we strike is no less likely to repeat his act."

"But he won't repeat it if we hit him hard enough," said Castle.

"He'll still tend to repeat it. He'll want to repeat it. We haven't really altered his potential behavior at all. That's the pity of it. If he doesn't repeat it in our presence, he will in the presence of someone else. Or it will be repeated in the disguise of a neurotic symptom. If we hit hard enough, we clear a little place for ourselves in the wilderness of civilization, but we make the rest of the wilderness still more terrible."[1]

Though the excerpt is fiction, it is a reflection of our reality. Our prison population is getting larger because we have not focused enough on altering potential behaviors. By effecting the Points as outlined in this plan we will provide means to altering potential behaviors.

To reduce the number of prisoners in our institutions, we must alter behaviors and develop programs to prevent crime and afford transitional programs to help facilitate individuals back into the main stream. For this to occur, prisoners must be afforded certain fundamental rights such as:

1. The right to personal safety. Current conditions in prisons are unsafe and in general, individuals are helpless to protect himself or herself.

2. Prisoners must be given the right to care, to include decent, clean housing, adequate diet, enough clothing, and medical care.

3. They must be afforded the right to personal dignity. We want them to function as model citizens when they come back into mainstream America. However, we don't provide the proper avenues to help them make an effective transition. It is very difficult to make the transition after living behind bars for years, especially when you live in an environment of humiliation where there is no self-respect, and no reinforced sense of self-worth.

4. They should be granted the right to work. It is irrational to deny a willing and able body the opportunity to work while he or she is in prison. This opportunity to work will enable them to meet their responsibilities for housing, and dependents care like other citizens.

5. They should have a right to self-improvement. To assist them in making a healthy transition back into the mainstream, again it must start in the prison by giving them an opportunity to receive an education, and provide vocational, recreational and artistic programs. We must always remember, the lack of these opportunities outside of the institutions drives poor people to criminality.

6. If Mandella can become President in South Africa, surely, a prisoner should have the right to vote in the United States, especially when they leave the institution.

7. Prisoners must have the right to a future and not three strikes you are out. Existing barriers should be removed and more contact with families and friend, and the general outside community should be encouraged.

Moreover, recommend transitional programs be established that afford convicts opportunities to participate during the last ninety days of their terms. These transitional programs should be designed to allow these individuals to leave the institutions early and permit them to live in a controlled environment at night, while receiving training and working in an un-controlled environment during the day.

This quote by Jeff Bingaman, former attorney general of New Mexico clearly states what we need to do:

"Prisons simply do not deal with the basic problems of crime in our society. Prison is a dehumanizing experience, and most persons come out the worse for being in. Nearly all criminals, even under the strictest sentencing practices will return to society. Even a well managed bureaucracy, necessary to run prisons, cannot change these basic truths....If New Mexico's heritage of rich and deep familial and community roots is to be realized, communities must play a part in housing, socializing and accepting persons who have violated the community's law. If New Mexico does not dramatically change its philosophy and practices about how to deal with criminals, there will be more tragedies and the need for more reports by Grand Juries, by Citizens' panels, and by the Attorney General. Ultimately, there will be more bureaucracy, more waste of taxpayers' money for architects and buildings, more crime and more human waste."[2]

If we wish to stop this human waste, we the free people in America must take action to turn this around. Like the campaign to increase the prisoners population by more of the same, we can use another approach and change this self-fulfilling prophesy. The prisoner population can be reduced by changing the overall approach to treating them while they are inmates and affording proper transitional programs.

The prisoners are not in position to correct this problem. It will take community- based organizations and people like you and I to take immediate action and demand that our current system be revised and action be taken that is designed to reduce the prisoners population. Once we carefully study this problem, we will discover that confluence of factors leads to criminality and action can be taken to address each root cause.

POINT 74 - ENSURING DUE PROCESS FOR JUVENILE OFFENDERS

Studies show that in a majority of cases, juveniles are not represented by counsel at the adjudicatory hearing. However, the Supreme Court's decisions of Re Gault, 387 U.S. 1 (1967), and other cases, have established a series of due process rights guaranteed to juvenile offenders, including the right to counsel. However, these rights are not always available.

According to the Office of Justice Programs, Office of Juvenile Justice and Delinquency Prevention (OJJDP): "In sum, there are major problems with access to and availability of counsel, and even when juveniles are represented, substantial questions are raised about the quality of that representation."

OJJDP is currently taking steps to increase juvenile offenders' access to legal services; and to improve the quality of preadjudicated, adjudicated, and dispositional advocacy for juvenile offenders.

Although, OJJDP is working to address this problem, immediate action is required by Black America now to ensure that African American youth receive due process especially, in light of the arrest rate for violent crime. In 1991 the violent crime arrest rate for black youth was 5 times higher than that of white youth (1,456 per 100,000 compared with 283 per 100,000). On a side note, the 5 to 1 ratio is extremely high, therefore, the low arrest rate of the white youth becomes suspect of personal discrimination on the part of the arresting officers. A number of other factors could contribute to this imbalance, i.e. black youth being stopped and questioned by officers more; the decision of the officers not to arrest the white youth for the similar infractions committed by the black youth. Nevertheless, current statistics suggest that this area must be closely monitored. More importantly, we must ensure that Black youth who are arrested receive the due process of the law.

Recommend the NAACP take immediate action to review and monitor this area. In addition, action should be taken on the local level to monitor the rate of arrest and to ensure all Black juvenile offenders receive due process. After careful evaluation, there may be a need to establish a group designed against the wrongful prosecution of juveniles.

In addition, recommend action be taken within the police department itself to ensure that personal discrimination does not occur in the enforcement of the law. This area can be addressed through human relations training (the need for human relations training for police officers is covered at Point 77) and a sound quality control program.

POINT 75 - REDUCING THE OPPORTUNITY TO COMMIT CRIME

We must reduce opportunities to commit crime by placing emphasis on developing effective neighborhood watch programs, and actively supporting of law enforcement activities. We must take measures to gain more support of the community by improving the law enforcement personnel public image. We must develop training for law enforcement personnel to this end. Moreover, we must create programs to divert youth or first time juvenile offenders from detention, incarceration experiences to community restitution and/or diversion programs activities.

POINT 76 - REDUCING OPPORTUNITIES TO SELL DRUGS

We must reduce opportunities to sell drugs by increasing activities designed to address the sellers, suppliers and the king pins. We must develop programs to gain more public support and confidence that they too can participate in the identification process of drug abusers or king pins without fear or reprisals. Reference Points 9 and 10.

POINT 77 - TRAINING LAW ENFORCEMENT OFFICERS

We must reduce discrimination by the police against African Americans and Hispanics. Premise: The police officers on the street are in key positions that determine when to charge, give traffic citations, and to arrest or not to arrest. Sometimes these decisions are arbitrary and discriminatory. In addition, some police officers will engage in improper conduct when they are deficient in certain human relations skills.

For over seventeen years my primary duties in the Air Force was that of a problem solver, working equal opportunity and treatment concerns, assessing human relations climates and training people in human relations. Prior to my retirement from the United States Air Force in 1989, I developed a special training course for law enforcement personnel while I was stationed at Los Angeles Air Force Base. I developed the course after an incident in 1987 occurred on base similar to the Rodney King's beating.

When this incident occurred the base security was handled by a local contractor. Many of the contracted employees were local police officers from the surrounding Los Angeles area who were moonlighting on base. After this incident, I'd look for the root causes and eventually, I had to conduct human relations training for these officers. During the training I became acutely aware of how ill-prepared they were in using the spoken word as a tool, especially when individuals failed to comply with their orders.

I remained in Los Angeles after my retirement. My concerns in 1989 about the numerous incidents involving the Los Angeles Police Department prompted me to assess the need for a more effective human relations training program. I developed a human relations program designed to meet the needs of the Los Angeles Police Department. I met with a sergeant at the Los Angeles Police Academy to present my program, but was unable to because he spent about three hours trying to convince me his program was outstanding already.

I kept communicating with the Los Angeles Police Department, and finally on April 10, 1990, (about 11 months, prior to the Rodney King Beating incident) I received a letter from Chief Daryl F. Gates who assigned a panel to evaluate my program. However, the panel never did evaluate my program.

I believe if the police officers were properly trained, the incident involving Rodney King and the police officers would have never escalated to the level it did.

More effective human relations training is needed to enable law enforcement personnel to effectively use human relations skills and to address the problem of discrimination that allows selective enforcement of the law. The training should be designed to:

- Increase police officers knowledge of their role in upholding federal, state and local laws, and local department policies on fair and equal treatment, including policies on sexual harassment.

- Give more definition on how to achieve and keep the promises made under the Law Enforcement Code of Ethics, which relate to human relations.

- Increase police offices' ability to manage cultural diversity.

- Increase the awareness of police officers on various aspects of human relations, including the following: (1) race relations, (2) openness (3) perceptions (4) discrimination (5) objectivity (6) attitude (7) non-verbal behavior (8) courtesy (9) compassion (10) arrogance (11) equal opportunity and treatment (12) sexual harassment (13) prejudice and (14) perspective.

- Provide police officers skills to manage personal anger and the anger of others.

- Enable police officers to use the transactional analysis approach to problem solving.

- Improve police officers' conflict resolution strategies.

- Enhance police officers' ability to allow the use of the spoken word to become a more effective weapon.

- Provide the police officer skills to achieve his or her individual responsibility for gaining and maintaining positive organization image through positive human relations.

- Improve internal communication and teamwork.

POINT 78 - EFFECTING OPERATION ROOT UP GANGS (OPERATION RUG)

Operation Root Up Gangs (Operation RUG) is a gang deterrence and prevention program. The long-term objective is to develop a mechanism to ensure the roots of the gang movement are identified and continuously addressed and then eradicated by the effected community.

The specific aims are:

(1) to regulate, evaluate, redirect, and coordinate all community activities designed to eradicate the roots of gangs. Through this coordinated proactive effort this operation institutes programs to provide leadership and raise funds to improve participating organization's effectiveness.

(2) Institute a "Personal Redirecting Program" for current gang members. Under this program, gang members can join and receive training to help prepare themselves for the job market through value clarification, education, counseling, job training, job readiness training, and job placement.

Operation RUG addresses the problem of neighborhoods throughout the United States being under siege and children who occupy them have been taken hostage by violence.

Children form gangs as surrogate families and use automatic weapons as a symbol of their deep feelings of helplessness and hopelessness. Behavior is an indicator of a child's emotions and low self-esteem. Thus, the surface actions of drive-by shootings, selling drugs for profit with no regard for human life and living with no regard for consequence, indicate a deep-seated detachment from morals, value and caring. Moreover, this shows that these young people lack self-worth and self-esteem.

There are tens of thousands of gang members throughout the United States. Driven by profits from the sale of illegal drugs or stolen goods, a societal underclass has been created. Thousands of American youth are killed every year in gang-related incidents.

In addition to even more disabling and life changing injuries, there are innocent by-standers, non-gang members and children-victims of gang initiated violence. Concurrently, car jacking is on the rise, often involving gang members targeting non-gang members and community residents. A report this year stated that black males are more subject to car jacking than any other group.

Consequently, innocent people are physically and emotionally killed in this cross fire. Danger has become a way of life for the young, but has driven resident to arm themselves, live behind bars and view the children of the neighborhood as the "enemy".

The "US" and "THEM" mentality allows the problem to grow deeper and larger and the symptoms of distrust, isolation, fear and lack of communication continue to permeate ever-increasing areas of neighborhoods throughout the country.

The very adults that could provide the attention, care, training, love and support become the victim and enemy. Our youth who need the guidance, protection, direction and boundaries become the victim and the enemy. The schism will continue to grow unless bridges are developed to re-establish that very natural bond between the young and the old.

Operation RUG, proposes just such a bridge so that the victims and the enemies become family and friend and the "US" and "THEM" become "WE".

Operation RUG converts a seemingly unmanageable problem into manageable components through sound and management principles. By developing a mechanism to expose the root causes of the gang movement, they can be continuously addressed and then eradicated by the people in the affected communities.

Throughout America, there are a number of community-based organizations addressing certain aspects of the problem, however, most do not address the root causes. There is no systematic mechanism that regulates, evaluates, redirects and coordinates all community activities to expose the root cause of gangs. Operation RUG puts ex-gang members in the resolution process and creating a cooperative spirit among community residents and community based organizations.

Past efforts have failed to:

(1) Address the root causes of gangs

- High Unemployment
- Minimum Wages
- Lack of Education
- Lack of Skills
- Lack of Positive Influence and Role Models
- Opportunity to Commit Crime
- Opportunity to Sell Drugs
- Action on Poverty
- Unstable Home
- Spiritual Void
- Demand For Drugs
- Gang Phobia
- Perceived Power
- Low Self-esteem

(2) Redirect gang members to positive achievements

(3) Involve ex-gang members in the resolution process

(4) Eliminate gang phobia

The past attempts at containment usually manifest as increased police presence, passage of more stringent (unenforceable) laws, use of battering rams on crack houses, marches, rallies, celebrity public service announcements and school assemblies. Containment is not a solution. Gangs must be eradicated.

Operation RUG establishes consortia to address each root, define functions and align community-based organizations accordingly. To facilitate management, the consortia are broken down in the following three categories:

Education and Opportunities

- High Unemployment
- Minimum Wages
- Lack of Education
- Lack of Skill
- Lack of Positive Influence and Role Models

Crime

- Opportunity to Commit Crime
- Opportunity to Sell Drugs

Social And Spiritual

- Action on Poverty
- Unstable Home
- Spiritual Void
- Demand For Drugs
- Gang Phobia
- Perceived Power
- Low Self-Esteem

Recommend the implementation of Operation RUG be throughout the United States. A copy of Operation RUG can be procured by contacting the author direct.

Drawing of the Roots of Gangs

POINT 79 - EMPOWERING THE COMMUNITY AGAINST CRIME

An effective police department goes hand and hand with empowering the community against crime. The police department must be a department that the community can trust. Some city officials believe that you must have an excessive number of police officers to provide adequate protection for the community. However, this is not always the case. A small well-trained police force with concern for law and order and the people in the community, can be much more effective than a large police force that the community can't trust.

When the community trusts the police force, the community does not hesitate in providing the police department needed information and assistance to uphold law and order. The community becomes the police departments additional eyes and ears. Therefore, the police department must take the lead in creating its public image and interact with the community it serves.

Neighborhood watch programs should be sponsored and promoted by the police department. Often community leaders take the initiative to establish neighborhood watch programs. Some programs are quite effective but when there is no central focus point that monitors and enhances the effectiveness of these neighborhood watch groups, they become reactionary, ineffective and eventually dissolve.

Recommend that police departments throughout America take the lead to enhance the effectiveness of neighborhood watch programs. Although, people in the community are responsible for managing neighborhood watch programs the leadership from the police departments is very important, especially in areas where the police image has suffered.

Cities throughout the United States should set goals to establish effective neighborhood watch programs.

Chapter VI Notes

1 Skinner, B.F., (1948), Walden Two, quoted by Cohen, Perspectives On Psychology: Introductory Readings, pp. 105 - 108

2 Dorsen, Norman, (1984), Our Endangered Rights:The ACLU Report On Civil Liberties Today, p. 232

CHAPTER VII

POLITICAL

In this chapter we examine ways to use our political power more effectively, to include the use of the vote and applying pressure through other means. Moreover, we explore ways to make politicians become more responsible and how to apply pressure on the movie industry to ensure that African Americans and Hispanics receive fair treatment.

POINT 80 - ENSURING JUSTICE IN ALL AFFAIRS

Voting for your candidate is not enough to ensure justice in all affairs. It takes a lot more than that. Dr. Henderson made it very plain:

"The message for African Americans is simple: remain politically active, vigilant and well informed on fiscal policy, or be placed further back in the budget line behind other priorities." [1]

Did you know - during the Supreme Court's 1988 -1989 term, more than a half dozen rulings, one after another erected a series of formidable barriers to blacks who must rely on the judicial system to protect them from employment discrimination.

Most of these rulings narrowed the interpretation of the civil rights laws and reversed established case law. These actions were on the most important congressional statues that protects minority rights in the area of economic: Section 1981 of the 1866 Civil Rights Acts and Title VII of the 1964 Civil Right Acts. With the passage of these acts and the Act of 1871 Congress intention were to address the pervasive problem of exclusion of blacks and other minorities from the economic mainstream of America.

Over the past two decades, the Court had been giving these laws a broad and liberal interpretation until 1988, when five members of the Supreme Court took a different approach.

In Patterson v. McLean Credit Union the court ruled that section 1891 did not protect a credit union employee from on-the-job racial harassment. The court held that section 1981:

"extends to only to the formation of contract, but not to the problems that arise later from the conditions of continuing employment" [2]

Moreover, the Court also ruled that the statute doesn't prohibit discrimination unless the promotion creates "a new and distinct relation between the employer and the employee."

This ruling, which narrowed the definition of relation had a disastrous effect on fair employment litigation. According to a study by the NAACP Legal Defense and Education Fund, between June 15, 1989 (the date of the decision) and November 1, 1989, at least 96 employment discrimination claims were dismissed because of Patterson, without serious consideration of the merits of those 96 complaints.

In general the Court during this period made it very difficult for victims of discrimination to show that certain employment practices violated their rights.

My point of this discussion is did you know that the Court made these rulings? If you did know about these rulings - what did you do to effect a change?

The National Urban League, Inc. publishes a book yearly entitled "The State of Black America". This is an excellent source of information that will enable you to remain politically active, vigilant and well-informed on fiscal policy, or be placed further back in the budget line behind other priorities.

There is a number of other things that you can do. For example, establishing an information community political phone net. This net could be established through a non-profit organization. The phone net could play an important part in keeping people informed of what is going.

In addition to a phone net, the community should be organized. Community-based organizations and churches must work together and have community forums, seminars, workshops and strategy sessions.

POINT 81 - INCREASING POLITICAL POWER

We must increase Black Americans and Hispanics political power through education - Black Americans and Hispanics must unite and organize a political coalition that empowers both groups. Moreover, within Black America, there must be a renewed sense of unity that will transcend economic status, geographic residence, and other tragedies that currently separate blacks from another black's plight.

The affluent African Americans must assist the lower class and underclass African Americans in realizing their potential political power. Through organization the poor can be heard. When this occurs, it will increase the overall African Americans political power. Working together, African Americans can make a difference.

African Americans must organize and effect a greater political influence at city halls, and in the state and federal governments. Although the civil rights statues do not expressly prohibit discrimination on account of poverty, they do prohibit discrimination on the account of race. Therefore, intergroup relations action must be conducted through the economic channel even though it may be basically concerned with race. Here I'm reminded of a popular saying during the 1960's: "What's the use of being able to sit down at a hamburg counter if you haven't got a dime."

We must increase our political power to address social and economic justice.

To effect this point, two aspects need to be carefully addressed (1) the poor who haven't used the political system by voting and the (2) upper class who are removed from the people who are in need.

First to address the poor who don't vote, there must be action to show them the power of their vote. It can start with something small, for example: effecting initiatives for cleaning up the alley ways, cleaning the streets, installing more street lights, tearing down old vacate buildings, or clearing lots that are currently being used as unauthorized land fills. The key is the poor people of the target communities must be part of this process of getting politicians to address these conditions that are impacting their lives in their community.

The involvement of middle and upper class African Americans is critical. Through an increased awareness campaign every effort should be made to reach the non-voting segment of the African American communities. We will discuss this process more at Chapter VIII.

POINT 82 - CREATING MORE EFFECTIVE POLITICAL LEADERSHIP AND LESS VACILLATION OF POLICIES

A change in administration, often means a change in programs. This method of running the affairs of this nation has cost America a lot in recent years. Consequently, African Americans, Hispanics, other minorities, and poor Whites have suffered dearly because of this ineffective leadership.

The government must learn that passing laws does not mean the passage of the law ends the condition. The Supreme Court desegregation decision in 1954 really didn't end desegregation and the passage of the Civil Rights Act of 1964 didn't end discrimination. In the same way, when programs come on line and receive funding, we can't look for over-night success in changing conditions that took years to manifest. In the past, programs have been cut and called failures, without giving these programs a chance to work.

Sarason summed it up like this:

> "Is it not equally amazing how many people really believed that if disadvantaged groups, like the blacks, were provided new and enriched educational experiences they would as a group blossom quickly in terms of conventional educational and intellectual criteria? Is it not pathetic how eager we were to believe that we possessed the knowledge to justify these expectations? What combination of ignorance and arrogance permitted people to proclaim that if we delivered the right kinds of programs and spent the appropriate sums of money we could quickly undo what centuries had built up? When the expectations that powered these efforts were obviously not being fulfilled, what permitted some people to conclude that perhaps the victim was in some ways different from (less endowed than) those in the dominant society? Why were they so ready to "blame the victim" instead of the thinking from which derived such an unrealistic time perspective?"[3]

In our efforts to change these conditions that are destroying America, we must realize that certain things will not change over-night. Nevertheless, we must continue to work our plan, re-evaluate, adjust, and effect. Therefore, our law-makers and other elected officials must learn from past mistakes. Though we have done a number of things correctly, we continue to make mistakes because we've failed to learn from our past ones.

Often when administrations change hands, the newcomers' conception of a problem or process determines his/her time perspective about how to influence or change it. Sometimes one's conception is faulty or one's time perspective poorly deduced, or both, nevertheless there is a relationship. Our leaders must learn to confront this relationship in a systematic and realistic way to prevent personal disillusionment and conflict. This will help enable our leaders to work in the best interest of the country.

America has elected a number of ineffective leaders who don't have the insight to lead this country or represent the people. It is becoming more apparent that some leaders value their political career interests more than what's in the best interest of the country. Nevertheless, Americans must call upon the politicians today and ask the government to take a new look at the way this country is being governed. America must tell these leaders that when they make decisions and pass laws, their actions must not be based on emotions or ploys to get votes. America, remind the elected officials, that they are in office to work in the best interest of the country and not in their own personal political interest.

Senator Paul Simon in his book "Let's Put America Back To Work" provides some inside information about politicians. In fact his insight and observations at a local public hearing confirm my suspicions. Simon states:

"For the last three decades, under both the Democratic and Republican administrations, we slowly drifted in the wrong direction. Although we are one of the lowest taxed societies in the industrial world - which is contrary to the public myth - political leaders of both parties have been reluctant to face the decision of either providing more revenue or curtailing growing services. Slowly the deficit grew. And grows. We got deep into the fiscal quicksand with the passage of the tax bill of 1981. It was offered by President Reagan in good faith, and accepted by Democrats, as well as the Republicans. People presented him with theory that you could spend more and reduce taxes, and the stimulation from the reduced taxes would produce additional revenue. He bought the concept."[4]

According to Simon, President Reagan assured Congress that by the passage of the 1981 tax bill, by Fiscal Year 1984, the budget would be balanced. However, he was off by $200 billion dollars. Moreover, by the fiscal year 1986, the deficit reached $230 billion, three times as high for one year as the deficit of any previous president.

Here is an example of ineffective leadership; leadership that failed to do their homework, leadership that fell to the pressure of special interest groups, who benefitted by the passage of the bill. (Senator Simon didn't vote in favor of this bill).

It is apparent that some elected officials are so concerned about being re-elected, their decisions are not always in the best interest of the country. The same thing can happen at local level as well. For example, recently I attended a city council meeting in Los Angeles. One of the items was approved by a 8 to 7 vote. Though the issue was approved, it became very clear to the spectators that this favorable vote was not in the best interest of Los Angeles, but based on personal political interests. In fact, this decision cost the tax payers, $2.5 million and in my opinion it undermined the integrity of the City Council.

Let's continue the discussion on ineffective leaders by examining a statement made by Senator Simon:

> "Part of our present difficulty has been caused by a simple thing that superficially sounds good: We have elected members of the House and Senate who have done what the voters want."[5]

I would take it just a little farther than that: we have elected people who have failed to keep the public informed of what's really going on in this nation. In fact, even today the nation as a whole is not aware of the true state of the economy, the real impact of crime, the fact that the affluent are the ones who benefitted from the most recent tax bills. America needs to know that we pay over $200 billion a year in interest alone. America needs to know that $200 billion is twice the amount of our overall budget of 1962. America needs to know that due to ineffective leadership: "Budget deficits averaged only 0.1 percent of GNP between 1950 and 1969; but during the 1980's, the deficits averaged 4 percent of GNP."

In 1987, Paul Simon attempted to inform America, and in 1992, Ross Perot attempted to inform America on the nation's problems, to no avail.

We are paying 200 billions dollar a year in interest. America must be told the truth. To address these problems facing Black America, we must address the serious problems that are facing America.

Though, poverty, crime, violence, the deficit, discrimination, and education all are serious problems, our greatest problems that confront America today are its ineffective leadership and an uninformed public. Currently, America has the resources and means to address poverty, violence and all interconnected problems, but the public needs to know what is going on. For example, the public needs to know that the affluent are the ones to benefit from these tax bills before they are passed. The public needs to know that many Americans may lose their jobs by the passing on NAFTA; and NAFTA mostly benefits the affluent.

Moreover, Americans need to know that we can resolve the unemployment problem, poverty and crime. Americans need to know that these problems are interconnected. The people need to know what it will cost if we resolve it now. America also needs to know, that if we fail to resolve these problems now, we will not only have "children at risk", but we will have "an America at risk".

Senator Paul Simon developed a plan to put America back to work. Our elected officials must study this plan. Here are some comments from a few individuals who have reviewed his plan:

"It is scandalous that we have so easily accepted 7 percent unemployment as the national norm. That number is an emblem of grinding hardship for millions of Americans who want to work and cannot find jobs.

But Paul Simon offers help. "Let's Put America Back to Work" is a virtual encyclopedia of the recent economic history of jobs and joblessness in the United States, and better than that, a rich blueprint of practical ideas for putting our people back to work. I like best his theme of cooperation among business, labor and government. I know this book will be influential in solving one of our most serious national problems."[6]

Governor Mario M. Cuomo (NY)

"Paul Simon is a worthy heir to an Illinois tradition. Like the late Paul Douglas, he thinks hard about important issues. In this thoughtful and provocative book, Senator Simon addresses the most intractable of our economic problems - persistent unemployment."[7]

Senator Edward M. Kennedy (MA)

"This is not a plaint. This is a plan: a common-sense, prairie-plain plan to put America back to work."[8]

Senator Daniel P. Moynihan (NY)

"The nation must applaud Paul Simon for calling attention to the great forgotten American problem - unemployment at level would have been thought intolerable a few years ago - and, more than that, for proposing sound, practical and productive remedy..."[9]

Professor Arthur Schlesinger, Jr.

"Senator Simon rightly argues that 7 percent (unemployment) is not the 'best' America can do and puts forward a practical proposal for doing much better. These are proposals to which every American ought to listen."[10]

Professor Lester C. Thurow

This is not a ploy for a presidential campaign for Senator Paul Simon. In fact I don't know if he is even interested in running again. But, after reading his book, and being a deep thinker myself, I'm able to recognize good work and sound and practical solutions that this work offers to America.

Recommend that our elected officials read it. Revise his plan, if necessary. Inform America of the costs and benefits, but let's not continue to lead this country into social chaos. Let's not continue to allow millions of Americans to live in poverty, go homeless, and to live in fear. Let's not allow racial tension to continue to build because of your inaction. America pays its politicians quite well, at least ten times the minimum wage, I might add. America deserves a lot more from them. In fact, ineffective leadership has been the downfall of great nations in the past, therefore, we the people call upon the elected officials today to lead. However, if you are a politician and you don't know how to lead, resign, so we can elect strong leaders.

To change many of these conditions that are impacting African Americans will take a lot of work. Sometimes we will get immediate results, and sometimes the results will take longer than anticipated. Nevertheless, we must develop programs that offer real solutions and then give them a chance to work. We must continue to use our time, talents, resources and money to change conditions that have taken hundreds of years to create.

We must take measures to ensure that we develop politicians to be our representatives to the government body and not the government representative to us, the people. Moreover, action must be taken to ensure that the public awareness level is increased to the point that more sound policy decisions are made, and provisions are established to give sound policies a chance to work, with less vacillation.

POINT 83 - USING THE MOVIE INDUSTRY TO EDUCATE

Recently there have been attempts to use the movie industry to educate people on certain conditions that confront us. Today we have a great need to use the movie industries like never before. Immediate action is needed to produce and promote programs that preserve and protect the black family. We must re-think sitcoms that are currently designed to be "humorous" however, the by-products promote discrimination, stereotypes, mistrust and destroy positive human relations.

Recommend that writers and producers act immediately and produce movies that are both educational with high commercial value. This is a challenge. However, if you perceive it, you can make it happen. Remember, our underdeveloped youth need you. There also should be an effort to educate the public of the state of America through the movie industry, to include the plight of the poor, homelessness and the unemployed.

The movie "The Flintstones" is a good example of a non-traditional way of educating America on its current state, though none of the published critics were able to focus on the educational value of the movie. Nevertheless, that is good because it will take a series of productions to make the needed impact. There must be more movies of this order. The goal must be to increase the awareness of as many Americans as possible aware of America's current state and the need for change. In addition to this goal, action must be taken to end the many acts of discrimination through movies and television productions.

Recommend a community-based be group organized in the Los Angeles area with mandate to effect this objective. OR the NAACP branch in Hollywood adopt an initiative to effect this point.

POINT 84 - APPLYING CONTINUOUS PRESSURE ON HOLLYWOOD AND THE MAJOR TELEVISION NETWORKS

There must be continuous pressure applied on Hollywood to ensure that Blacks and Hispanic are treated fairly in the movie industry and are given more meaningful roles that promote a more positive image in productions. In addition to productions, action must be taken to ensure that equal employment opportunities become a reality in these industries. We must remember that African Americans have some real political power in this area. Although, African Americans make up only about 12% of the national population, it is estimated that Black America purchased about 50% of the movie tickets. If Blacks are going to continue to spend money in this manner, African Americans, lets use our political power in this area and make a difference.

Recommend that this become a national interest item for the major civil rights organizations. On July 25, 1994, Reverend Jesse Jackson announced that the National Rainbow Coalition will take measures to ensure equality is a reality at major television broadcasting networks. He also called for a boycott of one of the major network in 1995. The network will be named after the facts are researched. On a side note: Reverend Jesse Jackson knows the important of collecting data prior to taking action against any institution. It is important that we realize the importance of researching the facts prior to taking action against firms.

To effect this Point, it will require increased awareness and a collective effort of all of the civil rights organizations, and every concerned American. To help facilitate this action, I recommend that the NAACP branch in Hollywood, the Brotherhood Crusade, Urban League, CORE in

Los Angeles, work very close with the Rainbow Coalition in planning the appropriate strategies.

This area requires continuous monitoring, even after 1995. It is very important that we remember, in all we do, we must work together in order to be effective.

POINT 85 - ALL OF OUR FREEDOM, HERE, AND NOW

As the late Dr. Martin Luther King, Jr. said: "We want all of our freedom, here and now." We must let America know that we must have all of our freedom, now. This campaign can be waged through demonstrations, rallies, letter writing, songs, raps and other actions as appropriate. It is very important that we effect this campaign because it will help rekindle a charge that has grown dim over the last two decades.

Black America, we must become more proactive and set a new tone for this nation. Our suffering has lasted far too long. In the past, there has been too much suffering in Black America and there is still too much suffering in Black America, today. We have had too much of a double share of the bad things in life, for too long. Today, the good things in life that America has to offer must become part of our now. Hope for the future and prosperity must become a part of our now. Jobs, business opportunities, loans, grants, and the liquidation of ghetto life, must become part of our now. Parity in income must become part of our now. Yes we must declare to America today, we must make a declaration by our action. We must take a "No Non-sense Approach" with America. Moreover, we must take a "No Non-sense Approach" with one another. We must unify to a level of unification, that would be second to none to any other group. We must come together and pave the way for a secure future for Black America. We must work together until social and economic justice becomes a reality.

However, prior to commencing the campaign, the African-American and Hispanic Communities must become educated on all issues. Let's become educated now.

POINT 86 - DEVELOPING POLITICAL POWER THAT IS READY TO MOBILIZE

African Americans must develop a political force that will ensure that issues of utmost concern to Black America are continuously addressed in every community throughout the United States. Today, we are fortunate in that we have had a number of lessons learned that were passed down to us from Dr. Martin King, Jr. and other leaders who are no longer with us. Moreover, we are truly blessed to have some of the leaders alive today who had personal experiences in the civil rights movement of the 1960's. Through the Power Pack, lessons learned from great leaders have also been shared. Here, we will develop the vehicle that is needed to propel us into the 21st century.

First, let's recap several important lessons learned:

(1) There is more power in socially-organized masses on the march than there is in guns in the hands of a few desperate men.

(2) We have developed many creative forms to assist in mobilizing our efforts to include: mass boycott, sit-down protests and strikes, sit-ins, refusal to pay fines and bail for un-just arrests, mass marches, mass meetings, prayer pilgrimage, bank-ins, phone-ins, faxes, and massive letter writing.

(3) We must cease internal fighting and turn outward to the enemy - using every form of mass action - and never let them rest.

(4) Marches must continue over a period of thirty to forty-five days to produce any meaningful results.

(5) Boycotts must be sustained over a period of several weeks and months to assure results.

(6) There is nothing quite as effective as a refusal to cooperate economically with the forces and institutions which perpetuate evil in our communities.

(7) People will work together and sacrifice if they understand clearly why and how this sacrifice will bring about change.

(8) Never assume that anyone understands. It is our job to keep people informed and aware.

(9) There must be a diversified approach to the problem. Organizations like the NAACP, Urban League, SCLC, CORE, ACLU and community-based organizations are very important in addressing solutions.

(10) "The most superficial look at history shows that no social advance rolls in on the wheels of inevitability. It comes through the tireless efforts and persistent work of dedicated individuals. Without this hard work, time itself becomes an ally of primitive forces and social stagnation. Unnecessary delays have already been suffered in the civil rights struggle through a lack of vigorous action."[11]

Martin Luther King, Jr.

(11) To address the problems of poverty, homelessness, and unemployment, there must be a grand alliance of African Americans, Hispanics and white Americans. We must not allow white extremists or black extremists to preclude this from happening.

(12) "The brunt of the Negro's past battles was borne by a very small striking force. Though millions of Negroes were ardent and passionate supporters, only a modest number were actively engaged, and these were relatively too few for a broad war against racism, poverty and discrimination. Negroes fought and won, but our engagements were skirmishes, not climatic battles.

No great victories are won in a war for the transformation of a whole people without total participation. Less than this will not create a new society; it will only evoke more sophisticated token amelioration. The Negro has been wrong to toy with the optimistic thought that the breakdown of white resistance could be accomplished at small cost. He will have to do more before his pressure crystallizes new white principles and new responses. The two forces must continue to collide as Negro aspirations burst against the ancient fortresses of the status quo."[12]

If the passage of bills was all it took for social and economic justice, I wouldn't have written this book and you would not be reading it now. However, we realize it takes a lot more than that. Here is another important lesson that Dr. King left us that I must share before I continue.

"One of the difficult lessons we have learned is that you cannot depend upon American institutions to function without pressure. Any real change in the status quo depends on continued creative action to sharpen the conscience of the nation and establish a climate in which even the most recalcitrant elements are forced to admit that change is necessary."[13]

On the above premise, this vehicle for social change is established. Now, more than ever before, we are becoming more aware of the work that we must do to achieve both social and economic justice. Awareness is key to establishing the force as we prepare to address the future skirmishes that will pave the way to win the climatic battle, whereby social and economic justice will become a reality.

Dr. King left with us some special instructions on how we must wage this climatic battle.

"This really means making the movement powerful enough, dramatic enough, morally appealing enough, so that people of goodwill, the churches, labor, liberals, intellectuals, students, poor people themselves begin to put pressure on congressmen to the point that they can no longer elude our demands.

Our idea is to dramatize the whole economic problem of the poor. We feel there's a great deal that we need to do to appeal to Congress itself. The early demonstrations will be more geared toward educational purposes - to educate the nation on the nature of the problem and the crucial aspects of it, the tragic conditions that we confront in the ghettos."[14]

The Points as outlined in the Power Pack will serve as one of our organized efforts to educate America. We first must become aware of decisions, proposed actions, events, laws, and plans that will impact our lives. As King stated: "When we confront our adversaries, we must be as armed with knowledge as they. Our policies should have the strength of deep analysis beneath them to be able to challenge the clever sophistries of our opponents. [15] Education without social action is one-sided value because it has no true power potential. Social action without education is a weak expression of pure energy.[16] After this level of awareness we must organize and then effect the plan. At Chapter VIII, there is a series of Points that address the organizing and effecting process.

Chapter VII Notes

1 Dewart, Janet, (1991), The State Of Black America, P. 78
"Budget, Taxes, And Politics: Options For the African-American
Community, Henderson, Lenneal J.

2 Patterson v. Mclean Credit Union, 105, L. ed. 2d 150, 109 S. Ct.
2363 (1989) quoted by Chambers in Black Americans And The
Courts: Has The Clock Been Turned Back Permanently?, Jullius .
Chambers, Esq., The State Of Black America p. 11

3 American Psychologist, November 1973, 28, pp. 962-71
"Jewishness, Blackness, and The Nature-Nurture-Controversy",
Seymour B. Sharon, published in "Perspective on Psychology" p.97

4 Simon, Paul, (1987) Let's Put America Back To Work p. 90

5 Ibid. 9

6 Ibid. Cover

7 Ibid. Cover

8 Ibid. Cover

9 Ibid. Cover

10 Ibid. Cover

11 Washington, James, M. (1986) A Testament Of Hope: The
Essential Writing Of Martin Luther King Jr., p. 111

12 Ibid. pp. 567, 568

13 Ibid. p. 188

14 Ibid. p. 66

15 Ibid. 110

16 Ibid. p. 110

CHAPTER VIII

ORGANIZING AND EFFECTING

This chapter brings the Power Pack together by developing the organization process that is needed to effect this plan. There are a total of 15 Points under this chapter. Each Point has been carefully selected and developed to enable the Power Pack to come alive and be put into action immediately.

POINT 87 - INCREASING UNITY

We must increase unity of African Americans and make America aware of the apparent failure of the United States government, in regard to addressing the roots of the problems that affect African Americans. The government has designed plans to deal with Blacks and growing problems by building more prisons, encampments, and implementing other measures that will ensure that African Americans will pose little or no threat to America in the future. Nevertheless, these efforts do not address root causes.

America must change its approach in addressing the problems impacting Black America. African Americans must take action now and let the people and the government of the United States of America know - that we will not be written off, and that we refuse to be treated the way this government has treated the American Indians. Whereby, now we find a people suffering continuing threats to their existence as distinct people.

America must clearly understand that we as African Americans will not allow this to happen to the Black people of this country. United we must stand fast in this resolve. Let's remind America, that we have pledged allegiance to the Flag of the United States of America and to the Republic for which it stands, one Nation under God, indivisible, with liberty and **justice** for all. And we, African Americans and Hispanics **demand justice and all of our freedom, now.**

POINT 88 - RE-ENACTING COMMUNITY

The actions of Mrs. Myrtle Faye Rumph (at Point 43) and the people working with the Al Wooten Jr. Heritage Center clearly show what a few people working together can do to reenact community.   Mrs. Myrtle Rumph action has truly recreated the sense of community that will make a difference in the lives of many young people and their parents. America can learn a lot from this accomplishment from this deed of Mrs. Rumph.

Re-enacting community will be one of our most difficult tasks because many people must make personal sacrifices.   Some have to come from their homes on the other side of town to help out.   Some people must come from behind the bars on their doors to help out.   The churches must become more involved in the community. Some people must begin to speak to people, people whom they haven't spoken to for years because their social status is below or above theirs.   Reenacting community will be a very difficult thing to do.

Dr. King encouraged us to look at ourselves and gave us the following advice:

"....The fact that so many Negroes have made lasting and significant contributions to the cultural life of America, in spite of these crippling restrictions is sufficient to refute all of the myths and half-truths disseminated by the segregationists.

Yet we cannot ignore the fact that our standards do often fall short. One sure sign of maturity is the ability to rise to the point of self-criticism. We have been affected by our years of economic deprivation and social isolation. Some Negroes have become cynical and disillusioned that they have lost that creative something called initiative. So many of us live above our means, spend money on nonessentials and frivolities, and fail to give to serious causes, organizations, and education institutions that so desperately need funds."[1]

The words of W. E. B. Du Bois is also very clear regarding this issue: "The community must be able to take hold of its individuals and give them such a social heritage, such present social teachings, and such compelling social customs as will force them along the lines of progress, and not into the great forest of death." [2]

Today, America finds itself in the "great forest of death." We must reenact community, the community that Du Bois spoke about. Many years ago we had that sense of community.   To reclaim   our communities we must take a critical look at them. Organize. Assess by asking questions. What's wrong? How can we fix it? What do we need? What resources do we have? We must prepare ourselves and then mobilize. The mobilization process is covered at Point 93.

POINT 89 - TEACHING THE PRINCIPLES OF NONVIOLENCE

There will be some difficult days ahead of us as we work this plan to achieve social and economic justice. We must prepare ourselves now to meet these challenges. To meet some of these challenges, it will cause for demonstrations, boycotts, marches and organization. Like King, I'm convinced that for practical as well as moral reasons, nonviolence offers the only road to social and economic justice for African Americans, Hispanics, poor whites and all other minority groups.

Today, there are some newly prosperous African Americans and prosperous white Americans who contemplate that the unemployable African Americans, the poor whites and Hispanics will live out their lives in the rural or the urban slums, silently and apathetically. This way of thinking is a mistake. In light of the riot/rebellion in Los Angeles in 1992, and assessing the work we must accomplish, we need to educate our people now on the art of nonviolence. Dr. King taught this art and it must be passed on now. Over the next several paragraphs I have blended the philosophy of Dr. King with mine's to chart the path for the future by using the art of non-violence.

We must not assume that people understand this art of nonviolence. They didn't understand in the 1960's until it was explained to them and they will not understand it today, unless they are taught.

King taught: Nonviolence demonstrations can not be organized around self-defense. He concluded that self-defense created more problems than it solved. Many individuals will not understand this. They must be taught, lessons learned must be shared.

When African Americans marched during the 1960's, the nation also marched to higher heights. King described it like this:

"It is always surprising that a few hundred Negroes marching can produce such a reaction across the nation. When marches are carefully organized around well-defined issues, they represent the power which Victor Hugo phrased as the most powerful force in the world, "an idea whose time has come." Marching feet announce that the time has come for a given idea. When the idea is a sound one, the cause a just one, and the demonstration a righteous one, change will be forthcoming."[3]

It is important that each demonstration has all of these conditions. The cause must be correct and just. Angry people cussing at mayor or the police chief, will not bring respect or dignity, nor will it help the causes.

We must continue to use marches in the future, and they must be designed to bring about the desired results. There have been hundreds of marches since the death of Dr. King. Many of those marches have not been effective. Here is an important lesson learned about marches that King left with us:

> "One march is seldom successful, and as a good friend Kenneth Clark points out in Dark Ghetto, it can *serve merely to let off steam and siphon off the energy which is necessary to produce change. However, when marching is seen as a part of a program to dramatize an evil, to mobilize the forces of good will, and to generate pressure and power for change, marches will continue to be effective."[4]

King also recommended that: (1) Marches continue over a period of thirty to forty-five days to produce a meaningful result (2) To be of sufficient size to produce some inconvenience to the forces in power or they go unnoticed (3) They must be larger enough to demand the attention of the press, for the press interprets the issue to the community at large and helps set the machinery for change.

Another nonviolence approach we must continue is the boycott. The boycott must be sustained over a period of several weeks and months to assure results.

Organization is our most powerful weapon, though it is very demanding. The most effective approach to produce change is to organize in units of power. There must be permanent groups established, such as an economic unit, tenant unit, laboring unit, anti-poverty unit, voting unit, and the unemployed unit, and so on. This is important to organize in this manner to protect their own interests and to produce change.

We must now organize the unemployed, to unionize the business within the ghetto, to bring tenants together into collective bargaining units and establish cooperatives for purposes of building viable financial institutions within the ghetto that can be controlled by African Americans.

Recommend that private foundations establish grants for the teaching of the nonviolence principles of Dr. King. It is imperative that our youth learn that violence in the street, like the riot/rebellion is not the answer. Moreover, recommend that the SCLC or another group adopt this training initiative and seek it very aggressively until we gain social and economic justice in these United States in America.

POINT 90 - MAKING THE CHURCH THE HEART BEAT OF THE COMMUNITY

When the Church is the heart beat of the community you will find the expression of agape love all around you. People in the community will not be afraid to reach out and help someone. People will not be afraid to say a kind word or walk the streets in the evening.

The black Church has always been looked upon to be the catalyst for change. It was the birthplace for education for African Americans, and has served as the focal point for community betterment for many years. However, today something is wrong. Yes, something is terribly wrong.

Dr. Martin Luther King, Jr. was only one man. He was a christian, but only one minister. When God worked through him, the black Church shined and it was truly the focal point for community betterment. It became the heart beat of the black community.

Today, has the heart beat of the community become the sound of guns? The beat that causes the Church to become silent and run cold. If we are to change the community for the better, it must come by way of the Church. No other force can do it.

Yes there are some black churches doing good things throughout the United States and making a difference. But the black Church must become one body and work together to address these problems. Ministers must come together and access where we are. We must transcend denominational barriers and religious barriers (Christian/Muslim) and realize that we serve one God. The Congress of National Black Churches, Inc. (CNBC) has 65,000 churches connected with it. Moreover, there are transcending eight historically black denominations, representing 250,000 church employees, and in excess of 19 million worshippers. Praise the Lord! Is this power? Or potential power? Martin Luther King, Jr. was only one man.

I believe that the harvest is still plentiful, but the laborers are still few. Therefore, this is potential power that needs collective consciousness and mobilizing. When that day comes this will be the true Church, the one that is built on the solid rock.

It is easy to write a very exciting combination of accomplishments that will evokes happy memories recalling victories in the past decade. However, I elected not to do that at this junction because we must not deceive ourselves. There is far too much pain to have celebrations in the real sense. We can't be satisfied with our old alliance that we have established because they haven't stood the real test. In the word of the Late Dr. Martin Luther King, Jr.:

> "Some churches recognize that to be relevant in moral life they must make equality an imperative. With them the basis for alliance is strong and enduring. But toward those churches that shun and evade the issue that are mute or timorous on social and economic questions, we are no better than strangers even though we sing the same hymns in worship of the same God."[5]

W. Franklyn Richardson wrote an outstanding article entitled: "Mission to Mandate: Self-Development through the Black Church" for "The State of Black America", 1994. In that article he mentioned many accomplishments of black churches to include their involvement in community investment. Here is a quote from his writing:

> "...History has taught that "we cannot live by prayer and fasting alone"; we need economic empowerment. The black church has awakened to the realization that we are our own greatest asset, and "community investment" is a strategy that can help people at the grass-roots level while providing models that can be used on a broader level. Community investment not only helps members of local congregations learn about poverty and wealth, examine their understanding of stewardship, and put capital at the service of the gospel," but it also serves as a way of mobilizing African Americans' consciousness and promoting the black church as a viable part of the African-American community."[6]

Richardson cites a number of success stories of how ministers have led their churches into business ventures. For example, one minister had a congregation of 200 members, of which 188 were on welfare. Nevertheless, through self-empowerment, today none of the members are on welfare. There are more of these success stories, but, there must be thousands of these type of successes throughout the church. We can build a strong alliance and support system, but, there must be a true resolve to that end. We must create a more solid foundation built on unity and mutual trust in order to realize the eradication of these conditions that inflict so much pain and suffering.

Recommend, you purchase a copy of the State of Black America, 1994 and read Richardson's work. Another document that is important for all churches to have was compiled by the National Congress for Community Economic Development, entitled: "Restoring Broken Places and Rebuilding Communities. This book contains a fairly extensive and diverse list of case studies of church base programs. A copy of this document will also assist you in enhancing your programs.

POINT 91 - BUILDING TRUST AMONG COMMUNITY-BASED AND NATIONAL ORGANIZATIONS

To address today's concerns, organizations must realize their common ground and petty competition must cease. Often it is rumored that some leaders have "sold out" to the power structure or have made opportunistic alliances with a political party to gain an individual advantage.

Leaders who sell-out should be criticized for their weakness. But we must ascertain that our criticism is founded. We must never criticize and put down another organization to gain an organization's advantage. When this occurs, there is no victory. It becomes disheartening defeat for all concerned. It works against social movement for social and economic justice.

By you reading this book up to this point it is apparent that you would like to become as informed as possible to enhance your effectiveness in achieving social and economic justice for the many people who are suffering today. Effective organizations are key to accomplishing this mandate.

We have had considerable legislation to be passed over the last thirty years. However, since the death of Dr. Martin Luther King, Jr., our organizations have not been truly effective in bringing life to those legislation. We must take a serious look at this and take measures to ensure that this is corrected and never happens again.

Let's ponder over this statement by Dr. King: "We made easy gains and we built the kind of organizations that expect easy victories, and rest upon them. It may seem curious to speak of easy victories when some have suffered and sacrificed so much. Yet in candor and self-criticism it is necessary to acknowledge that the torturous job of organizing solidly and simultaneously in thousands of places was not a feature of our work."[7]

As we look back over the past twenty years, we must agree that self-criticism is in order because we have lost some of our civil rights gains due to inaction. Today, many don't view the African Americans as a serious political force, however, a force that comes together to some extent at times to address crises. Increased awareness will clearly show Black America that the crisis is now.

Achieving social and economic justice must be worked daily and we must be prepared to mobilize at any time. However, first we must be organized. King suggested that we have people tied together in a long-term relationship instead of evanescent enthusiasts who lose their experience, spirit and unity because they have no mechanism that directs them to new tasks.

Unfortunately, at times African Americans, like other Americans allow self to get in the way of progress. We become too competitive when it's time to become cooperative. We fail to trust one another. When this occurs there is expression of self-hate, suspicions and intolerance of each other. This is a weakness that we must overcome.

It is very important that we learn from the wisdom that Dr. King left us. I strongly suggest that we take every opportunity. Here is another opportunity:

> "Negro leaders suffer from this interplay of solidarity and divisiveness, being either exalted excessively or grossly abused. But some of those leaders who suffer from lack of sustained support are not without weaknesses that give substance to criticism. The most serious is aloftness and absence of faith in their people. The white establishment is skilled in flattering and cultivating emerging leaders. It presses its own image on them and finally, from imitation of manners, dress, and style of living, a deeper strain of corruption develops. The kind of Negro leader acquires the white man's contempt for the ordinary Negro. He is often more at home with the middle-class white man than he is among his own people, and frequently his physical home is moved up and away from the ghetto. His language changes, his location changes, his income changes, and ultimately he changes from the representative of the Negro to the white man into the white man's representative to the Negro."[8]

The NAACP, Urban League, SCLC and CORE have many years of experience that must be shared with other organizations. In addition to sharing experiences, these organizations also must make a self-evaluation and make necessary adjustments to maximize their effectiveness and alertness. Today, it is important to have organizations that permeate mutual trust, incorruptibility and militancy.

Today it is imperative we realize that we haven't won the war, for we have only won small skirmishes. The big battle is yet to come. In fact, history will show you that our "general" was killed on April 4, 1968. We need another general of the nonviolent movement, with even an more organized force than we had during the 1960's. Organizations must organize, educate their members and community on the "big picture" and how their mission relates to this "big picture".

Locally, we must establish strong coalitions to create strong intergroup relations, build trust, reduce competitiveness, and create a more cooperative spirit. To address certain concerns, consortia should be established, composed of community-based organizations, churches, schools, individuals and government agencies.

In addition to these actions, there is a need for non-profit organization development training programs. Often, organizations will form after a crisis. Though the cause for formation is often worthy, leadership skills are often lacking for stability. To address this problem, action must be taken to assist these grass root organizations during their period of start-up.

There must be non-profit organizations organized with the specific mandate to assist organizations with the development training that is needed to become a viable organization. Grants should be sought from the city, county and private foundations to provide this much needed service.

In respect to the trust factor, we must first admit that this is a problem. Once we admit it we can resolve it. We must conduct workshops and seminars designed to this end. Recommend that concerned wealthy individuals help finance activities to this end throughout the country.

POINT 92 - DEMONSTRATING CONCERN FOR PEOPLE OF THE COMMUNITY

Over the past decade the civil rights movement appears to have stalled because of lack of interest and concern. Past gains were lost because of inattentiveness, the lack of awareness and involvement. There are a number of elderly individuals who feel so alone in our communities. Young people are seeking out gangs to find a sense of belonging. How could this happen among people who care and love one another?

Let's revisit a statement that was made by W. E. B. Du Bois, but on this visit we will look at these words from a different perspective:

> "The community must be able to take hold of its individuals and give them such a social heritage, such present social teachings, and such compelling social customs as will force them along the lines of progress, and not into the great forest of death."[9]

Let's break this statement down into words or thoughts to bring about greater understanding of what is required of us and how we can proceed in turning this profound statement into reality. In my experience, a statement like this remains as "literature" and "just good sounding words", if it is carefully deciphered.

The first thought: **The community.** The word community has many connotations and usages. I suggest in this text, let's look at community as a population rooted in one place whose members are interdependent on a daily basis and perform many activities that satisfy the population's economic and social needs.

In this sense a community can be a small town of one of the largest cities in the United States. This population that is rooted in one place **must.** In this text **must** is a verb, it expresses a command, a requirement, and an obligation.

Let's continue to reconstruct the statement of Du Bois.

The community must **be able to hold**...The word **able** means: having sufficient power, skill, or resources to accomplish an object. The thought **to hold** means: to have or maintain in grasp.

The community must be able to hold **of its individuals....** The word **individuals:** the elderly, the young, the good students, the not so good students, the model citizens, the ex-convicts, the youth at risk, the gang members. The word individuals is inclusive of all who reside in the community.

Let's continue. The community must be able to hold of its individuals **and give them.** The word **give** means: to bestow, to provide, to contribute, to donate. And **them;** the elderly, gang members, good students, not so good students, etc.

The community must be able to hold of its individuals and give them **such a social heritage, such present social teachings, and compelling social customs as will force them along the line of progress.**

I will not continue to break down this statement in the same fashion. However, my real point is that far too often we look at the work of great writers as literature only and miss the real messages.

To bring the profound statement of Du Bois to reality, it will take real concern for every individual that lives in your community. We also must realize that we are dependent upon one another. We must use all of our skills, talents and resources, to include money, to hold on to or to maintain these individuals in our grasp. Moreover, we must give (donate, contribute, and provide) them with much, not a small amount, but such a social heritage, such present social teaching, and compelling social customs as will force them along the line of progress.

To present social teachings, we must know our social heritage. If it is compelling social customs, we must be living them ourselves and be active role models.

Therefore, we have a charge to keep. We must not only talk it, but we must live it. We are the ones that can turn these conditions around, however, we cannot do it by locking ourselves behind bars in our homes, nor can we do it by flight. We must realize in order for Black America to be strong, we must work together and be concerned for one another. Our history shows us what it is like to be torn apart by brute force. It was brute force that was used to enslave us for many years. Now, it is a psychological force that is causing use to become weak and unwilling to take a stand for justice because we have lost hope in our people and lost hope in our ability to make a difference.

Now, it is a new day. I can see a light, and many smiling faces, mobilizing to turn this dismal state of affairs around.

POINT 93 - MOBILIZING AND USING OUR RESOURCES

Black America has more resources today than at anytime in the history of this country. However, we have failed to properly mobilize these resources. Failure of mobilization of the available resources was a key point made by Dr. Jeff P. Howard in his article entitled: "The Third Movement; Developing Black Children for the 21st Century". This article was published in a book entitled: State of Black America, 1992. Below is a quote from Dr. Howard's article:

> "Failure of mobilization - The available resources within black communities, the assets available to us with which we could take charge of our situation, have not been mobilized to address the problems of development of the mass of Black children. Failures of mobilization are functions of psychological and organizational problems, and these too, are remediable."[10]

Here is a reprint of Black resources as described by Dr. Howard:

- Educated people. Nearly 13 percent of our population is college-educated. These people are engaged in every sector of American institutional and economic life. As of 1989, 23.4 percent of 18-24-year-olds are enrolled in institutions of higher education. Twenty-six percent are majoring in social sciences and psychology. In 1989, blacks earned 5.7 percent of all bachelor's degrees awarded, 5.1 percent of all medical degrees and 4.9 percent of all law degrees.

- An institutional base, including 67,000 churches, human service agencies in every city focused on health care, youth services, and community action. The people who operate these institutions understand the community and its people.

- School systems run with significant black participation, and in many cases, outright control. Many urban systems have black superintendents, majority black school boards, and predominantly black faculty. As of 1985, there were 15,036 black faculty in higher education in America.

- Black colleges, with a long history of service that include training key leadership in the previous movements for change. There are 99 "historically black" colleges in the United States.

- National organizations, including the National Urban League, the NAACP, fraternities, sororities, and various professional organizations.

- Political leadership at the local, state, and federal levels in a position to fight for strategic policies and legislation favorable to the interests of black children. As of January 1988, there were over 6,829 black elected officials in the United States. Recent elections bring the total in the U.S. Congress to 40, including the first black woman elected to the Senate.

- Corporate professionals in banks and other financial institutions, local companies, and multinational corporations. These people operate in the functional heart of the economic structure of society. They are in product development and design, manufacturing, marketing, finance. They are in a position to learn how things work and how to get things done.

- Black women near or at parity with whites in earnings given comparable educational backgrounds. For every $1,000 a white person with four years of college earns, a black woman with four years of college earns $1,002.

- Professional women. Among employed black women, 63 percent are in professional positions, and 55 percent of those are in managerial positions.

- Professional people positioned in government, foundations, and other local and national not-for-profit institutions. Over a third of all black lawyers work for governmental departments, as do 30 percent of black scientists.

- Individuals who are well-positioned in the huge, worldwide sports and entertainment industries. There has been important recent progress in black ownership and control in this arena.

- Small businesses whose annual receipts average $50,000. Approximately $425,000 of this nation's small businesses are owned by African Americans.

- Disposable income, money that must be regarded a critical source of potential contributions to a cause the people embrace. Nearly 30 percent of black families earn over $35,000 with 14.5 percent earnings over $50,000. Blacks make up 7.8 percent of the total personal income earned in this country. There are three blacks on the Forbes list of the 400 richest men and women in the United States.

In addition to the above list, there are millions of African Americans with the talent, time, and other resources. Moreover, there are the African American Elderly, whom we have cast aside. Again, we have more resources today than we have ever had in the past. The questions are: (1) Do we have the resolve? (2) Do we understand all issues?

(3) Do we know the action we need to take? (4) Do we believe that we can do it? and lastly (5) Are we willing to make personal sacrifices and do it?

The issues are many. Many more than the 101 points outlined in this book. Nevertheless, the most pressing issue is the survival of African Americans. In spite of all the current resources that were just mentioned, we are still at risk as a people, if we fail to mobilize.

In Dr. Martin Luther King, Jr's. book entitled:"Where Do We Go From Here?", he summarized the problem as follows:

> "The many thousand of Negroes who have already found intellectual growth and spiritual fulfillment on this path know its creative possibilities. They are not among the legions of the lost, they are not crushed by the weight of centuries. Most heartening, among the young the spirit of challenge and determination for change is becoming an unquenchable force.
>
> But the scope of struggle is still too narrow and too restricted. We must turn more of our energies and focus our creativity on the useful things that translate into power.
>
> ....It must become a crusade so vital that civil rights organizers do not repeatedly have to make personal calls to summon support. There must be a climate of social pressure in the Negro Community that scorns the Negro who will not pick up his citizenship rights and add his strength enthusiastically and voluntarily to accumulation of power for himself and his people."[11]

In 1967, King posed the following questions: (1) How shall we turn the ghettos into a vast school? (2) How shall we make every street corner a forum, not a lounging place for trivial gossip and petty gambling, where life is wasted and human experience withers to trivial sensations? How shall we make every houseworker and every laborer a demonstrator, a voter, a canvasser and a student?

He answered these questions with this statement: "We must utilize the community action groups and training centers now proliferating in some slum areas to create not merely an electorate, but a conscious, alert and informed people who know their direction and whose collective wisdom and vitality command respect."[12]

It will take ordinary people with the courage to meet these challenges, people who believe in God. People who love people, people not looking for a savior, but people with faith in themselves and other people, with the resolve to make it happen and a clear understanding of the mission.

POINT 94 - INCREASING AWARENESS AND INVOLVEMENT

To increase awareness and involvement we need strong leadership. We don't need rabble-rousers, but we need leaders that are calm and yet positive. There is no place for misguided emotionalism. The problems are too complex and too serious. Though we are faced with situation after situation that may cause one to become bitter, bitterness cannot become the fuel for this movement. So let's not become bitter. Nor can falsehood, hate or malice become our guide.

By reading this book your awareness should have increased, however, it must not stop there. Now you must help to ensure that others are just as aware as you are. Tell them where they can purchase this book. Don't withhold information that can empower others. Increased awareness is one of the factors that is needed to bring us together, however, it will take strong leadership with a sense of direction and the right spirit that we keep us together.

We must be lead by the right spirit. Dr. King reminded us not to become victimized with a philosophy of "black supremacy". And our aim must never be to defeat or humiliate the white man, but to win his friendship and understanding.

The Urban League takes pride in trying to keep us aware of what's going on in Black America through its yearly publication of: "The State of Black America". Purchase these books yearly. After you make a purchase read it, and tell a friend so they can do the same thing. This new awareness should help guide you on the issues you need to address. You must always remember, you are not alone in this struggle. Today we have a number of organizations involved, both locally and nationally.

The NAACP is the oldest civil rights organization in this country. With their help over the years, we have been able to obtain a number of victories through the courts. We must support the NAACP in its efforts, both nationally and locally. These organizations can be best supported by you becoming an active member, involved and aware of every decision made by the courts regarding human or civil rights.

In addition to these organizations, there are other organizations that you may wish to become involved in such as CORE, SCLC, The Rainbow Coalition, sororities, fraternities or a local organization. Regardless of how you become involved you must be aware of the issues and remain focused.

We can lose focus when organizations aren't working together and we become victims of the "drum major instinct" that Dr. King warned us about. An instinct that causes us to want to be important, to surpass others, to achieve distinction, and to lead the parade. This instinct is okay to have as long as it's not perverted. Today, we don't have time to allow a perverted quest for attention, recognition, or importance to become our reasons to get involved. For if these are the reasons for your involvement, I ask you, what happens when you stop receiving the attention, recognition, or the sense of importance? There must be a more important reason than any of these.

Today, there is a number of more important reasons to become involved. I believe one of the most important ones is the fact that the future of Black America is at state because our children are being underdeveloped and we have the resources, ability, and power to change this around by our involvement. If we should keep this in mind, we won't lose focus and become perverted in our actions.

You may agree that the reason stated above is a very important reason, however, you still have the drum major instinct. Dr. King addresses this desire by paraphrasing what Jesus said to his disciples:

> "Oh, I see, you want to be first. You want to be great.
> You want to be important. You want to be significant.
> Well you ought to be. If you're going to be my disciple,
> you must be." But he reordered their priorities, and said,
> "Yes, don't give up this instinct. It's a good instinct if you
> use it right. It's a good instinct if you don't distort it and
> pervert it. Don't give it up. Keep feeling the need for being
> important. Keep feeling the need for being first. But I
> want you to be first in love. I want you to be first in moral
> excellence. I want you to be first in generosity. That is
> what I want you to do."[13]

POINT 95 - DEVELOPING TASK FORCES/COUNCILS LOCALLY AND NATIONALLY

In order to properly assess, manage, and take appropriate preventative or corrective actions in our quest for social and economic justice for African Americans, we must have task forces/councils nationally and locally throughout the United States.

These task forces/councils should be composed of trained individuals; individuals who are available to mobilize within minutes locally and within hours nationally. Properly trained individuals could help prevent incidents like the Los Angeles riot of 1992. Prior to the riot, Los Angeles had become a breeding ground for racial tension and violence. However, there was no effective leadership to properly manage the climate.

While I was in the military, one of my primary duties was to take measures to ensure that we didn't have riots on the installations that I was assigned. I was trained to perform this duty and I worked this area for over seventeen years. During the 1970's, I was hand-picked to go to a base in the south after someone fire bombed the wing commander and base commander's cars and a black security police officer took control of the command post with an M-16. Incidents of this type on military bases, you didn't normally hear about them in the press. However, our military was not immune to these type of incidents. After being picked for this special assignment, it was my responsibility to go there and restore calm and provide the wing commander direct support to create meaningful human relations programs and to ensure equal opportunity and treatment was afforded to base personnel on and off base. My efforts helped to create a model program for the command in less than one year. There were a number of other trained individuals like myself who had the same type of training and duties.

I believe that we need to train individuals and provide them with the needed skills to assess and take preventative measures throughout the United States. This training should be similar to the training that was provided to the military human relations personnel. At the beginning of the riot in Los Angeles, in 1992, I responded to Florence and Normandie, as a concerned citizen. However, when I got there it was already out of control. I attempted to summon help to no avail. Nevertheless, I took my car and positioned it across the street to preclude traffic from going north on Normandie to Florence for a while, and for two hours from about 5 O'clock P.M. to 7 P.M., I worked the intersection just south of Florence trying to prevent individuals from going into the impact area. Another individual worked the area with me. I was also able to calm some people down and kept them from becoming involved in the riot.

During the riot I travelled the streets of Los Angeles to include April 29, 30 and May 1st. I made my assessment and I assisted in restoring peace wherever I could. My small business burned down in the riot, but that did not keep me from making a special report to the nation of my observations and findings in the height of the riot. A friend of mine made a thirteen minute video of my report to the nation. This report did not contain any of the riot's scenes. However, it was a very candid report on what was happening, and why it was happening. Moreover, it offered solutions on how to stop the violence in Los Angeles and throughout the United States, and how to prevent it from reoccurring. The report was sent to President Bush, Governor Pete Wilson and Mayor Tom Bradley.

A trained human relations/crisis prevention response team and an effective police department would have made a big difference in Los Angeles. In fact, there were a number of actions that could have been taken to prevent the riot, however, Los Angeles lacked the required leadership.

We don't have to create new organizations to train and employ these task forces/councils, but, we can support the organizations that we have like the NAACP, Urban League, SCLC and CORE. Nevertheless, there must be a new mandate to create these forces.

Though some of you may not see the immediate need for these trained mobile individuals, in time you will see the need especially as we move forward on the Power Pack. An active civil rights movement necessitates preparedness. Moreover, in an inactive civil rights movement where there is social and economic injustice, you are bound to have incidents, and continued tension. There is an immediate need today for these trained human relations/crisis prevention persons to assist our school in maintaining stable climates.

To finance this undertaking will require more donations and increased memberships in the organizations that decide to take on this added responsibility. Funding also should be solicited from private foundations and the federal state and local government.

POINT 96 - DISCOVERING COMMON GROUND

Finding common ground is very important when developing teams that are willing to work together. In our search we must ask meaningful questions. The more people we wish to involve the more questions we need to ask. Nevertheless, we start to exclude people. We should review your objectives and ask ourselves: "How does the exclusion help the cause?"

If we wish to involve only African Americans in this search for social and economic justice, common ground may have been discovered at point 94: "The future of Black America is at stake because our children are being underdeveloped and we have the resources, ability, and power to turn this around by our involvement." However, working on this premise alone will not be enough to obtain social and economic justice in America.

African Americans must realize that the brunt of African American's past battles were won by a very small striking force. Though millions of African Americans were ardent and passionate supporters, only a modest number were actively engaged. Before Dr. King's death, he clearly pointed out that these were only skirmishes that we had won. For the broad war against racism, poverty and discrimination more African Americans must become involved. And African Americans must put aside all of our differences and work together and build alliances with other groups.

There are some whites who are guilt-ridden and fear if the African American attains power, they would with restraint or pity act to revenge the accumulated injustices and brutality of the years. We as African Americans must show the white Americans that they have nothing to fear. We must forgive now and find common ground. Hopefully, they will become true alliances with common interests. This is the type of unity that is needed to win the war on poverty.

It is very important that the Hispanics, Asian Americans, African Americans and white Americans realize we must work together, as one nation. We must work together, to address the needs of every group, every man, woman, boy or and girl, and the unborn.

America must realize that Black America is not only at risk, but America is at risk. When we realize this, at that point we would have discovered common ground.

Hopefully, by reading this book, you have discovered your reason to become involved, and now you are inspired to take immediate action to ensure that social and economic justice become a reality here in the United States, and in this century.

POINT 97 - CREATING AND MAINTAINING COMMUNITY INVOLVEMENT

There must be a new wave of positive activities that the entire community can become involved in. The focus of these activities should be designed to create better intragroup relations and to address the many concerns that are impacting the community. There must be much talk and much action to include events of all types, workshops, seminars, plays, concerts, marches, demonstrations, protesting, vote registration drives, job fairs, business expo's, career days, sharing with neighbors day, community clean-up, boycotts, singing, dancing, and socializing together.

We must create a new day, a new awareness and appreciation for one another. We must turn our streets of violence to those learning centers. We must begin to share our love for one another like never before in the history of this country.

Details must be developed to effect this new way of thinking, but it should become a nation-wide movement, whereby, every city throughout the nation is on the same wave line. A common theme, like the "Power Pack" should be used. The rappers can help us set the tone and reach the young people. Nevertheless, the energy must flow from a higher plane.

America we can do it, and we can do it now. It will be fun, educational and spiritual. Through this sense of unity we will achieve both social and economic justice. We will become a force that nothing in this world can stop.

POINT 98 - RESTORING PRIDE BACK TO THE COMMUNITY

At Point 23, we covered aspects of this subject with an extensive commentary. Here I will not repeat the commentary nor will I make another. However, I suggest that you read Point 23 again now, if you have any questions as to why restoring pride is necessary.

My concern here is about the act of doing it - making it happen. To restore pride back to the community let's start with each one of us as individuals. What we think about and what we do is very important to this process. Now, allow me to become personal.

When you see individuals at the gas stations asking to pump gas in your car for money - what do you think? - what do you do? When you see gang members standing on street corner selling drugs - what do you think? - what do you do? When you hear about or see another senseless killing on radio or television - what do you think? - what do you do? When you see people sleeping outside in the streets - what do you think? - what do you do? When you see rundown homes, apartment buildings, and unkept lawns - what do you think? - what do you do?

Let's continue. When you hear people talking about one another - what do you think? - what do you do? When you see prostitutes standing out on street corners - what do you think? - what do you do? When you hear about the need for volunteers to tutor children in reading, math and science - what do you think? - what do you do? When you hear about another unjust law being contemplated - what do you think? - what do you do? When it is election day - what do you think? - what do you do?

This list can go on and on. The bottom line, restoring pride back to the community is about positive thoughts and doing the right thing to effect those thoughts. The pride of the community is the sum total of the pride of the people who live in the community. In this sense, when you help someone else - you help yourself.

POINT 99 - EVALUATING PROGRAMS

There must be an evaluation program established to evaluate the goals and objectives of each point of the Power Pack. From these 101 Points there will be hundreds of initiatives that must be managed and effected. An effective evaluation is essential to this process. Without one, the overall effectiveness of the movement could be undermined. Though individuals intentions may be notable, some may lack the leadership to carry out their proposed solutions. Evaluation must take place at six different levels to include personal/individual, local community organizational, national organizational, local governmental, state governmental and federal governmental.

Personal/Individual Level.

At the personal/individual level, it is an individual responsibility to monitor their personal involvement and the involvement of their family members. Recommend that each individual review each Point of this plan and assess their strengths and weaknesses. Use their strengths and work to build the areas of weakness. Decide on the areas that he/she could best serve his/her community and become involved as appropriate.

Although individuals can't be involved in every initiative in the community, it is important to stay abreast of what's going on in the community and throughout the nation. Therefore, it is recommended that individuals maintain an evaluation check list of the Power Pack.

Local/Organizational Level.

Like individuals, most organizations can't be involved in each Point of the Power Pack and maintain its effectiveness. Therefore, organizations must decide how to allocate their resources and their level of involvement. Nevertheless, there is a lot of work to accomplish and each Point must be addressed at a local level. Therefore, it is imperative that all organization efforts are coordinated with other organizations to improve the overall effectiveness. Working together and sharing resources is essential.

Recommend that organizations also maintain an evaluation check list of the Power Pack and develop a system to evaluate its effectiveness.

National Organizational Level.

At this level, organizations like the NAACP, Urban League, SCLC, and CORE, the National Black Corpus and religious organizations to include all denominations, the Muslim Leaders and the Nation of Islam. Recommend at the national level, these organizations increase their interaction and coordination with one another. Work to maintain a cooperative working relationship to effect these Points.

Recommend that a National Power Pack Review Council be established to evaluate the overall effectiveness of stated goals and plan strategies for future actions. Recommend representation from each national organization.

Local, State, and Federal Government Level

It is also very important that the federal government keep abreast of what is going on throughout the United States regarding fair and just treatment. I recommended to President Bush in 1992 after the riot in Los Angeles that he designate a period for a "Basic Equality Review" throughout America. Today, I'm making the same recommendation to President Clinton and future Presidents of the United States.

The period of review should be designated to reaffirm the government's commitment to discover and address concerns, by assessing the criminal justice system and all aspects of our basic quality of life. The end result of this period of observation should be to create affirmative programs that will be enacted to achieve a higher quality of life for all Americans.

The review should be structured in a manner to allow state and local government to implement such review. However, uniform guidelines should be developed by the federal government. In addition, the review should be flexible in order to allow state and local government to implement programs as needed during the review period. Recommend that the review be conducted every four years and the period of review should be from 6 months to one year.

Moreover, at the local, state, and federal level, action could be taken to monitor and to help facilitate the effectiveness of the Power Pack by commissioning individuals or groups to that end.

POWER PACK 101 POINT CHECKLIST

POINT NO.	AGENCY RESPONSIBLE	PHONE	COMMENTS

THE 101 POINTS OF THE POWER PACK

Awareness

Point 1   - Ending Psychological Warfare and Racial Discrimination
Point 2   - Educating the People
Point 3   - Increasing Unity

Social

Point 4   - Eliminating Poverty
Point 5   - Enhancing the Quality of Life
Point 6   - Empowering the Homeless
Point 7   - Resolving the Hunger Problem
Point 8   - Reducing the Level of Violence
Point 9   - Reducing the Substance Abuse Problems
Point 10   - Reducing the Demand For Drugs
Point 11   - Understanding the Gang Problem
Point 12   - Reducing Gang Phobia (Fear of Gangs)
Point 13   - Improving Black Men and Black Women Relationship
Point 14   - Empowering the Black Men
Point 15   - Providing Pre-Marriage Counseling
Point 16   - Improving the Family Unit Through the Churches,
             Videos and Movies
Point 17   - Domestic Violence Prevention/Intervention Programs
Point 18   - Reducing the Rate of Divorce Through Communication
Point 19   - Reducing Health Problem Through Education And Care
Point 20   - Reducing the Rate of AIDS
Point 21   - Conducting Stress Management Classes
Point 22   - Restoring A Sense of Pride and Concern
Point 23   - Maintaining A Sense of Pride
Point 24   - Learning From the Elderly
Point 25   - Reducing the Number of Unstable Homes
Point 26   - Showing Our Young People That We Can Get Along
Point 27   - Redirecting Our Talents From Being Self-Centered to
             Concern for One Another
Point 28   - Educating African Americans and Hispanics on How to
             Deal With Anger
Point 29   - Building Morality Through Rap
Point 30 -   Educating the Musicians, Rappers and Producers On
             the Damaging Impact of the Negative Messages
Point 31   - Teaching Life Coping Skills to Our Young People
Point 32   - More Effective Socialization Process
Point 33   - Establishing Teen Parenting and Skill Developing Program
Point 34   - Providing Sex Education For Youth 11 to 13 Years of Age
Point 35   - Addressing the Needs of Our Young People Who Have
             Been Institutionalized
Point 36   - Empowering the Inter-cities Resolve
Point 37   - Ensuring Safe Communities For Our Youth

232

Point 38 - Maintaining Clean Communities
Point 39 - Ensuring Landlords Maintain Properties that Are Rented to the Elderly and Low-income Individuals

Education and Opportunities

Point 40 - Developing Black Children For the 21st Century
Point 41 - Raising Self-Esteem
Point 42 - Reducing School Drop-out Rates
Point 43 - Improving Education Opportunities
Point 44 - Addressing the Needs of Our Children In the Public School System
Point 45 - Creating A Safer Public School Environment
Point 46 - Training Public School Teachers On How to Work With Today's Youth
Point 47 - Developing Effective Mentors' Programs
Point 48 - Creating Effective Homework Assistance Programs
Point 49 - Developing Videos/Movies On the Importance of A Good Education
Point 50 - Developing Effective Workshop For Young People on Various Life Skills Training
Point 51 - Promoting Basic Skill Development (Remedial Training)
Point 52 - Establish Redirecting Training For Current Gang Members
Point 53 - Increase College Enrollment/Completion And Preparing For The New Information Era

Economic

Point 54 - Revising Our Economic System
Point 55 - Achieving Parity In Receiving Loan From Banks For Blacks and Hispanics
Point 56 - Improving Business Opportunities
Point 57 - Increasing the Market for Black Business
Point 58 - Enhancing Black on Black Business Relationships
Point 59 - Ensuring the Highest Quality of Services By Black Businesses
Point 60 - Creating Assets And Establishing Financial Investment Groups (FIG)
Point 61 - Building Trust Among African Americans
Point 62 - Promoting Black-Owned Businesses
Point 63 - Enhancing Your Personal Credit Worthiness

Equal Employment Opportunity

Point 64 - Creating A More Effective EEOC
Point 65 - Reducing the Processing Time For Complaints Filed
  With the EEOC
Point 66 - Educating Employers and Employees on the
  "Destructive Perception of Discrimination Cycle"
Point 67 - Improving Equal Employment Opportunities Through
  Human Relations Training
Point 68 - Adjusting to the Job Market
Point 69 - Effecting Job Readiness Training
Point 70 - Creating A Job Market/Placement Services for
  Individuals With Felony Convictions
Point 71 - Increasing Employment Opportunity For Youth

Criminal

Point 72 - Reducing Crime In Our Communities
Point 73 - Reducing the Number of Prisoners
Point 74 - Ensuring the Due Process For Juvenile Offenders
Point 75 - Reducing Opportunities to Commit Crime
Point 76 - Reducing Opportunities to Sell Drugs
Point 77 - Training Law Enforcement Officers to Protect and
  Serve
Point 78 - Effecting Operation Root Up Gangs (Operation RUG)
Point 79 - Empowering The Community Against Crime

Political

Point 80 - Ensuring Justice in All of Our Affairs
Point 81 - Increasing Political Power
Point 82 - Creating Less Vacillation On Policies By Politicians
Point 83 - Using the Movie Industries to Educate
Point 84 - Applying Continuous Pressure On Hollywood
Point 85 - All of Our Freedom, Here, and Now
Point 86 - Developing Political Power That Is Ready To Mobilize

Organizing And Effecting

Point 87 - Increasing Unity
Point 88 - Reenacting Community
Point 89 - Teaching The Principles of Nonviolence
Point 90 - Making the Church the Heart Beat of the Community
Point 91 - Building Trust Among Community Based And National
  Organizations
Point 92 - Demonstrating Concerns For People of the Community
Point 93 - Mobilizing and Using Our Resources
Point 94 - Increasing Awareness and Involvement
Point 95 - Developing Task Forces/Councils Locally and Nationally

234

POINT 100 - EFFECTING THE POWER PACK

You have had the opportunity to examine the extent of the problem that we are facing in America. We've examined these conditions from several different perspectives, to include legal, social science, economics, theology, political science, politicians, and the grass roots.

Actions to address some of these Points may be already underway in your community. If so, of course that is good. Nevertheless, it is important that the action agencies interact with other action groups in the community. There also must be a means to determine the effectiveness of the organizations in addressing these problems. If there is no organization in the community that provides this type of service, you may wish to start one and seek funding from your city, state, or private foundation for the operation.

To successfully implement these 101 points, first the community needs to become educated. This is covered under Point 2. Increased awareness is very important. This awareness can be increased by book reviews in news papers, radio and television talk shows. The cable TV is also an excellent media.

Next, ensure that the governor of your state, the mayor and members of your city council receive copies of this book.

A meeting needs to be held among all community leaders on implementation. Ensure that all community organizations have an opportunity to participate. Select a lead organization or a coordinator for Power Pack. Prior to implementation, there must be an assessment of current community organizations efforts. Much excitement must be created, centered around these Points. Hold seminars, workshops and town hall meetings.

Establish consortia to address each Point, as appropriate. Define functions and align community organizations accordingly. Inform the city government of your action and gain the city support at the onset. Ensure that all community-based organizations have an opportunity to participate.

As an individual, recommend that you go through the process as outlined at Point 99.

We have a lot of work to do, however, we as a team can to it. We must unify our efforts to ensure victory. As you begin to read the last Point of the Power Pack, I ask that you just reflect on the bigger picture, not necessarily the work that we have to do, but the joy and happiness that social and economic justice will bring to a people who have lost hope in themselves and in one another. The part that you play is vital to bring the full measure of social and economics to God's people in the United States.

POINT 101 - TRANSCENDING RELIGIOUS, RACIAL AND SOCIAL STATUS BARRIERS TO AGAPE LOVE

Agape love quite often was a subject that Dr. King spoke on and wrote about. It is important to speak about it because the vehicle, (the Power Pack) is fueled only by agape love and without it the engine will not start.

Before we discuss agape love, let's discuss transcending religious and racial barriers. During this 20th century, I believe that Malcolm X was a man who was able to transcend these barriers to a great extent. Let's first review some of the earlier teachings that led him to developing the mind set of hating white men. In the book entitled "Malcolm X", as told by Alex Haley, there is an account of how he was mis-educated to believe that the white man was the devil. As Malcolm was mis-educated, countless others have been, to include the way some white men were mis-educated about the black man. In general, some white people were taught that black people were inferior to whites and slavery was justified because the black man was cursed. This mis-education was reinforced by the misuse of scriptures from the Holy Bible. Fortunately, many have risen above those thoughts.

In order to transcend from any point, I believe that first you must discover where you are and recognize the road you've travelled to get there. Next, you must make a conscious decision on where you want to go. Then, you can select the road to travel to rise above the limitations that keep you bound. Here is a reconstruction of some the of literature Malcolm X received from the followers of the Honorable Elijah Muhammad which contributed to Malcolm X's education, and mis-education as well:

> "...history had been "whitened" in the white man's history books, and that the black man had been "brainwashed for hundreds of years" Original Man was black, in the continent called Africa where the human race had emerged on the planet Earth."[14]

Under the same doctrine, Malcolm X was taught that the white men had committed the greatest crime in human history by trafficking black flesh from Africa. Consequently, millions of black men, women, and children were brought in chains on slave ships to the west. They were also cut off from all knowledge of their own kind, their language, religion, and past culture, until the black man in America was the earth's only race of people who had absolutely no knowledge of his true identity.

History should be taught. However, Malcolm was not only taught history. He was taught to hate. When you mix the facts regarding the way black people were treated by some of the white men in America with hatred, and then label white men as devils, and combine this with the stereotyping of white people, the by-product is bitterness and hatred. This type of teaching is very destructive.

Some of you may question why I put this quote in this book at my closing? The excerpts are not included to cause confusion; however, they are here to bring about understanding so that we can begin to work together. If you examine these excerpts carefully, you will find that everything mentioned is actually true, with the exception that the white man is portrayed as being the devil. Today, when we look at the situation in Rwanda, we can clearly see that doing devilish acts are not about the color of one's skin. It's about what we believe and what we do. To make a transformation from hate, especially when you have been oppressed for so long, is quite a difficult task. Moreover, it is also difficult to transcend when you feel threatened that you will lose something that you have. We must overcome the by-products of oppression and the fear of losing the status of white supremacy.

Prior to the death of Malcolm, it appeared that he lost his hostility for white men and he expressed his willingness to work with them. This quote is Malcolm X's answer to the question: What do you think is responsible for race prejudice in the U.S.?

"Ignorance and greed. And a skillfully designed program of miseducation that goes right along with the American system of exploitation and oppression.

If the entire American population were properly educated - by properly educated, I mean given a true picture many whites would be less racist in their feelings. They would have more respect for the black man as a human being. Knowing what the black man's contributions to science and civilization have been in the past, the white man's feelings of superiority would be at least partially negated. Also, the feeling of inferiority that the black man has would be replaced by a balanced knowledge of himself. He'd feel more like a human being, in a society of human beings.

So it takes education to eliminate it. And just because you have colleges and universities, doesn't mean you have education. These colleges and universities in the

American education system are skillfully used to miseducate."[15]

For us to really work together, we must understand one another and not toy with one another. America has toyed with the African Americans far too long. And African Americans have toyed with each others far too long. We must stop playing with people. When we stop playing with people, we can build trust, respect, and meaningful working relationships.

Some of us may wish to forget this portion of our history. However, we must never forget it. We must learn from it, both the Black and White Americans, and then forgive. It is quite painful to realize that after all of these years in America, African Americans have not received the full measure of social and economic justice. And today, even the white poor are victims of the same system. The bottom line is, something is still wrong in America today when over 35 million people live in poverty, one percent of the population owns as much of the country's assets as the bottom 80%, and when the top 5 percent of the income earners make more than the bottom 40 percent. America, we can't continue in this vein. We must work together and change our current state in order for this country to survive.

America is a land of the free. As Paul reminded the Christian in the scriptures as recorded in Galatians 5:13-15, allow me to remind my fellow Americans of the same.

> "As for you, my brothers, you were called to be free. But do not let this freedom become an excuse for letting your physical desires control you. Instead, let love make you serve one another. For the whole Law is summed up in one commandment: "Love your neighbor as you love yourself." But if you act like wild animals, hurting and harming each other, then watch out, or you will completely destroy one another."

After completing my research on the first 100 Points, I discovered another interesting comment that was made by Malcolm X. Allow me to share it here because it's most appropriate:

> "In my thinking, if the students in this country forgot the analysis that has been presented to them, and they went into a huddle and began to research this problem of racism for themselves, independent of politicians and independent of all the foundations (which is a part of the power structure), and did it themselves, then some of their findings would be shocking. But they would see that they would never be able to bring about a solution to racism in

this country as long as they're relying on the government to do it..."[16]

This document, the Power Pack was not written as just an idea or something to read and throw aside. Nor, was this document written for radio talk shows to mock. It was written to bring about an understanding. An understanding that is needed now in this great nation as we press ahead into the 21st century. Without this discernment, America is headed for social chaos at a level not experienced in this country since the civil war. The rapid escalation of the riot in Los Angeles bears witness that America is not immune to self-destruction.

America is being ripped apart because of the personal gains of a few people. America is also being ripped apart because of the failures of the politicians . Americans have been under-estimated by politicians who believe they can continue to keep America in the dark while we pay over $200 billion annually in interest on borrowed money. Americans need to know these facts.

Two social scientists, Piven and Cloward, in a historical assessment of government welfare programs, have determined that the government institutes massive aid to the poor only when the poor constitute a threat.[17] Eitzen states: "When large numbers of people are suddenly barred from their traditional occupations, they begin to question the legitimacy of the system itself. Crime, riots, looting, and social movements aimed at changing existing social, political, and economic arrangements become more widespread. Under this threat, the government initiates or expands relief programs in order to diffuse the social unrest. During the Great Depression, Piven and Cloward contend, the government remained aloof from the needs of the unemployed until there was a surge of political disorder. Added proof for Piven and Cloward's thesis is the contraction or even abolition of public assistance programs when stability is restored."[18]

America doesn't need another great depression. We have enough people who live in a state of depression now. America doesn't need more riots and social upheavals. However, America needs strong leadership, and a government that is for the people and by the people.

Politicians must realize that the future of America must outlast their political careers. Every American can agree (with the exception of a few elected officials, perhaps) that the future of this country is more important than the future of any elected official. Therefore, politicians, don't toy with us, give us the facts.

America, there are only a few politicians who will tell you the true nature of the problems facing America internally. Without first educating you, the people of the conditions of America, politically speaking, politicians realize if they should build their platform on correcting the problems of America, they would be committing political suicide. However, without conveying the full extent of the problems to America, America itself could be destroyed from within. This does not have to occur, however, to stop these destructive internal activities, we need an informed America and strong leadership.

There is a number of barriers that separate us. Our belief, Hindu-Moslem-Christian-Jewish-Buddhist, our race, our values, political parties and our social status. In spite of all of our differences there are at least three things that we all have in common, we all live in America, we are human beings, and the same God created everyone of us. Realizing these factors, now we must decide what are we going to do to make America the best possible place to live on earth since we have also been blessed with the resources to make this a reality.

It is apparent that we can not continue under the same false pretense that we have used for years, i.e. that everything is all right, these people are bad people, they are lazy, they don't want to work, etc. Today, with the aid of modern technologies, America can't hide the truth. We can't hide millions of people sleeping on our streets. We can't hide 35 to 50 million people living below the poverty line. We can't hide injustice, like the beating of Rodney King. If we could, America would continue to conduct business as usual, however, today it is no longer possible.

Let's remember that the same God who made us - also loves us. God loves the affluent, like the poor. God loves the African Americans, like the White Americans, Hispanics, Korean Americans, Japanese-Americans, Native Americans and all other Americans. However, God does not love the evil things that we do to one another. We must create better human relations programs in America - People of difference cultures and beliefs must learn how to live with one another. We can't realize our full potential as a nation until America develops strong intercultural relations. This will not happen on its own, but we must make it happen through increased awareness, training and social interactions.

Like we know that God loves us. We must love one another in the same way. King described it like this:

> "Agape is more than romantic love, agape is more than friendship. Agape is understanding, creative, redemptive, good will to all men. It is an overflowing love which seeks nothing in return. Theologians would say that it is the love of God operating in the human heart. So that when one rises to love on this level, he loves men not because he likes them, not because their ways appeal to him, but he loves every man because God loves him. And he rises to the point of loving the person who does an evil deed while hating the deed that the person does..."[19]

As we create much needed understanding, and are earnest with one another, recognize the real problems that we are confronted with in America and begin to really work those problems, we will find that a person should not be judged by the color of their skin. We also will find that the poor don't have to continue to be poor and the rich will be willing to become even more richer, however, at a slower pace.

My fellow Americans, you have your charge. Now tell a friend about the Power Pack.

Chapter VIII Notes

1 Washington, James M., (1986), A Testament Of Hope: The Essential Writings Of Martin Luther King, Jr., p. 149

2 Cited by Floretta Dukes McKenzie, Ph.D. and Patricia Evans, "The State Of Black America", (1991), "Education Strategies For The 1990s"

3 Washington, James M. (1986), A Testament Of Hope: The Essential Writings Of Martin Luther King, Jr., p. 59

4 Ibid. p. 60

5 Ibid. p. 607

6 Richardson, W. Franklyn, Mission To Mandate: Self-Development Through The Black Church, The State Of Black America, (1994) p. 119

7 Washington, James M., (1986), A Testament of Hope: The Essential Writing Of Martin Luther King, Jr., p.307

8 Ibid. p. 613

9. Cited by Floretta Dukes Mckenzie, Ph.D. , "The State Of Black America, (1991) p. 106, "Education Strategies For The 1990s"

10 Howard, Jeff P. The Third Movement: Developing Black Children For the 21st Century", The State Of Black America, (1992), The National Urban League

11 Washington, James M. (1986), A Testament Of Hope: The Essential Writings Of Martin Luther King, Jr., p. 610

12 Ibid. p. 611

13 Ibid. 265

14 Haley, Alex (1973), The Autobiography Of Malcolm X, p. 162

15 X, Malcolm, (1965), Malcolm X Speaks, p. 146, from an interview on January 18, 1965, printed in Young Socialist, March, 1965

16 Ibid. p. 221, From interview, Young Socialist, March-April 1965

17 Eitzen, D. Stanley, (1983), Social Problems, p.47, quoted from Frances Fox Piven and Richard A. Cloward, Regulating The Poor (New York: Pantheon, 1971)

18 Ibid. p. 47

19 Washington, James M. (1986), A Testament Of Hope: The Essential Writings Of Martin Luther King, Jr, p. 46

REFERENCES

Akbar, Na'im, 1984, Chains and Images of Psychological Slavery, Jersey City, New Jersey, New Mind Productions

Allen-Hagen, Barbara and Melissa Sickmund, Ph.D., "Juveniles and Violence: Juvenile Offending and Victimization", "OJJDP, Fact Sheet #3, July 1993

Barrineau, H. E. III, 1989, "Civil Liability In Criminal Justice"

Berghe, Pierre L. van den, 1990, "State Violence and Ethnicity"

Berne, Eric M.D., 1967, "Games People Play", New York, New York, Grove Press, Inc.

Breitman, George, 1992, Malcolm Speaks, New York, N.Y., Pathfinder Press

Chambers, Julus L., Esq, "Black Americans and the Courts: Has the Clock Been Turned Back Permanently?", The State of Black America, fifteen edition

Charlesworth, Edward A., Nathan, Ronald G., 1984, New York, New York, Ballantine Books, a division of Random House

Cohen, Ira S., 1975, Perspectives On Psychology, Introductory Readings, New York, New York, Praeger Publishers, Inc.

Dewart, Janet, 1987, The State of Black America 1987, New York, New York, National Urban League, Inc.

Dewart, Janet, 1988, The State of Black America 1988, New York, New York, National Urban League, Inc.

Dewart, Janet, 1989, The State of Black America 1989, New York, New York, National Urban League, Inc.

Dewart, Janet, 1990, The State of Black America 1990, New York, New York, National Urban League, Inc.

Dewart, Janet, 1991, The State of Black America 1991, New York, New York, National Urban League, Inc.

Dewart, Janet, 1992, The State of Black America 1992, New York, New York, National Urban League, Inc.

Dewart, Janet, 1993, The State of Black America 1993, New York,

New York, National Urban League, Inc.

Dewart, Janet, 1994, The State of Black America 1994, New York, New York, National Urban League, Inc.

Dorsen, Norman, 1984, "Our Endangered Rights - The ACLU Report On Civil Liberties Today", New York, New York, Pantheon Books, a division of Random House, Inc.

Feld, Barry, "Justice By Geography: Urban, Suburban, and Rural Variations in Juvenile Justice Administration, "The Journal of Criminal Law and Criminology, Vol. 82, No. 1, Spring 1991

Harris, Thomas A., M.D., 1973, "I'm OK-You're OK", New York, New York, Avon Books

Herbert, James I. 1989. "Black Male Entrepreneurs and Adult Development"
McCaghy, 1976, "Deviant Behavior"

Jacob, John E. "Black America, 1989: An Overview", The State of Black America, fifteenth edition

Kairys, David, 1993, "With Liberty and Justice For Some", New York, Pantheon Books, a division of Random House, Inc.

Kawasaki, Guy, 1993, Hindsights, Hillsboro, Oregon, Beyond Words Publishing, Inc.

Keniston, Kenneth, 1977, "All Our Children, The American Family Under Pressure", New York, N.Y., Carneigie Corporation of New York

Kunjufu, Jawanza, 1984, Developing Positive Self-Images & Discipline in Black Children, Chicago, Illinois, African-American Images

Feld, Barry, "In Re Gault Revisited: A Cross State Comparison of the Right to Counsel in Juvenile Court," Crime and Delinquency, Vol. 34 No. 4, 1988

McClelland, Peter D., 1990, "The American Search For Economic Justice", Cambridge Massachusetts, Basil Blackwell, Inc.

McMurray, Georgia L. "Those of Broader Vision: An African-American Perspective on Teenage Pregnancy and Parenting", The State of Black America, fifteen edition

Meltzer, Milton, 1986, Poverty In America, New York, New York, William Morrow and Company, Inc.

Naisbitt, John and Aburrdene, Patricia, 1985, Re-inventing the Corporation, New York, N.Y., Warner Books, Inc.

Nason, Leslie, 1964, Help Your Child Succeed In School, New York, New York, Cornerstone Library Publications

Nieli, Russell, 1991, "Racial Preference and Racial Justice - The New Affirmative Action Controversy", Lanham, Maryland, National Book Network

Primm, Beny J., Drug Use: Special Implications for Black America, The State of Black America, 1987.

Richard, James, R. and Weiss, Bernd W., 1977, Dubuque, Iowa, Kendall/Hunt Publishing Company

Richmond, Elmore Jr., 1990, Richmond's Guide To Effective Human Relations and Problem Solving, Los Angeles, California, Authors Unlimited

Rossi, Peter H., 1989, "Down and Out in America, The Origins of Homelessness", Chicago Illinois, Chicago Illinois, The University Of Chicago Press

Scheele, Adele, Ph.D., 1979, "Skill For Success", New York, New York, Ballantine Books, a division of Random House

Sherraden, Michael, 1991, "Assets and the Poor, A New American Welfare Policy", Armonk, New York, M. E. Sharpe, Inc.

Simon, Paul, 1987, "Let's Put America Back To Work", Chicago Illinois, Bonus Book, Inc.

Sitkoff, Harvard, 1993, "The Struggle For Black Equality"

Sterba, James P., 1988, "How To Make People Just"

Swinton, David H., Ph.D., "The Economic Status of Black Americans During the 1980s: A Decade of Limited Progress, The State of Black America, fifteenth edition

Walter L. Updegrave, "Race and Money'" Money, December 1989,p.152

Washington, James M., 1986. A Testament Of Hope, The Essential Writings Of Martin Luther King, Jr., New York, New York, Harper & Row

Welsing, France Cress, 1991, "The IsisPapers, The Key To The

Colors", Chicago, Illinois, Third World Press

West, Cornel, 1993, Race Matters, Boston, Massachusetts, Beacon Press

INDEX